GOETHE'S **Faust**

GOETHE'S Faust

TRANSLATED BY BARKER FAIRLEY

UNIVERSITY OF TORONTO PRESS

©University of Toronto Press 1970
Toronto and Buffalo
Reprinted 1972
Printed in the United States of America
ISBN 0-8020-6153-2 (paper)
ISBN 0-8020-1668-5 (cloth)
LC 74-151823

Performing rights for the English stage version
by Barker Fairley and Peter Raby may be arranged through
Gilbert Parker, Curtis Brown, Ltd.
60 East 56th Street, New York, New York 10022

This book has been published with the help of a grant
from the Humanities Research Council of Canada,
using funds provided by the Canada Council

TRANSLATOR'S NOTE

Goethe's *Faust* was published separately in two parts,
Part I ending with the Gretchen episode (p. 82). Part I is
an unbroken series of scenes, while Part II is in five acts.
In the present translation division into acts and parts has been dropped
and the scenes are numbered continuously from first to last.

GOETHE'S Faust

ILLUSTRATED BY RANDY JONES

DEDICATION

You shifting figures, I remember seeing you dimly long ago, and now I find you coming back again. I wonder should I try to hold on to you this time. Have I the inclination, have I the heart for it? You draw closer out of the mist. Very well then, have your way. The magic breeze that floats along with you fills me with youthful excitement.

You bring back joyful days and joyful scenes and you recall many folk who were dear to me. Early love, early friends rise from the past like an old tale half-forgotten. The pain comes back and with it the lament that life should be so wayward, so confused, and I go over the names of those good people who left this life before me, cut off by some ill chance from further happiness.

Those that I wrote for then will not see what follows now. The friendly throng is dispersed; the early responses have died away. I write now for the unknown crowd whose very approval I dread. If there are any now alive who were pleased with my verses, they are scattered far and wide.

And a great desire seizes me – a desire I have not felt for years – to return to this solemn realm of the spirit. My song resumes hesitantly, insecurely, like an Aeolian harp. I am shaken through and through. The tears come freely and my heart is softened. All my world now seems far away, and what was lost has become real and immediate.

PRELUDE ON THE STAGE

The director, the poet, the clown

DIRECTOR

Tell me, you two, you've stood by me so many times when things were bad. What luck do you think we shall have on this tour of ours through the country? The crowd is so easy-going I'd like to please them. The posts are up and the stage is ready. And there they are, all sitting with their eyes wide open, looking forward to a treat and perhaps a real surprise. I usually know how to satisfy them, but I've never been so much at a loss as now. Of course, they're not used to seeing the best, but they've read an awful lot. We want something lively, something novel, and it has to be pleasant too, and not meaningless. For I must say I like the sight of people streaming in crowds to the tent, thrusting in bursts like birthpangs through the narrow gate, and fighting their way to the box office all in broad daylight at four in the afternoon or earlier. Yes, breaking their necks almost to get a ticket, like starving men in a famine at a baker's door. No one but a poet can work this miracle on such a mixed public. My friend, do it today.

POET

Don't talk to me about the vulgar mob, the seething vortex that sucks you in against your will. The very sight of it paralyses me. Lead me rather to the quiet nook that is my heaven, the only place where a poet can be happy and can cultivate his precious gift among those who love and cherish him.

The verses, good or bad, that spring to his lips from deep within him are crowded out in the rough-and-tumble of the day. You have to wait for years to see them in their true light. Showy things are just meant for the moment, but whatever is really good comes through to posterity.

CLOWN

Posterity, I hate the word. What if I were to talk about posterity? Who would amuse people now? They want their fun and they're going to get it. Having a lad like me on hand is worth something, isn't it? If you know how to reach your audience, you'll never quarrel with it, and the bigger it is, the easier they are to work on. So be a good boy and do your best. Give us something with all sorts of imagination in it, give us wisdom, good sense, feeling, passion, if you like, but don't forget there has to be some clowning too.

DIRECTOR

Plenty of action, that's the first thing that's needed. People want to use their eyes, they want to see. If you keep the scene moving all the time, if you keep them staring and gaping, it's more than half the battle. They'll love you. Give them lots of stuff and you'll appeal to lots of people. Everyone will be free to make his choice. If you offer plenty there'll be this or that for so many of them and they'll all go home contented. Whatever piece you do, do it in pieces. With a mixed grill you can't miss. It's easy to think up, easy to stage. If you present them with an artistic whole, what's the use? They'll only take it in snatches anyway.

POET

You don't know what a cheap trade that is, unworthy of a true artist. Botchwork, the lowest of the low, that's what you've come down to. *page 3*

DIRECTOR

Talk like that doesn't bother me. If a man wants to be effective, he must use the right tools. Just remember what sort of people you're addressing. It's not hardwood you have to split, it's soft. One of them comes because he's bored and another comes from gorging at the dinner table. And, what is worse, quite a lot of them have just been reading the newspaper. They come with their minds on something else, the way you go to a carnival. It's curiosity at most that brings them along. The ladies come in their finery and this helps too without costing us anything. What are you poets dreaming of in your ivory towers? Don't give yourself illusions about a full house. Take a closer look at our patrons, coarse cold-hearted people, one hoping for a game of cards after the play, and another for a wild night in bed with a girl. You silly fools, there's no sense in tormenting the nine muses here. I tell you, give us plenty, pile it on, and you can't go wrong. Just get them all mixed up, they're hard to please. What's got you now? Are you in pain, or is it ecstasy?

POET

Off you go, and get someone else to do your dirty work. Do you expect a poet wantonly to trifle away his greatest gift, nature's gift to his humanity, merely to oblige you? By what power is it that a poet masters the elements and moves the hearts of all men? Is it not the sense of harmony extending from him to embrace the world? Without him nature is like an endless thread, indifferently, discordantly turning on the spindle, no harmony in it. Who is it that breaks up the monotony, enlivens it, gives it rhythm? Who is it that can take a single thing and make it part of the great chorus extolling the universe? Who is it that blends storms and tempests with the human emotions or mingles the glow of sunset in our thoughtful moods? Who scatters all the spring flowers in the paths where lovers walk? Who makes the meagre laurel into a crown of honour for all who deserve it? Who assures us there are gods in council on Olympus? It is the power of man as revealed in the poet.

CLOWN

All right. Get to work with it, this pretty gift of yours. Try it on a love-story. You know how it goes. You meet someone, you feel something, you stick around, and bit by bit you get involved. You're all happiness and then trouble comes. First the rapture and then the misery, and before you know where you are you have a whole romance. Write us a play on these lines. But scoop it up out of real life, life at the full. Everybody lives it, few know it. And it's interesting, no matter where you scratch it. Variety, colour, confusion, error, and a grain of truth. That's the right brew, it suits everyone. The handsome young folk will turn up, tense with expectation. The sentimental ones will get their fill of melancholy. You'll touch life at many points and so each of them will learn about himself. They're young, they're ready to laugh, ready to cry. They're still growing, they still have their ideals, their illusions. You can appeal to that. Adults are so set in their ways you can never please them. But the young will always be grateful for what you offer.

POET

Then give me back the days when I was like that, the days when a fountain

of song welled out of me, one song after another, and never stopped. The
world was veiled in mist; the budding branch was a miracle of promise; the
valleys were clothed with flowers, thousands of flowers, for me to pluck.
I had nothing, yet I had enough – the urge towards truth and the joy of
illusion. Oh, give me back those driving passions – the deep happiness that
hurts, the force of hate, the power of love. Oh, make me young again.

CLOWN

Youth, my friend, is what you may need in the stress of battle, or in love
when pretty girls hang on your neck and won't be repressed, or if you're
running a race and see the winning-post so near and yet so far, or on riotous
nights, first whirling in the dance and then feasting and drinking till daybreak. But when it comes to playing the old familiar tune and doing it
boldly, yet gracefully, and setting yourself a task and working it out in a
happy, casual way, that, old gentlemen, is your job and we respect you for it.
They say old age makes us childish, but it isn't so. Old age brings out the
true child in all of us.

DIRECTOR

We've had arguments enough, what we want now is action. You're wasting
your time over these compliments when we might be doing something
useful. What's the good of talking about being in the mood or not in the
mood. The mood never comes to those who hesitate. If you pretend to be
poets make your poetry do what you tell it to do. You know what we want.
We want strong drink, so on with the work. We've no time to lose. What
you don't do today, you won't find done tomorrow. Tackle something
within your reach and go at it with a will. Once started, you won't want to
let go and you'll work on because you're committed.

You know that in the German theatre each of us is free to experiment.
Today you can be lavish with scenery and all the furnishings. You have sun
and moon at your disposal and stars in plenty. Water, fire, rocks, beasts,
birds – we're not short of any. So on this little stage of ours you can run
through the whole of creation and with fair speed make your way from
heaven through the world to hell.

PROLOGUE IN HEAVEN

The Lord. The heavenly host. Then Mephistopheles. The three archangels step forward

RAPHAEL

The sun resounds among the singing spheres with its ancient music and, thundering loud, completes its course. The angels cannot fathom it, but the mere sight gives them strength. The great, the incomparably great, works of creation are splendid as on the first day of the world.

GABRIEL

And with speed incredible the earth revolves in its glory, the radiance of paradise alternating with deep and dreadful night. Sea-floods storm at the base of the rocks, and sea and rocks alike are whirled in the swift motion of the spheres.

MICHAEL

And tempest on tempest rages from sea to land, from land to sea, forming a chain of mightiest energy. Dread lightnings flash before the thunderclap. But your messengers, O Lord, revere the gentler processes.

ALL THREE

The angels cannot fathom it, but the mere sight gives them strength. And all your mighty works are splendid as on the first day.

MEPHISTOPHELES

Since you, O Lord, are receiving once more and wish to know how we're getting on, here I am again among those present. You've never made me feel unwelcome in the past. Only you must forgive me, I can't talk big. If I tried, you'd laugh at my rhetoric. But I forget, you haven't laughed for a long time. On the sun and the planets etcetera I've nothing to report. I only see the life of man – how wretched it is. These little lords of creation haven't changed in the least. They're just as queer as they were on the first day. It would be better for them if you hadn't given them the light of heaven. They call it their reason and all they use it for is to make themselves more bestial than the beasts. With your Grace's permission, they seem to me like those long-legged grasshoppers that make their little flying jumps and then settle in the grass and sing the same old song. If only they would stay in the grass. But they bury their noses in all the dirt they find.

THE LORD

Is this all you have to say to me? Must you always come complaining? Is there never anything on earth that you approve of?

MEPHISTOPHELES

No, sir, I find it pretty bad there, as I always have. Men's lives are so miserable I'm sorry for them. Poor things, I haven't the heart to plague them myself.

THE LORD

Do you know Faust?

MEPHISTOPHELES

What? The professor?

THE LORD

He is my servant.

MEPHISTOPHELES

Well, I must say, he has his own way of serving you. The common food and drink is not for him. There's an unrest in him that drives him off the map. He half knows how crazy he is. He claims that heaven ought to yield him the pick of the stars and earth its uttermost delights. And nothing, near or remote, can ever satisfy him.

THE LORD

I admit he's not yet rid of his confusion, but I shall soon lead him into the light. The gardener knows when he sees the tree in leaf that flower and fruit will follow in due season.

MEPHISTOPHELES

What will you wager? I'll take him from you yet, if you give me permission to lead him gently my way.

THE LORD

You're free to do that for the rest of his days. Striving and straying, you can't have the one without the other.

MEPHISTOPHELES

Much obliged. I've never enjoyed having to do with the dead. Rosy cheeks are what I like. I've no use for corpses. I'm like a cat with a mouse.

THE LORD

Very well, I leave it to you. Draw his mind away from its true source and, if you can get a grip on him, set him on your downward path. And confess in the end to your shame: man in his dark impulse always knows the right road from the wrong.

MEPHISTOPHELES

Good enough. But I shan't be long over it. I'm not afraid of losing my bet. If I succeed, you must allow me to celebrate my triumph. I'll make him eat the dust and enjoy it, like my old friend, the serpent.

THE LORD

I give you complete freedom, as I always have. I've never hated your sort. Of all the negative spirits your roguish kind gives me the least concern. It's so easy for men to slump and before long they want to do nothing at all. So I don't object to their having your company. You act as a stimulant and so serve a positive purpose in spite of yourself.

But you, the true sons of heaven, I bid you rejoice in the living beauty of the world, its growth, its love. Seek in your minds for what is permanent in its change.

The heavens close, the archangels withdraw

MEPHISTOPHELES *alone*

I like to see the old man now and then, and I take good care to keep in with him. It's nice of so great a personage to talk to the devil himself in this human way.

scene 1 NIGHT

A high, narrow, vaulted Gothic chamber

FAUST *sitting at his desk, restless*
Look at me. I've worked right through philosophy, right through medicine and jurisprudence, as they call it, and that wretched theology too. Toiled and slaved at it and know no more than when I began. I have my master's degree and my doctor's and it must be ten years now that I've led my students by the nose this way and that, upstairs and downstairs, and all the time I see plainly that we don't and can't know anything. It eats me up. Of course I'm ahead of these silly scholars, these doctors and clerics and what not. I have no doubts or scruples to bother me, and I snap my fingers at hell and the devil. But I pay the price. I've lost all joy in life. I don't delude myself. I shall never know anything worth knowing, never have a word to say that might be useful to my fellow men. I own nothing, no money, no property, I have no standing in the world. It's a dog's life and worse. And this is why I've gone over to magic, to see if I can get secrets out of the spirit world and not have to go on sweating and saying things I don't know, discover, it may be, what it is that holds the world together, behold with my own eyes its innermost workings, and stop all this fooling with words.

Oh if this were the last time the full moon found me here in my agony. How often have I sat at this desk among my books watching for you in the deep of night till at last, my melancholy friend, you came. Oh to be out on the hilltops in your lovely light, floating among spirits at some cavern's mouth or merging into your meadows in the dimness. Oh to be clear, once and for all, of this pedantry, this stench, and to wash myself in your dew and be well again.

But where am I? Still a prisoner in this stifling hole, these walls, where even the sunlight that filters in is dimmed and discoloured by the painted panes, surrounded from floor to ceiling by dusty, worm-eaten bookshelves with this sooty paper stuck over them, these instruments everywhere, these beakers, these retorts, and then, on top of that, my family goods and chattels. Call that a world?

Is it any wonder that your heart should quail and tremble and that this ache, this inertia, should thwart your every impulse? When God created man he put him in the midst of nature's growth and here you have nothing round you but bones and skeletons and mould and grime.

Up then. Out into the open country. And what better guide could I have than this strange book that Nostradamus wrote. With its help I shall follow the movement of the stars. Nature may teach me how spirits talk to spirits. It is futile to brood drily here over the magic signs. You spirits, hovering about me, hear me and answer. *He opens the book and sees the sign of the macrocosm*

What a vision is this, flooding all my senses with delight, racing through my nerves and veins with the fire and the freshness of youth. Was it a god who set down these signs that hush my inner fever, fill my poor heart with happiness, and with mysterious power make visible the forces of nature about me. Am I myself a god? Such light is given to me. In these pure lines I see the working of nature laid bare. Now I know what the philosopher meant: 'The spirit-world is not closed. It is your mind that is shut, your heart that is inert. Up, my pupil, be confident, bathe your breast in the dawn.' *He contemplates the sign*

Oh what a unity it is, one thing moving through another, the heavenly powers ascending and descending, passing the golden vessels up and down, flying from heaven to earth on fragrant wings, making harmonious music in the universe. What a spectacle. But ah, only a spectacle. Infinite nature, how shall I lay hold of you? How shall I feed at these breasts, these nurturing springs, for which I yearn, on which all life depends? When these are offered, must I thirst in vain? *He turns the pages angrily and sees the sign of the Earth-spirit*

How differently this sign affects me. You, Earth-spirit, are closer to me, warming me like wine and filling me with new energy. I'm ready now to adventure into life, endure the world's joy and the world's pain, wrestle with its storms, and not lose courage in the grinding shipwreck. See, the room is clouded, the moon is hid, the lamp goes out, vapours rise, redness flashes, terror comes down on me from the vaulted roof. You spirit that I have sought, I feel your nearness. Reveal yourself. My whole being gropes and struggles towards sensations I never knew. My heart goes out to you. Reveal yourself. You must, though it costs me my life. *He seizes the book and spells out the mysterious sign, a red flame flashes, and the spirit appears in the flame*

SPIRIT
Who calls?
FAUST *with face averted*
Appalling.

SPIRIT

You sought me mightily, you sucked and pulled long at my sphere. And now?

FAUST

Ah! I cannot face you.

SPIRIT

You begged breathlessly to see me, to see my face, hear my voice. I yield to your implorations. Here I am. And now, you would-be superman, what abjectness is this? Where now is your spirit's call? Where is the heart that swelled to world-size, created its own world, and cherished it rapturously, thinking itself the equal of us spirits? Where are you, Faust, whose voice came to me with such pressure, such urgency? Is this Faust, shattered when my breath reaches him, a worm wriggling away in terror?

FAUST

Must I give in to you, you flame-shape? Yes, here I am. This is Faust, your equal.

SPIRIT

In floods of life, in storms of action, I range up and down. I flow this way and that. I am birth and the grave, an eternal ocean, a changeful weaving, a glowing life. And thus I work at the humming loom of time, and fashion the earth, God's living garment.

FAUST

You busy spirit, roaming the wide world, how close I feel to you.

SPIRIT

You are not close. You are not equal. You are only equal to what you think I am. *disappears*

FAUST *collapsing*

Not equal to you. Me created in God's image. And not even equal to you. (*A knock*) Oh, death. That's my famulus knocking. Oh that at the supreme moment this dull creeping fellow should spoil my wealth of visions.

Wagner in his nightcap with a lamp in his hand. Faust turns in annoyance

WAGNER

Forgive me. I heard you declaiming. From a Greek tragedy, I've no doubt. This is an art. I wish I was better at it. It's worth a lot nowadays. They do say an actor could teach a parson.

FAUST

Yes, if the parson's an actor, as may sometimes be the case.

WAGNER

Oh, dear me. When a man is stuck in his study all the time and only sees the world on holidays, from far away, through a telescope, you might say, hardly that, how is he to persuade them of anything?

FAUST

You'll never do this, if you don't feel it. If it doesn't come from deep down and win the hearts of your hearers with energy unforced. Oh yes, stay put in your chairs, paste your clippings together, concoct a stew from other men's tables, blow the petty little flames from your ashheaps to entertain the simple-minded, if that's what suits you. But you'll never move and unite the hearts of men, unless your own heart is behind it.

But the delivery, the technique, is what makes a good orator. I realise how much I have to learn.

FAUST

Make your living honestly. Don't be a bell-tinkling fool. Intelligence and good sense can be left to speak for themselves. If you really have something to say, do you have to hunt for words and phrases to say it? These smart speeches of yours, packed with titbits from everywhere, are as unrefreshing as the wind in autumn rustling the dry leaves.

WAGNER

But art is long, God knows, and this life of ours is short. I often lose heart in my studies, and lose confidence too. There's so much to master before you can get back to the sources. And, poor fellows, we snuff out before we're halfway through.

FAUST

Manuscripts. Is that the sacred spring to quench your thirst for ever? You'll never find true refreshment unless it comes from within you.

WAGNER

You must pardon me, though. It's a great satisfaction to enter into the spirit of the times, to see what a wise man once said and then to consider what wonderful progress we've made since.

FAUST

Oh yes, wonderful indeed. Past ages, my friend, are a book with seven seals. What you all call the spirit of the times is just your own spirit with the times reflected in it. A sorry sight it often is, I must say. One glance is enough to make you run. A garbage can and a lumber-room. Or, at best, a blood-and-thunder play with excellent moral saws and sayings, good enough perhaps for a puppet-show.

WAGNER

But the world around us, the human heart and mind. Everyone wants to know about it.

FAUST

Know about it. What sort of knowing? Who'll tell you the honest truth? The few men who really knew and didn't keep what they knew to themselves but told the world what they felt and saw have been burned and crucified from the beginning of time. But excuse me, friend, it's very late, we must stop now.

WAGNER

I could have stayed up all night, conferring with you so intellectually. But tomorrow is Easter Sunday and you must allow me to come and ask you one or two more questions. I've kept my nose to the grindstone and I know a lot, but I want to know everything. *off*

FAUST *alone*

Strange they don't lose hope altogether, always busy with things that don't matter, digging greedily for treasure and happy when they come across an earthworm.

To think that this prosaic voice sounded here in my room when the air was thronged with spirits. But for once, you miserable wretch, I'm grateful to you. You saved me from despair that was not far from destroying   *page 11* me. This apparition was so tremendous, it made a dwarf of me, a nothing.

Shaped in God's image, was I? Conceitedly indulging in the clear light of heaven, thinking I was soon to look into the mirror of eternal truth after leaving mortality far behind me. What presumption. Imagining I was greater than the angels, able to move of my own accord in nature's veins and create like one of the gods. Oh, the punishment. One thundering word has brought me low.

Equality with you I cannot claim. I had the strength to summon you, but not the strength to hold. In that supreme moment I felt at once so great and so small. And then ruthlessly you thrust me back into uncertainty, the common lot of men. Who will tell me what next to do, or what not to do? Shall I abandon my quest or not? The things we do cramp us not less surely than the things that are done to us.

Our noblest thoughts soon lose their purity in the dross that invades them. Then mere comforts suffice and ideals are despised. The lofty sentiments that were the breath of life to us are smothered in the earthly rubble.

Time was when your imagination with bold and hopeful flight would reach out into infinity, but when, in the whirligig, misfortunes come, then little room is all the room it needs. Care at once lodges deep in the heart, clothing itself in endless disguises and bringing disquietude and those mysterious pains. Whatever crosses our mind, nothing is free from it – fire, water, dagger, poison, family, property. You quake at the thought of what doesn't happen and you weep for the loss of what you never lose.

I'm not like the gods. I know it now. I'm like the worm, wriggling in the dust, the worm that feeds on the dust and is crushed to nothing by the passing foot.

What is it but dust, this high wall shutting me in with its hundred compartments? And all this rubbish, these countless moth-eaten trivialities that beset me? Can I be expected to find what I want here? Am I to read in a thousand books that men have always been harassed and that one of them was happy here or there? You empty grinning skull, what have you to say to me? All you can say is that your poor brain like mine once groped for the light and the truth only to go grievously astray at the close. As for these instruments, they mock me, these wheels and cogs and rollers. I stood at the gate, they were the keys. Complicated enough, but they didn't lift the latch. You can't pluck nature's veil, she stays a mystery in full daylight. What she doesn't choose to reveal you can't force out of her with screws and levers. These old things are only here because they were my father's, I never used them. This parchment has been gathering soot from my smoky lamp for years. Better by far, it would have been, to squander the little I had than to go on sweating here under the weight of it. What you inherit from your forebears isn't yours unless you do something with it. Things unused are a sore burden. Only your creativeness moment by moment can turn them to account.

But now this flask here? Can it be magnetic? Why does it suddenly rivet my attention, easing and clearing my mind, like moonlight flooding the dark forest?

Come down, you rare, you sacred draught, you tribute to man's cunning, you blend of subtle poisons, quintessence of opiates.

Show your master what you can do for him. I look at you, my pain is less. I take hold of you, my stress relaxes. The flood-tide of my spirit ebbs and ebbs, and the high sea beckons. The great waters sparkle at my feet. A new day invites me to new shores.

A fiery chariot comes swinging down for me. I'm ready to follow a new course, ready for a new activity in a purer sphere. What exaltation, what divine joy. And what a reversal, deserved or not. A worm and now this. Yes, turn your back on the sweet sunlight. Tear open the gates that others shrink from approaching. The time has come to show by your deeds that man in moral courage is equal to the gods, bold enough to face that dark horrific cavern and force his way to the narrow passage, girt with flames of hell, and do it serenely, even at the risk of lapsing into nothingness.

And now I take this long-forgotten crystal loving-cup down from its old case. I remember how it figured at family parties and how the guests were amused when the pledger did his duty, invented a rhyme to interpret the decorations, and emptied the cup at a draught. There is no friend of my youth to pass it on to this time, nor any need for rhyming. This is a drink that soon intoxicates, the drink that I prepared, the chosen drink darkening the brimming cup. I pledge it with all my heart to the new day. *He puts the cup to his lips. Church bells and choir*

CHOIR OF ANGELS

Christ is risen. Joy to the mortal no longer swathed in fleshly ills, inherited, insidious, ruinous.

FAUST

What heavy bourdon, what high note is this, that pulls the glass from my lips with such force. Do these deep bells announce the Easter festival? Is this the choir singing the comforting words, first sung by angels at the darksome grave, giving assurance of a new faith, a new covenant?

CHOIR OF WOMEN

We, his faithful ones, anointed and laid him in shrouds, and now he is no longer here.

CHOIR OF ANGELS

Christ is risen. Happy the lover of mankind, his sad and saving ordeal passed.

FAUST

Why do you seek me in the dust, you heavenly notes, strong and gentle at once? Ring out elsewhere for weaker men. I hear your message well enough, but I lack the faith, the faith that fathers your miracle. I don't aspire to those regions whence your message comes. And yet, these sounds, known to me from early years, call me back to life. I remember sabbaths when in the stillness the kiss of heavenly love was granted me. In those days the pealing bells were full of promise and to utter a prayer was a rapture of delight. A strange, sweet yearning would draw me out into the fields and woods where floods of tears gave birth, it seemed, to an inner world. This is the song that ushered in the merry games of childhood and the festive springtime, so free, so happy. Memory, piety, holds me from this last step of all. Ring out, sweet bells. My tears come. Earth has won me back again.

CHOIR OF DISCIPLES

He that was sublime in life has gone up from the sepulchre and is beginning now to share the joy of creation. Master, we who languish here on earth bemoan your fortune.

CHOIR OF ANGELS

Christ is risen out of corruption. Rejoice and free yourselves. Go forth and praise him in good works, promising blessedness. Then the master will be near, he will be among you.

scene 2 OUTSIDE THE TOWN-GATE

People of all sorts out for the day

SOME JOURNEYMEN
Why go that way?
OTHERS
We're going to the Huntsman.
THE FIRST ONES
But we want to go to the Old Mill.
ONE
I say, go to Riverview.
SECOND
The road there's so dull.
THE SECOND ONES
What'll you do?
THIRD
I'll go with the rest.
FOURTH
Come on up to the village. That's where you're sure to find the prettiest girls and the best beer. And a good scrap too.
FIFTH
You never have enough. Is your hide itching for the third time? I don't want to go there. I hate the place.
SERVANT GIRL
No, I'm going back home.
ANOTHER
We're sure to find him beside those poplars.
FIRST
That's no fun. It's you he'll walk with. You're the only one he dances with. What's that to me?
THE OTHER
He won't be by himself today for sure. He told us Curly was coming with him.
STUDENT
The way those wenches step out. They're hefty. Come on, let's join them. That's what I like – a maid in her Sunday best, a good strong beer, and a nippy tobacco.
GIRL
Just look at those nice boys. It's a shame. They could have anyone they
wanted and they go running after those servant girls.

SECOND STUDENT *to the first*

Not so fast. There's two others coming. Nicely dressed. One of them lives next door. I've taken a real fancy to her. They're just strolling along. They'll let us pick them up.

FIRST STUDENT

No, I don't want to be put on my best behaviour. Come on quick or we'll lose the others. The hand that wields a broom on Saturdays will fondle you best on Sundays.

TOWNSMAN

No, I don't approve of our new mayor. Now he's appointed, he's getting bolder every day. And what is he doing for the town? Aren't things getting worse all the time? We have to toe the line more than ever and pay bigger taxes too.

BEGGAR *singing*

Good sirs, fair ladies, so gay, so shining, pray look on me and ease my lot. Let me not grind my organ here for nothing. If you don't give, you won't be happy. This is a holiday, make it a good day for me.

ANOTHER TOWNSMAN

I know nothing better on Sundays and holidays than talking about war and rumours of war when the nations are at one another's throats far off in Turkey and places. You stand at the window and empty your glass and watch the boats gliding downstream, then go home in the evening in good spirits, thankful for peace and peaceful times.

THIRD TOWNSMAN

Yes, neighbour. I'm with you there. Let them split one another's heads and all go topsy-turvy, so long as things stay just the same at home.

OLD WOMAN *to the girls*

Oh, how smart you are, you pretty creatures. You could turn anybody's head. But go easy. Don't put on such airs. I know how to get you what you want.

GIRL

Come on, Agatha. I take good care not to be seen with those old witches. But on St Andrew's night she did show me my future lover.

THE OTHER

She showed me mine in a crystal, like a soldier, in riotous company. I keep a look-out for him, but I've had no luck.

SOLDIERS *singing*

High-walled castles and haughty girls, these we assail. A bold endeavour, a great reward. Death or delight, we follow the trumpet. Girls or castles, surrender they must. A bold endeavour, a great reward. And the soldiers march away.

Faust and Wagner

FAUST

The ice is gone in the brooks and rivers under the sweet spring's quickening glance. And the valleys are green with hope. Old winter, the dodderer, has shrunk into the hills, streaking the sprouting meadows with impotent hail. But the sun will have no whiteness, where all is thrust and growth. She wants colour everywhere. Being short of flowers, she makes the gay crowd serve. Turn round here on the rise and look back at the town. See the motley throng pouring out through the dark gate into the sunlight. They all love it. They're celebrating the resurrection, because they're resurrected themselves, out of cramped houses, stuffy rooms, out of the toils of trade, the weight of roofs and gables, the narrow streets, the church darkness. Back into the daylight. See how soon they scatter among the fields and plots. See these boats all dancing in the river, wherever you look. And here this last boat setting out loaded to the gunwale. You can make out the colour of the dresses sprinkled right up the hillside. And now I can hear the noise of the village. This is the people's heaven, young and old contentedly saying: Here I can be free, here I am human.

WAGNER

It's an honour to go for a walk with you, professor, and profitable too. But I would never come here alone, because I can't bear any coarseness. I hate this fiddling and shrieking, and this skittle-alley. They make an infernal noise and call it enjoyment, call it singing.

Peasants under the linden tree

Dance and Song

The shepherd put on his best for the dance. And smart he looked in his gay jacket. They were dancing like mad round the linden tree. There was no room there. Hooray, hooray, on went the fiddles.
He pushed his way in and bumped a girl with his elbow. She whipped round and yelled 'Stupid.' Hooray, hooray. Don't be so rough.
Round and round they went, this way and that way. Skirts were flying. They got hot and rested arm in arm. Hooray, hooray. And hip to elbow.
And don't make so free. Lots of girls have been had. But he got her off to one side all the same. They could just hear the noise of the dance. Hooray, hooray, on went the fiddles.

OLD PEASANT

It's nice of you, doctor, to come among us common folk today and not feel above it, you being so learned a scholar. So take this drink in our best cup with our compliments. We don't want it just to quench your thirst. We hope that for every drop that is in it a day will be added to your life.

FAUST

I accept this refreshment with thanks and drink to the health of all of you.

The people gather round

OLD PEASANT

Indeed it was right of you to come on this happy day. I remember what you did for us once in evil days. There's many a one here now whom your father saved from the fever when he stopped that epidemic. You were a young man then. You went into all the houses. Many never came out alive, but you did. You stood a lot. You helped us and God helped you.

Your health, sir, we wish you a long life to go on helping us.

FAUST

Bow down to him from whom help comes. *He passes on with Wagner*

WAGNER

What satisfaction it must give you to be revered by all these people. Lucky is he who can derive such advantages from his talents. They all come running and enquiring. Fathers show you to their little boys. The fiddling stops, the dancers stop. They line up when you move on. Caps fly in the air. It wouldn't take much and they'd go down on their knees as if the sacred host was coming.

FAUST

It's only a few steps further to that rock where we'll rest a while. I often used to sit here alone with my thoughts, tormenting myself with prayer and fasting. I was firm in my faith then and full of hope. And with sighs and tears and wringing of hands I believed I could force the Lord in heaven to end the plague. The approval I get from these people is a mockery to me now. If only you could read in my heart how little my father and I deserved the approval. My father was a quiet gentleman who studied nature in his own queer way, but honestly enough. He joined a society of alchemists who went in for the black kitchen, laboriously mixing opposites in search of remedies. A red lion was wedded in a warm liquid to the lily, then the two were distilled again and again over an open flame till finally the young queen appeared in many colours. This was our remedy. The patients died. No one asked any questions. With our hellish drugs we did more harm in this part of the country than the plague. I administered the poison myself to thousands, they pined away, while I have lived to see the time when they praise their murderers.

WAGNER

You shouldn't let it bother you. If you carefully and conscientiously practise the arts that have been handed on to you, it's all that can be expected. A man who respects his father will be glad to learn from him and if he in his turn can add to science his son will profit.

FAUST

What a sea of confusion and error we live in, finding no use for the knowledge we have and lacking the very knowledge we need. There is solace in the mere thought of escape. But why spoil this happy hour with such lamenting? See how the evening rays pick out the little houses in their green setting. The day is over and the sun is almost gone, speeding away on its life-giving journey. And now I long for wings to lift me off the ground and let me follow it. Then I should have the quiet earth ever below me in an eternal sunset, with all the heights aflame and the valleys at rest and the silvery streams turning to gold. Not the grim mountain with all its chasms would check my marvellous flight. And next the great ocean would come in sight with the day's warmth lying in its bays. If the sun seems near to sinking, a burst of new energy carries me after it, to drink its eternal light, the day always before me and the night behind, the heavens above me and the waves beneath. A lovely dream, but not for long. The body has not wings to match the spirit's wings. Yet it is natural for our feelings to soar upward and onward, when *page 17* we see the lark trilling its song, a speck lost in the blue, or the eagle in hilly country floating above the pines, or the heron over flats and lakes winging its way to roost.

WAGNER

I've had some queer thoughts myself, but I never wanted to do that. You get your fill of woods and fields so quickly. And I've no desire to fly like a bird. What I like is the pleasures of the mind that carry you from page to page and from book to book and make winter evenings a delight. You're snug and warm in every limb and, with an old parchment spread before you, it's heavenly.

FAUST

This is the force that drives you. You don't know the other force, and I hope you never will. As for myself, there are two of me, unreconciled. The one clings to the earth with its whole body sensually, while the other soars with all its might to the abodes of the blest. If there are spirits about, ranging and ruling in the atmosphere, come down to me out of this golden light, and transport me where life is rich and new. If I only had a magic carpet to take me abroad I wouldn't part with it for anything, not for the costliest of gowns, not even for a king's mantle.

WAGNER

Don't summon those spirits that throng the air and threaten us with danger on every hand. We know them too well. In the sharp North wind they attack us with their arrowy tongues or they eat out our lungs in the withering East. In the South they come out of the desert to blaze down on our poor heads and the West wind only refreshes in order to flood our fields and drown us out. They're all ears, because they're full of mischief. They do what we ask, because they like to fool us. They pretend to come from heaven and they lie with the tongues of angels. But let us push on. The colour has all faded from the scenery, it's chilly now and damp. Home's the place after dark. But what are you standing and staring at so? There's nothing to see here in the twilight.

FAUST

Do you notice the black dog running there in the stubble?

WAGNER

Oh yes. I saw it a while back. It's just a dog.

FAUST

Look again. What do you think it really is?

WAGNER

A poodle, following us the way dogs do.

FAUST

Don't you see that he's circling us and getting nearer and nearer? If I'm not mistaken, there's a streak of fire trailing behind him.

WAGNER

All I see is a black poodle. Your eyes must be deceiving you.

FAUST

I believe he's drawing magic snares round our feet and wants to come to terms with us.

WAGNER

He's just confused, because he finds we're strangers and not his master.

The circle is narrowing, he's not far away.

WAGNER

There you see. He's no ghost. He's just a dog like any other dog, whining and lying down and wagging his tail.

FAUST

Come here. Stay with us.

WAGNER

A silly creature. You stop, he's at your service. You speak to him, he jumps up at you. Throw something away, he'll fetch it. He'll fetch your stick out of the water.

FAUST

You must be right. It's just his tricks, no trace of a spirit.

WAGNER

Even a philosopher might enjoy having a well-behaved dog. Some student has trained him well, he'll do you no discredit. *They enter the town-gate*

scene 3 FAUST'S STUDY

FAUST *entering with the poodle*
It's dark now in the fields and everywhere. Night has come, bringing its strange intimations and premonitions. Our better self is awakened, our unruliness, our dangerous impulses abated. Thoughts of love begin to stir in me, love of mankind, love of god.

Be quiet, poodle. Don't run about so. What are you sniffing at in the doorway? Lie down behind the stove, I'll give you my best cushion. You entertained us nicely with your antics when we came down the hill. Now let me make you comfortable as my guest. You're welcome to stay if you don't make a noise.

This is the time when a man feels clear in his own mind, sitting in his den with the friendly lamp burning. Reason raises its voice again and hope revives. You long to reach the springs of life, you long for the source.

Poodle, stop your whining and growling. There's no place for these animal noises beside the lofty music that I hear within me. We know that if people don't understand a thing they ridicule it, they complain about the good and the beautiful because it embarrasses them. Is the dog going to follow suit?

But ah, in spite of myself my inner contentment is beginning to fail. Why must the flow so soon give out and leave us thirsting? I've seen it many times. But there's another way, if we put our trust in the supernatural and yearn for revelation. And where does the light of revelation burn better and brighter than in the New Testament? I must look at the original without delay and see if I can render it honestly in my beloved German. *He opens a volume and begins*

The text reads: In the beginning was the word. But stop. What about this? I can't rate the word nearly as high as that. I'll have to translate it some other way. Unless I'm mistaken, the true reading is: In the beginning was the mind. But let's not be in a hurry with the first line. Can it be the mind that creates the world? Surely we ought to read: In the beginning was the *page 19* energy. But no sooner do I write this than something tells me not to stop there. And now I see the light and set down confidently: In the beginning was the act.   •

Poodle, if you and I are to share the room, you'll have to stop your yelping. I can't do with so bothersome a companion. One of us will have to go. I'm sorry. You can't be my guest any longer. The door's open. Off with you. But what do I see? Can it be natural? Can it be real? This poodle is swelling so. It can't be a poodle. It's more like a hippopotamus. Eyes of fire and dreadful jaws. What a spectre I brought home with me. But I'll get you. The key of Solomon is the thing for the likes of you.

SPIRITS *on the landing*

There's someone trapped in there. Don't go in. Stay out. The old devil's caught like a fox in a trap. But watch. Float about for a minute and you'll see he'll get loose. Help him if you can. He's done us many a good turn.

FAUST

First I'll go at him with the spell of the four elements.

Let the salamander glow, let the undine writhe, let the sylph disappear, let the cobold toil.

No man could be master of the spirits, if he didn't know the elements, their strength and their properties.

Salamander, disappear in flame; Undine, rustle and collapse; Sylph, shine like a meteor; Cobold, bring help, come out and make an end of it.

None of the four is in the beast. There he lies grinning at me. I haven't hurt him yet. But I'll make you sit up with a stronger one.

Fellow, are you a fugitive from hell? Then look at this sign, before which the black angels bow down.

He's swelling up with bristling prickles.

You base creature, can you read his story here, the never begotten, the ineffable one, filling the heavens, wantonly transfixed.

Caught behind the stove, he's swelling like an elephant, filling the whole room, turning into cloud. Don't go through the ceiling. Lie down at your master's feet. You see I'm as good as my word. I'll roast you with holy fire. Don't wait till I give you the threefold light. Don't wait till I turn on the strongest of my arts.

MEPHISTOPHELES *the cloud fades, he comes out from behind the stove, dressed like a wandering scholar*

What's the noise about? What can I do for you, sir?

FAUST

So you were the poodle, were you? A wandering scholar. Very amusing.

MEPHISTOPHELES

I salute the learned gentleman. You certainly made me sweat.

FAUST

What's your name?

MEPHISTOPHELES

I call that a silly question, coming from a man who holds words in such contempt and cares only for depth and nothing for appearance.

FAUST

With birds like you one can usually tell the nature by the name, and tell it only too clearly, if your name happens to be lord of the flies, or liar, or destroyer. Well, who are you?

MEPHISTOPHELES

A part of the force that always tries to do evil and always does good.

FAUST

You're speaking in riddles. Explain.

MEPHISTOPHELES

I am the spirit that always negates, and rightly so, since everything that comes into existence is only fit to go out of existence and it would be better if nothing ever got started. Accordingly, what you call sin, destruction, evil in short, is my proper element.

FAUST

You call yourself a part and yet you look like a whole.

MEPHISTOPHELES

I'm just speaking the modest truth. I know that man in his silly little world thinks he's a whole, or usually does. But I am part of the part that was everything in the beginning. Part of the darkness that gave birth to light. Light that in its arrogance challenges Mother Night and claims the possession of space. But, try as it may, it will never succeed, because it can't free itself from objects. It flows from objects, it beautifies objects, it is intercepted by them. And so, when we get rid of objects, we shall get rid of light as well. I hope it won't be long.

FAUST

Now I see what you're up to. You can't destroy on a big scale, so you're working on a small.

MEPHISTOPHELES

Yes, and not achieving much either. This thing, this clumsy world, confronting nothingness, I haven't been able to get at it yet. After all the pounding waves, the storms, the fires, the earthquakes, land and sea stay just as they were. And as for that cursed brood of men and animals, I can do nothing with them. To think how many of them I've buried already and yet there's always some new blood circulating. Always. It's enough to drive you mad. Germs spring up by the thousand in earth, air, or water, dry or wet, warm or cold. If I hadn't reserved fire for myself, there'd be nothing I could call my own.

FAUST

So you are pitting that cold malignant devil's fist of yours against the power of creation, against the life-force that never halts. A futile endeavour. Better try something else, you crazy son of Chaos.

MEPHISTOPHELES

We must certainly look into this. I'll have more to say about it another time. Do you mind if I go now?

FAUST

I can't see why you ask. We're now acquainted. Come and see me when you like. Here's the window. There's the door. And there's always the chimney.

MEPHISTOPHELES

Unfortunately there's a little thing that stops me going out. The mandrake's foot in the doorway.

FAUST

What? The pentagram? Does that bother you? Tell me then. If this blocks you, how did you get in? Can devils be fooled?

MEPHISTOPHELES

Take a look. It isn't well drawn. You see, the corner pointing out has a break in it.

FAUST

A lucky accident. So, by pure chance, you're my prisoner.

MEPHISTOPHELES

The poodle never noticed when it came running in. Now it's different. The devil can't get out.

FAUST

Why don't you go through the window?

MEPHISTOPHELES

It's a rule among ghosts and devils. They have to go out the way they came in. Going in, we can choose. Going out, we're tied.

FAUST

So even hell has its laws? I like that. We might come to terms with one another.

MEPHISTOPHELES

What we promise we keep, to the full. No haggling. But it isn't simple. We'll talk about this some day soon. For the present, I beg you please to let me go.

FAUST

Oh, stay another minute and chat with me.

MEPHISTOPHELES

Let me go now and I'll soon be back. Then you can ask all the questions you like.

FAUST

I didn't try to trap you. You walked into the trap yourself. A man doesn't catch the devil every day. Better hang on to him when he has him.

MEPHISTOPHELES

If you wish, I'm prepared to stay and keep you company, provided you allow me to entertain you in my own way.

FAUST

Excellent. Do what you choose, only let it be pleasant.

MEPHISTOPHELES

You'll get more sensuous pleasure from my entertainment than in all the dull round of the year. What these gentle spirits sing, the lovely scenes they show, is not just empty magic. Nose and palate will get their share. You'll be delighted. No preparation is needed. We're all assembled. Begin.

SPIRITS

Let the vaulted ceiling lift, the dark clouds scatter, and the friendly blue sky appear, with milder suns and sparkling stars. Hosts of angels pass by in the air, awakening our desire. Their robes and ribbons fill the landscape, cover the arbours where lovers unite. Vines sprout, grapes pour into the presses, rivers of foaming wine trickle through the clean rocks, leave the heights, spread into lakes, with green shores sloping, birds drink delight, fly towards the sun and the happy isles rocking in the waves, with jubilant choirs singing, dancing in the meadows. Some climb the hills, others swim, others float in the air, all finding life and divine happiness.

He's off. Well done, you airy youngsters. You've performed your duty and sung him to sleep. Thank you for the concert. You, Faust, are not the man to keep the devil in your grasp. Play on him now with sweet dreams, plunge him into depths of illusion. But to burst this threshold's spell I need a rat's tooth. And I shan't have to wait long. There's a rat rustling here, he'll hear me at once.

The lord of rats and mice, of flies, frogs, bugs, and lice commands you to come out of hiding and nibble this threshold where I'm putting a drop of oil. There you are. And now to work. The corner that blocks me is the forward one here. Another bite and it's done.

Now, Faust, dream away till we meet again.

FAUST *waking*

Have I been duped a second time? Is this all I have from my rendezvous with spirits? Did I just see the devil in a dream and lose a poodle?

scene 4 FAUST'S STUDY

Faust. Mephistopheles

FAUST

A knock. Come in. Who's pestering me now?

MEPHISTOPHELES

It's me.

FAUST

Come in.

MEPHISTOPHELES

You have to say it three times.

FAUST

Oh well then, come in.

MEPHISTOPHELES

That's the way. I trust we shall hit it off together. You see, I want to cheer you up and so I've put on the costume of a nobleman, red with gold braid, a cape of stiff silk, a cock's feather in my hat, and a long rapier. And I want you to wear the same, so that you may feel completely on the loose, free and ready to find out what life is like.

FAUST

No matter what I wear, I shall feel the misery of our petty, earthly existence just the same. I'm too old to take it lightly, too young to back down altogether. What has the world to offer me? Renunciation. You can't do this, you can't do that. This is the eternal refrain that rings and jangles in our ears hour by hour all our life long. When I wake in the morning, I wake with horror. I could shed bitter tears to think of the day beginning that will not grant me one thing I wish for, no not one, the day that with senseless carping will nip all pleasure in the bud and thwart every generous impulse with its ugliness and its mockery. When I lie down on my bed at night I am full of fears. There will be no repose, wild dreams will come to terrify me. The divinity that resides in me, master of my powers, can shake me to the depths,   *page 23* but that is all. It effects nothing outwardly. And so life to me is a burden, and death what I desire.

MEPHISTOPHELES
And yet death when it comes is never wholly welcome, never.

FAUST
Oh happy the man whom death reaches at the moment of victory to twine the bloody laurels about his brow, or it finds him after the mad whirl of the dance lying in a girl's embrace. Oh would that I had collapsed and died in ecstasy under the earth-spirit's impact.

MEPHISTOPHELES
Someone I know didn't drain his draught on that particular night.

FAUST
Spying round is your game, it seems.

MEPHISTOPHELES
I don't know everything, but I know a lot.

FAUST
I was fooled. Sweet, familiar music, thoughts of happy days, awoke what was left of the child in me and lifted me out of my horrible confusion. But not again. Now I put my curse on everything, the decoys, the enticements, that confront us on every side, all the trumpery and flattery that detains us in this vale of misery. I curse the high and mighty notion the mind has of itself; I curse the dazzle of the outer world that assails our senses; I curse the dreams we dream, the hypocrisy of them; I curse the illusion that our names can last and make us famous. I curse property in every form, be it wife and child or man and plough. I curse Mammon, whether he incites us to action with promise of rewards or smoothes the pillow for us in our lazy moments. I curse the winecup and its comforts. I curse love and its heights. I curse hope. I curse faith. And, most of all, patience I curse.

SPIRIT CHORUS *invisible*
    Alas, alas for the lovely world destroyed. A demi-god has shattered it with a mighty blow. See, it is falling, crumbling. We carry the remnants over into limbo and lament the beauty lost. Man in your strength build it again. Build it better. Build it in your heart. Begin a new life with clear mind and let new songs be sung.

MEPHISTOPHELES
These are my lesser minions. Note how shrewdly they urge you to be active and cheerful. They want to draw you out of your stagnant solitude into the wide world.

    Stop playing with this misery that gnaws at your life like a vulture. Any company, the meanest, will make you feel that you're a man among men. Not that I propose to thrust you among riff-raff. I'm not one of the great, but if you care to join forces with me for life, I shall be happy to oblige you on the spot. I'll be your companion and, if I suit, I'll be your servant, your slave.

FAUST
And what have I to do in return?

MEPHISTOPHELES
There's plenty of time for that.

FAUST
Not a bit of it. The devil's an egoist and not disposed to help others free

MEPHISTOPHELES

I pledge myself to your service here and will always be at your beck and call. If we meet over there, you can do the same for me.

FAUST

Over there is no concern of mine. If you can shatter this world to pieces, let the other come. My joys and sorrows belong to this earth and this sunlight. When I part with them, the rest can follow, whatever it is. There may be top and bottom in that other place; people there may go on loving and hating. I simply don't care.

MEPHISTOPHELES

I see no difficulty in that. Come, agree. My tricks will delight you. I'll show you things no one has ever seen before.

FAUST

You poor devil, what can you have to show me? Did the likes of you ever comprehend the mind of man and all its great endeavour. But come on. Perhaps you have food that never fills you; red gold that trickles through your fingers like quicksilver; a game at which you can't win; a girl who while lying in the arms of one lover with the wink of an eye picks up someone else; honours that lift you to the seventh heaven and then go out like shooting stars. Come along with your fruit that rots in the hand when you try to pick it, and your trees that grow new leaves and shed them every day.

MEPHISTOPHELES

There's nothing there that I don't feel equal to. Entertainments like those are just in my line. But, my friend, the day will come when we shall want to relax and savour a good thing quietly.

FAUST

If ever I lie down in idleness and contentment, let that be the end of me, let that be final. If you can delude me into feeling pleased with myself, if your good things ever get the better of me, then may that day be my last day. This is my wager.

MEPHISTOPHELES

Agreed.

FAUST

And shake again. If ever the passing moment is such that I wish it not to pass and I say to it 'You are beautiful, stay a while,' then let that be the finish. The clock can stop. You can put me in chains and ring the death-bell. I shall welcome it and you will be quit of your service.

MEPHISTOPHELES

Consider what you're saying. We shan't forget.

FAUST

Quite right. I haven't committed myself wildly. If I come to a stop, if I stagnate, I'm a slave. Whether yours or another's, what does it matter?

MEPHISTOPHELES

There's the doctoral dinner this very day. I shall be there as your servant. But, to meet all emergencies, could I have a word in writing?

FAUST

So you want it in writing, do you, you pedant? Don't you know the worth of a man, the worth of a man's word? Isn't it enough that my given word is   *page 25* to rule my life for the rest of my days? I know that, when you see the world raging along like so many torrents, you may well ask why a mere promise should bind me. But this is the way we are. We cherish the illusion and cling to it, it keeps us clear, and clean-spirited, and responsible. But a parchment all filled out and stamped is a spectre that everyone dreads. The written word dies, leather and sealing-wax take over. What do you want, you devil? Bronze, marble, parchment, paper? Shall I write with a style or a chisel or a pen? Take your choice.

MEPHISTOPHELES

Why do you get so heated and exaggerate so when you start speechifying? Any scrap of paper will do. Only you must sign with a drop of blood.

FAUST

If this really satisfies you, we'll go through with the tomfoolery.

MEPHISTOPHELES

Blood. Blood is special.

FAUST

Don't be afraid of me breaking the contract. My full effort and energy is what I promise. I aimed too high. I'm only fit to be in your class. The great Earth-spirit has rejected me. Nature is closed to me. I can't think. I'm sick of learning, have been for ages. Let us spend our passions, hot in sensual deeps. Let us have miracles galore, all the miracles, round us in magic veils. Let us plunge into the rush of time, the race of events, hit or miss, pain or pleasure, just as it comes, always on the move, always doing something. It's the only way.

MEPHISTOPHELES

We don't make any restrictions. If you like to flit about, here a nibble, there a nibble, or just sample things on the high run, well and good. I hope you'll like it. Only help yourself and don't be bashful.

FAUST

Am I not telling you that it's not a question of enjoyment? A whirl of dissipation is what I seek, this and nothing else, pleasures that hurt, torments that enliven, hate that is instinct with love. Having got the desire for knowledge out of my system, I mean to expose myself to all the pain and suffering in the world. Nay more. All that is given to humanity, total humanity, to experience I desire to experience in my own person, the heights and the depths of it, the weal and the woe, to enlarge myself in this way to humanity's size, and to smash up with the rest of humanity in the end.

MEPHISTOPHELES

Mark my words. I've been chewing at this old leaven for thousands of years. In the short space of a lifetime no man will ever digest it. This totality, this whole, is God's affair and no one else's. I can assure you of that. You see, he dwells in eternal light, us devils he thrusts into darkness, and all you are fit for is day and night, half and half.

FAUST

But my mind is made up.

MEPHISTOPHELES

Good enough. There's only one thing I'm afraid of. Time is short and art is long. Take my advice. Engage a poet. Let him turn on his imagination and

load you with all the virtues and distinctions – the courage of the lion, the
speed of the stag, the hot blood of Italy, the endurance of the North. Let him
solve the problem of combining generosity with cunning, and plan a young
man's impulsive love-affair for you. I'd like to know the gentleman. I'd call
him Mr Microcosm.

FAUST

What am I then, if it isn't possible to reach the peak of humanity, as I so
vehemently desire?

MEPHISTOPHELES

You are what you are. Put on as many wigs as you like, and boots a yard
high, you'll never be bigger than you are.

FAUST

So it was all to no purpose – I feel it now – that I took on me the whole
treasury of the human mind. No new strength has been awakened in me.
I'm no larger than I was, no nearer to the infinite.

MEPHISTOPHELES

My dear sir, you're looking at things in a conventional way. We must do
better than that, or the joys of life will escape us. Hang it. You have your
hands and feet, you have a headpiece and a codpiece. And anything else you
can enjoy is yours, isn't it? If I can afford a coach and six, isn't their energy
mine? I can ride around as proudly as if I had twenty-four legs. So come,
no more ruminating. Let us set off together. I tell you, when you talk this
theoretical stuff, you put me in mind of a donkey on a barren heath, led
round and round by an evil spirit, while all the time there's nice green grass
near by.

FAUST

How do we begin?

MEPHISTOPHELES

We just get out of here. Out of this torture chamber. What sort of a life is
this, boring yourself and these young men? Leave that to your portly neighbour. Why go on threshing straw? After all, you daren't tell them the best of
what you know. I can hear one of them outside on the landing.

FAUST

I can't possibly see him.

MEPHISTOPHELES

The poor boy's been waiting a long time. He deserves a friendly word. Lend
me your cap and gown. I shall look well in them.
He puts them on Now leave it to me. I only need a quarter of an hour.
Meanwhile make yourself ready for our tour.

Faust off

MEPHISTOPHELES *in Faust's gown*

Keep it up. Go on despising reason and learning, man's greatest asset. Let
me entangle you in my deceits and magic shows and I'll get you for sure.
This man was born with a spirit that drives him on incessantly and will not
be curbed. All at such a pace that he overleaps the common pleasures. I'll
drag him through a round of riotous living, where everything is shallow and
meaningless, till I have him at my mercy like a fly on a fly-paper. I'll dangle

food and drink before his greedy mouth. He'll beg in vain for refreshment. He'd be sure to go under anyway, even if he hadn't given himself to the devil.

A student enters

STUDENT
Excuse me, sir, I'm a newcomer, wishing to introduce himself to a man respected and revered by everyone.

MEPHISTOPHELES
I appreciate your courtesy. As you see, I'm a man no different from others. Have you called on anyone else?

STUDENT
Please be kind to me, advise me. I'm young and eager. I have a little money, enough. Mother would hardly let me leave home. I want to study something worthwhile, now I've come so far.

MEPHISTOPHELES
Well, you're in the right place.

STUDENT
Honestly, I feel like pulling out again. I'm not happy in these big buildings, these walls. It's so shut in. You don't see a tree, not a blade of grass. And sitting in the lecture room my head goes round, I nearly pass out.

MEPHISTOPHELES
It's all a matter of habit. A child doesn't immediately take to the breast, but before long it feeds lustily. At the breasts of wisdom you'll find your appetite growing every day.

STUDENT
I'll cling to her neck with delight. But how do I get there?

MEPHISTOPHELES
First you must tell me what faculty you choose.

STUDENT
I want to be a really learned man. I want to master nature and science and earth and heaven, all of it.

MEPHISTOPHELES
You're on the right track there, but you'll have to apply yourself.

STUDENT
I'm heart and soul in it, but I'd like a little relaxation on summer holidays.

MEPHISTOPHELES
Time flies so fast you mustn't waste it. But with a little method you can save time. And therefore, my friend, I advise you to begin with a course in logic. There they'll put you through your paces, lace your mind up tight in a pair of murderous jackboots and set it crawling ponderously along the straight road, not flitting about all over the place like a will-o'-the-wisp. And they'll tell you and tell you again that things you used to do in one, like eating and drinking, have to be done now in a one-two-three. Our thinking apparatus, you know, works like a weaver's loom, where a single tread starts a thousand connections, the shuttles go back and forth and the threads flow invisibly. And then a philosopher comes and proves that it had to be so. The first statement was thus and so, and the second was thus and so, and that's

why the third and the fourth are thus and so. If the first and the second weren't there, there'd never be a third and fourth at all. This impresses his hearers, but it doesn't make weavers of them. If they want to discuss a living thing they begin by driving out the spirit, and this leaves them with the parts in their hands, lifeless and disconnected. The chemists call it manipulating nature, but they're fooling themselves.

STUDENT

I don't quite follow you.

MEPHISTOPHELES

You'll soon find it easier, once you learn to simplify and classify.

STUDENT

It all makes me feel as stupid as if I had a mill-wheel going round in my head.

MEPHISTOPHELES

Next, and above everything else, you must have a go at metaphysics and make sure you profoundly comprehend the things that don't fit into the human brain. Whether a thing fits or doesn't fit, there's always an excellent word for it. Attend regularly, for your first term, five lectures every day, be there on the dot, do your homework and your preparation carefully so as to be sure afterwards that the professor said nothing that wasn't in the book. But mind you write everything down, as if it was the Holy Ghost himself dictating to you.

STUDENT

You don't need to tell me twice. I know the value of that. If you get a thing down in black and white you can take it home with you and not worry.

MEPHISTOPHELES

But what about a faculty?

STUDENT

Well, I know I don't want to study law.

MEPHISTOPHELES

I'm with you there. I know what that stuff's worth. Laws and statutes, inherited like a disease, dragging on endlessly from generation to generation and from place to place, sense turning into nonsense, benefaction into bane and boredom. A pity you have to be someone's grandson. About the rights and privileges you're born with they never have a word to say.

STUDENT

You make me hate the stuff more than ever. How lucky I am to get your advice. Now theology attracts me.

MEPHISTOPHELES

I don't want to lead you astray. But this is a subject where it's not easy to keep on the right track. There's so much poison concealed in it and you can hardly tell the poison from the cure. The best way here again is to keep to one man and take his word. Swear by what he says. But stick to words anyway. Then you'll find your questions answered and your doubts removed. You'll join the church of the know-it-alls.

STUDENT

But a word has to mean something. It must have a concept behind it.

MEPHISTOPHELES

I grant you that. But you mustn't be fussy about it. Because when you run out of concepts a word can come in very handy. You can argue with words, believe in words, you can do nearly anything with words, make them into a whole system, and you can't rob them of an iota.

STUDENT

I'm afraid I'm taking up a lot of your time. But there's one thing more. Could you give me a lead on medicine? Three years is so short a time and the field is so vast. A hint or two is a great help.

MEPHISTOPHELES *aside*

I'm sick of this sobriety. I'll have to play the devil again.

Aloud

Medicine is easy to grasp. When you've finished studying the universe, you'll find you just have to let it go its own sweet way as before. Your science won't help you much. You learn what you can. But see that you make the most of your opportunities. That's the thing. You're well set up, you're not backward. If you trust yourself, others will trust you. Above all else learn to manage women. There's one treatment that will cure all their manifold troubles. And if you make some show of honesty, you'll have them where you want them. It's useful to be an M.D., it wins their confidence and makes them think you're an expert. You'll be able to feel around for little things right away that others have to wait years to lay their hands on. You'll know how to give her the right look, ardent but cunning, and squeeze her pulse and take her round the hips to see how tightly she's laced.

STUDENT

This sounds better. At least you know what you're at.

MEPHISTOPHELES

My friend, all theory is gray, the tree of life is golden-green.

STUDENT

I assure you, it's all like a dream. Might I trouble you again some day and hear more of your wisdom?

MEPHISTOPHELES

I'll gladly do what I can.

STUDENT

I can't leave without asking you to sign my autograph book. Please.

MEPHISTOPHELES

Very good. *He signs and returns the book*

STUDENT *reads*

'Eritis sicut Deus, scientes bonum et malum.' *He closes the book reverently and leaves*

MEPHISTOPHELES

Just follow my motto and my old crony, the serpent, and you'll land yourself in trouble sooner or later, whether you're made in God's image or not.

Faust enters

FAUST

Where do we go now?

MEPHISTOPHELES

Wherever you like. We'll see the little world and then the great. Just think, you're going to get the whole course without paying a penny. It'll be fun and profitable too.

FAUST

But how am I to lead a gay life with this long beard? It'll all be a failure.

I've never been at home in the world. In company I feel so small. I shall always be ill at ease.

MEPHISTOPHELES

My friend, you'll get over that. Just have more confidence in yourself and you'll be all right.

FAUST

How do we start? I don't see your carriage and horses anywhere.

MEPHISTOPHELES

We'll spread my cloak, it'll carry us through the air. But you mustn't bring a heavy pack on this bold venture. A little hydrogen, supplied by me, will send us up. Quickly and easily if we travel light. Congratulations on your new career.

scene 5 AUERBACH'S TAVERN IN LEIPZIG

A merry company, drinking

FROSCH

What! Nobody drinking? Nobody laughing? And all these long faces? This won't do. You're fire and flame mostly. Today you're like a heap of wet straw.

BRANDER

It's your fault. You're so flat yourself. Can't you give us some fooling, some filth?

FROSCH *pours a glass of wine over his head*

There you have both.

BRANDER

You dirty swine.

FROSCH

Well, you asked for it and you got it.

SIEBEL

Out you go, if you start quarrelling. Come on, let's sing a hearty song, all together. Oho, oho.

ALTMAYER

Ouch. I can't stand it. He's splitting my ears. Hey, cottonwool.

SIEBEL

That's the true bass, when it echoes from the vault.

FROSCH

Right. Out with them that can't take a joke. Oho, oho.

ALTMAYER

Doh. Ray. Me. Fah.

FROSCH

We're all tuned up. *sings*

The Holy Roman Empire. Oh, poor thing. How does it hold together?

BRANDER

That's a miserable song, a nasty song, a political song. Woof. You can think yourselves lucky when you wake up in the morning that you don't have to worry over the Holy Roman Empire. Me, I thank my stars I'm not an emperor or his chancellor. But we need a head man here. Let's elect a pope. You know what a man has to have to be a pope, don't you?

FROSCH *sings*

Dame nightingale, fly. Fly to my sweetheart. Give her my love.

SIEBEL

None of that. You and your sweetheart.

FROSCH

Yes, give her my love, and kisses too. You can't stop me. *He sings*

Unbar the door in the quiet night when my lover is waiting. Bar it again in the morning early.

SIEBEL

Okay. Sing all you want about that girl of yours. I'll have the laugh yet. She made a fool of me. She'll do it to you. I'd give her a goblin for a lover to flirt with at the cross-roads. Let an old billy-goat on his way home from the Brocken bleat at her as he trots past. A decent man of flesh and blood's too good for her. I'd smash her windows in. That's all I have to say to her.

BRANDER *rapping the table*

Listen to me, fellows. You all know I have the savvy. We have lovers sitting here. I ought to treat them to something special, just for them. Part of a good night's fun. Now listen to this. One of the latest songs. Mind you come in on the refrain. *He sings*

There was a rat lived in the cellar, feeding on lard and butter. Gave itself a tidy paunch and looked like Dr Luther. The cook put poison down for it. The poison griped and twisted it, like love-pangs in the belly.

CHORUS *shouting*

Like love-pangs in the belly.

BRANDER

It rushed around, rushed up and down, and drank at every puddle, gnawed the whole house and scratched at it, it didn't help it any. It got the jitters, jumped about, the pain was more than it could stand, like love-pangs in the belly.

CHORUS

Like love-pangs in the belly.

BRANDER

In broad daylight its throes were such it ran into the kitchen, dropped by the stove and twitched and lay, in torture, hardly breathing. The naughty cook just laughed and said: The creature's had its medicine now, like love-pangs in the belly.

CHORUS

Like love-pangs in the belly.

SIEBEL

The fun those louts are having. A real art, I call it, to scatter poison for the poor rats.

BRANDER

You seem to favour them.

ALTMAYER

Look at the fat one with a bald head. He thinks the bloated rat is him exactly. His troubles make him as quiet as a lamb.

MEPHISTOPHELES

What I must do now, first and foremost, is find some good company for you to let you see how smooth and easy life can be. Here they make every day a holiday. They're not brainy, but they like their comforts and each of them dances in his little round like a kitten chasing its tail. They're as happy as larks, provided they don't have a headache and the landlord isn't pressing for cash.

BRANDER

You can see they're travellers. They look so queer. I'll bet they've just arrived.

FROSCH

By golly, you're right. Good for Leipzig. It's a regular little Paris, civilized and civilizing too.

SIEBEL

What do you think they are?

FROSCH

Just leave it to me. Drinks round once and I'll pump them dry like drawing a child's teeth. They must be well-born, they look so proud and dissatisfied.

BRANDER

Quacks, I'll bet they are.

ALTMAYER

Maybe.

FROSCH

Watch me. I'll give 'em the works.

MEPHISTOPHELES *to Faust*

These people never can spot the devil even when he has them by the collar.

FAUST

Good day, gentlemen.

SIEBEL

Good day to you.
Sotto voce, looking sideways at Mephistopheles
What is it makes him lame in one foot?

MEPHISTOPHELES

May we join you? The company will be good, though we can't expect the same of the drink.

ALTMAYER

You must be very hard to please.

FROSCH

I suppose you were late leaving Rippach. Did you have supper with Jack Ass?

MEPHISTOPHELES

We didn't stop this time. But we had a word with him last time. He had a lot to say about his cousins and sends you his best. *He bows to Frosch*

ALTMAYER *sotto voce*

There you see. He's no fool.

SIEBEL

A sly dog.

FROSCH

Just wait. I'll get him yet.

MEPHISTOPHELES

If I'm not mistaken, we heard you singing excellently in chorus. **Singing must sound well in this vault.**

FROSCH

Are you by any chance a pro?

MEPHISTOPHELES

No, I haven't the voice, but I have the liking.

ALTMAYER

Will you sing us a song?

MEPHISTOPHELES

As many as you wish.

SIEBEL

But no old stuff. Something new.

MEPHISTOPHELES

We're just back from Spain, the land of wine and song. *He sings*
    There once was a king and he had a great big flea.

FROSCH

Jesus, do you hear that? A flea. Do you get it? A flea. I'll say that's something.

MEPHISTOPHELES *sings*
    There once was a king and he had a great big flea.
    It might have been his very son, he doted on it so.
    And he sent for his tailor and gave him his orders:
    Measure this junker and dress him in full.

BRANDER

Yes, and you tell the tailor to watch his step, if he values his head, and not give him crinkles in his pants.

MEPHISTOPHELES
    So now there he was, arrayed in silks and satins.
    Ribbons on his coat and a cross on it too.
    He was made a royal minister and wore a great star.
    And his brothers and his sisters, they were big folk at court.
    And all the lords and ladies were eaten alive,
    the queen and her lady's maid bitten up and chewed.
    They didn't dare nip them, they didn't dare touch them.
    Let them come biting us, and we nip them and we squash them,
    we squash them as we please.

CHORUS *with a shout*
    Let them come biting us, and we nip them and we squash them,
    we squash them as we please.

FROSCH

Bravo. That was swell.

SIEBEL

May all the fleas be squashed.

BRANDER

Like this. Finger and thumb. And then quick.

ALTMAYER
Here's to freedom. Here's to wine.

MEPHISTOPHELES
I'd be happy to drink to freedom, if only your wines were a little better.

SIEBEL
Don't say that to me again.

MEPHISTOPHELES
I'm afraid the landlord will object. But if not, I'd like to give you gentlemen something out of our own cellar.

SIEBEL
Go right ahead. I'll vouch for it.

FROSCH
If you have something good, we'll give you credit for it. But don't let it be a mere sip. If I'm to judge, I need a real mouthful.

ALTMAYER *sotto voce*
Looks like they're from the Rhine.

MEPHISTOPHELES
Let me have a gimlet.

BRANDER
What do you want a gimlet for? You don't mean to say you've brought the barrels with you?

ALTMAYER
There's a basket of tools behind there.

MEPHISTOPHELES *taking the gimlet. To Frosch*
Now tell me what you'd like.

FROSCH
How come? Are you offering us a choice?

MEPHISTOPHELES
You can have whatever you wish.

ALTMAYER *to Frosch*
Ha. Ha. You're licking your lips already.

FROSCH
Good. If I can choose, I'll have a Rhine wine. I'll stick to the fatherland every time.

MEPHISTOPHELES *boring a hole in the table where Frosch is sitting*
Give me some wax to cork with quickly.

ALTMAYER
It's just a conjuring trick.

MEPHISTOPHELES *to Brander*
Now it's your turn.

BRANDER
I want champagne, and sparkling.

*Mephistopheles bores, one of them has made the corks
and is sticking them in*

BRANDER
You can't find all you want at home. Often a good thing comes from abroad.   *page 35*

If you're a true German you can't stand the French, but you like to drink their wines all the same.

SIEBEL *as Mephistopheles approaches him*
I must confess I don't care about your dry wines. Give me a real sweet one.

MEPHISTOPHELES *boring*
I'll give you Tokay.

ALTMAYER
Look here, good sirs, you're fooling us.

MEPHISTOPHELES
Come now. That would be a bit risky with gentlemen like you. Quick. Tell me. What wine shall I give you?

ALTMAYER
Any you like. Don't ask me.

After the holes are all bored and corked

MEPHISTOPHELES *with strange gestures*
The goat grows horns, the vine grows grapes. The grapes are juicy, the vine is woody. The wood table can yield wine too. A natural miracle, believe it you.

ALL *drawing the corks. The wine chosen fills the cups*
Oh, what a well-spring, all for us.

MEPHISTOPHELES
Take care not to spill any of it.

They drink repeatedly

ALL *singing*
We're happy as cannibals, happy as swine, hundreds of swine.

MEPHISTOPHELES
See how free these people are, see what a good time they have.

FAUST
I wish we could pull out now.

MEPHISTOPHELES
Wait a minute. You'll see their swinishness come to a head beautifully.

SIEBEL *drinking carelessly, spills some wine on the floor and it bursts into flame*
Help. Fire. Help. All hell's blazing.

MEPHISTOPHELES *exorcising the flame*
Gently my elemental friend.
To Siebel
This was only a touch of purgatorial fire.

SIEBEL
What's all this? Just wait. I'll make you pay for this. You don't seem to know who you're dealing with.

FROSCH
No more of this. I tell you once is enough.

ALTMAYER
We'd better get rid of these chaps quietly.

SIEBEL
Mister, do you think you can play your monkey-tricks here?
MEPHISTOPHELES
Be quiet, you old tub. ·
SIEBEL
Broomstick, yourself. Are you going to insult us now?
BRANDER
Let's beat them up.
ALTMAYER *draws a cork out of the table and flames come out*
I'm on fire. I'm on fire.
It's witchcraft. At him. He's fair game.

They draw their knives and close in on Mephistopheles

MEPHISTOPHELES *solemnly*
False words, false forms, new meanings, new places. Be here and there.

They stand in astonishment and stare at one another

ALTMAYER
Where am I? What a lovely land.
FROSCH
Vineyards, can it be?
SIEBEL
And grapes under my nose.
BRANDER
Here in this green arbour, what vines, what grapes.

He seizes Siebel by the nose. The others do likewise and raise their knives

MEPHISTOPHELES *as above*
Illusion, free their eyes. Mark how the devil plays his pranks.

He disappears with Faust, the men spring apart

SIEBEL
What's happened?
ALTMAYER
What?
FROSCH
Was that your nose?
BRANDER *to Siebel*
And I'm still holding yours.
ALTMAYER
There was a shock went right through me. Bring me a chair. I'm all in.
FROSCH
Tell me, whatever was it?
SIEBEL
Where's that fellow? If I get hold of him I'll finish him.

ALTMAYER
I saw him sailing out of the cellar-hatch astride of a tub. I've such a drag in my legs. (*turning to the table*) My. Do you think that wine's still running?
SIEBEL
It was all a trick, an illusion.
FROSCH
I really thought I was drinking wine.
BRANDER
And what was that with the grapes?
ALTMAYER
And they say there's no such thing as miracles.

scene 6 WITCH'S KITCHEN

A low hearth with a cauldron on the fire. Various figures are seen in the steam rising from it. A she-ape sits by the cauldron, skimming it and seeing that it doesn't boil over. Her mate is sitting beside her with the little ones. Walls and ceiling are covered with the strangest appurtenances of a witch's household. Faust. Mephistopheles

FAUST
This insane witchcraft disgusts me, I find it revolting. Are you telling me that I shall get rejuvenated in this idiotic collection of junk? Am I to take an old hag's remedy? Is this foul brew going to lift thirty years off my back? It's a poor look-out for me if you can't think of something better. It's hopeless, I give up. But isn't there a natural way. Isn't there some healing balm that man has discovered?
MEPHISTOPHELES
Now you're talking sense. There is a natural way. But that's another story, and a curious one.
FAUST
I want to know.
MEPHISTOPHELES
Well, I'll tell you a way. It'll cost you nothing, no witches, no doctors. Go right off into the country and start digging and hoeing. Keep yourself, and keep your thoughts, strictly confined in a small circle. Eat the simplest food. Live with your cattle as cattle. Don't be above manuring the field you plough with your own dung. If you want to stay young till you're eighty, believe me, this is the best way to do it.
FAUST
I'm not used to that sort of thing. I can't come down to handling a spade. And that narrow existence doesn't suit me.
MEPHISTOPHELES
Then it has to be the witch.
FAUST
Why her? Can't you concoct the potion yourself?
MEPHISTOPHELES
A nice waste of time that would be. I could be doing a host of things, I could

build a thousand bridges, meanwhile. This is a job that calls for patience
as well as science. A strange and complicated process. The draught takes
years before it's potent. The devil taught her how to make it, but the devil
can't make it himself.

Seeing the apes

Look, what dainty creatures. This is the girl and this is the boy. (*to the
apes*) Your mistress seems to be away.

THE APES

Left by the chimney, to feast with company.

MEPHISTOPHELES

How long is she usually out on the spree?

THE APES

Just as long as we sit here warming our paws.

MEPHISTOPHELES *to Faust*

How do you find them?

FAUST

As gross as anything I ever saw.

MEPHISTOPHELES

Now for me, a chat like this is just what I enjoy. (*to the apes*) Tell me, you
monkeys, what are you stirring the pot for?

THE APES

We're making thin soup for beggars.

MEPHISTOPHELES

Then you have a large public.

THE APE *comes towards Mephistopheles obsequiously*

    Quick, throw the dice, and let me win, and make me rich. I'm badly off.
    If I had cash, I'd have sense too.

MEPHISTOPHELES

How happy the ape would be, if he could buy lottery tickets.

In the meantime
the young apes have been playing with a big ball
which they roll forward

THE APE

    This is the world. It rises and falls, and never stops rolling. It rings like
    glass, so easy to break. It's hollow inside. It's shiny here. And shinier
    there. I'm quick on my pins. Take care, my son, and keep away. You might
    get killed. The thing's of clay. The clay can break.

MEPHISTOPHELES

What's the sieve for?

THE APE *lifting it down*

If you were a thief, I'd spot you at once.

He runs to the she-ape and lets her look through it

Look through the sieve. Do you recognise him and daren't name him?

MEPHISTOPHELES *moving towards the fire*

And what's the pot for?

THE TWO APES

    The silly sot. Doesn't know the pot. Doesn't know the kettle.

MEPHISTOPHELES
Don't be so rude.

THE APE
Here, take the whisk and sit you down. *seats Mephistopheles in the armchair*
FAUST *who has been standing in front of a mirror, going close to it and then stepping back*
What can this be? A magic mirror? And what a marvel of a woman. O Love, lend me your swiftest wings and take me where she is. Oh, I can't get close to her. If I try, she fades away. How beautiful she is, how unbelievably beautiful, reclining there. The quintessence of all that is heavenly. To think the earth has this to show.

MEPHISTOPHELES
Naturally, if God works his head off for six whole days and then claps his hands at the finish, there must be something mighty good there. Go on gazing at her as long as you wish. I can find you a sweetheart like that. The man that gets her for keeps can count himself lucky.
Faust goes on staring at the mirror. Mephistopheles stretches out in the armchair and plays with the whisk
Sitting here, I feel like a king on his throne. I have the sceptre in my hand. All I need is a crown.

THE APES *after executing all sorts of intricate dance-movements, they bring a crown to Mephistopheles with shouts*
Oh, be so good and glue the crown, with blood and sweat.
Clumsily they break the crown into two pieces and jump about with them
Now we've done it. We talk and watch, and listen and rhyme.

FAUST *looking into the mirror*
I'm beside myself.

MEPHISTOPHELES *pointing to the apes*
My head's beginning to go round too.

THE APES
And if we're lucky, and if it sorts, our rhymes are thoughts.

FAUST *as above*
I'm going out of my mind. Let's get out of here.

MEPHISTOPHELES *still in the armchair*
At least you must admit these poets are honest.

The cauldron, which the she-ape has been neglecting, begins to boil over. This produces a big flame which reaches up the chimney. The witch comes riding down through the flame with a great shriek

THE WITCH
Ouch, ouch, you ape, you swine, curses on you, forgetting the pot and singeing me.
Catching sight of Faust and Mephistopheles
What's this? Who are you? What do you want? Hell-fire take you.

She dips the spoon in the cauldron and throws flame on Faust, Mephistopheles, and the apes. The apes whine

Smash, smash. Broken glass. A pretty mess. It's all a joke. Just beating time, to your stinking tune.

The witch starts back in a rage

Don't you know me, you bag of bones? Don't you know your lord and master? I could just light into you and your monkeys and make mincemeat of you all. Have you no respect for my red doublet? Can't you see my cock's feather? Did I try to hide? Must I tell you who I am?

THE WITCH

O sir, forgive my rudeness. But you're not letting anyone see your hoofed foot. And where are your two ravens?

MEPHISTOPHELES

I'll let you off this time. I know we haven't seen one another lately. And culture has put its finger on the devil as on everyone else. You won't see the northern spectre any more. No more horns and tail and claws. As for this horse's hoof of mine, it would tell against me. That's why for years I've padded my calves. Lots of young men do it.

THE WITCH

Fancy Satan, my lord Satan, come to see me again. It makes me all dithery.

MEPHISTOPHELES

Woman, don't call me by that name.

THE WITCH

Why not? What's the matter with it?

MEPHISTOPHELES

Relegated to the book of fable long ago. But it hasn't helped mankind in the least. They've got rid of the evil one, but the many evil ones are still with us. Just call me Baron and it'll be all right. I'm a man of the world, like others. If you doubt my noble birth, here's my escutcheon. *He makes an indecent gesture*

THE WITCH *laughing immoderately*

Ha, ha. That's just like you. You were always a rogue, you rogue you.

MEPHISTOPHELES *to Faust*

Take note of this, partner. This is the way to handle witches.

THE WITCH

Well, gentlemen, what will you have?

MEPHISTOPHELES

A good-sized glass of you know what. But let it be your oldest. The older it is, the better.

THE WITCH

Gladly. There's a bottle of it here that I sometimes take a nip of myself. It's turned quite mellow. I'm pleased to oblige.

Quietly But if your companion drinks it unprepared, it might be the death of him, as you know.

MEPHISTOPHELES

He's a good friend of mine. I want him to get the benefit. Make it the best you have. Draw your circle, do your incantations, and then give him a glassful.

scene 6   *The witch with strange gestures draws a circle and puts fantastic things inside it. The glasses begin to hum and the cauldron rings, making music. Finally she fetches a big book and brings the apes into the circle, using them as a desk. They also hold the torches. She beckons to Faust to join her*

FAUST *to Mephistopheles*
This is going too far. These silly contraptions, these lunatic gestures, this crassness, this falsity. I've seen it all and I despise it.
MEPHISTOPHELES
Come, come. Take it lightly. Don't be so critical. She has to perform some hocus-pocus, if the stuff is to work. *He pushes Faust inside the circle*
THE WITCH *declaiming from the book with great emphasis*
Know this, know this. Make one a ten. And let two go. Make an even three. Your fortune is made. Then lose your four. Turn five and six into seven and eight. So says the witch. That's all there is. And nine is one and ten is nothing. This is the witch's two-times-two.
FAUST
The old woman seems to be off her head.
MEPHISTOPHELES
There's plenty more to come. The whole book's like this. I know it well. Lost a lot of time over it. You see, a complete contradiction is a mystery to wise and foolish alike. It's an old trick, spreading lies with three-in-one and one-in-three. You're safe with that, and can talk and teach undisturbed. Who wants to argue with fools? Usually people think when they hear words there must be some meaning in them.
THE WITCH *continuing*
The power of science, hidden from the world. If you don't think, you get it given, no trouble at all.
FAUST
What rubbish is she talking now? I can't endure it any longer, it's like a pack of fools, talking all at once.
MEPHISTOPHELES
Enough, enough, most excellent sibyl. Come, give us your potion and brim the cup. It won't hurt this fellow. He's a man of many promotions. He's had good drinks before.
THE WITCH *with much ceremony pours the potion into a cup*
When Faust puts it to his lips, there is a slight flame
MEPHISTOPHELES
Down with it. You'll be glad of it. A man that's pals with the devil doesn't need to fear a little fire.

The witch breaks the circle and Faust steps out

MEPHISTOPHELES
Come on out with me now. You mustn't rest.
THE WITCH
I hope it'll agree with you, sir.
MEPHISTOPHELES *to the witch*

If I can do you any little service, remind me at the Walpurgis.

Here's a song. If you sing it now and then, it'll help.
MEPHISTOPHELES *to Faust*
Come away with me now. You have to perspire freely, so that the drink works both ways, inwards and outwards. I'll show you then how a gentleman can enjoy his leisure. We'll set Cupid hopping about and you'll soon be delighted.
FAUST
Just let me have another look in the mirror. That woman was so very lovely.
MEPHISTOPHELES
No, no. You'll soon have the fairest of the fair right in front of you. (*aside*) Any woman will be a Helen to him with this drink under his belt.

scene 7 STREET

Faust. Gretchen passing by

FAUST
May I? May I walk with you, O fairest lady?
GRETCHEN
I'm not a lady, I'm not fair. I can go home by myself. *She disengages herself and goes off*
FAUST
By God, there's a beauty for you. I never set eyes on the likes. Such a good girl, so pure, but she knows how to cut you too. Those bright red lips and shining cheeks, as long as I live I'll never forget them. The way she dropped her eyes would break a man's heart. And that quick temper, well, that was priceless.

Enter Mephistopheles

FAUST
Listen here. You must get me that girl.
MEPHISTOPHELES
Which girl?
FAUST
She just went past.
MEPHISTOPHELES
What? Her? She's just been to confession. The priest couldn't find a thing. I slipped close by and overheard them. An innocent creature, no need to confess at all. I can't do anything with her.
FAUST
She's over fourteen, isn't she?
MEPHISTOPHELES
You talk like a regular John Thomas, flattering yourself that any favour, any flower you fancy is yours to pluck. But it can't be done, not always.
FAUST
Stop your preaching, Mr Sermonizer. I tell you this. If that sweet young   *page 43*

thing doesn't sleep in my arms tonight, we part company. I'll give you till the stroke of twelve.

MEPHISTOPHELES
Please be reasonable. I need at least a couple of weeks just to reconnoitre.

FAUST
Let me have a couple of hours and I could seduce one like her and not need the devil to help me.

MEPHISTOPHELES
You talk just like a Frenchman. But don't take it hard. What's the good of having your pleasure point-blank? The fun isn't nearly as great as when you've worked on her in all sorts of ways and got her going. You can read about it in those Italian tales.

FAUST
I don't need them to get me going.

MEPHISTOPHELES
Now, to put it bluntly, this pretty girl of yours isn't to be had in a hurry. You can't take her by storm. We have to use our wits.

FAUST
Get me something of hers. Take me to her bedroom. Get me a scarf she wears or, closer to my desire, get me one of her garters.

MEPHISTOPHELES
To let you see that I'll do what I can, we'll not lose a minute. I'll take you to her bedroom this very day.

FAUST
Shall I see her? Shall I have her?

MEPHISTOPHELES
No, she'll be at a neighbour's. But you'll be able to feast your senses there and think of the delights that await you.

FAUST
Can we go at once?

MEPHISTOPHELES
It's too early yet.

FAUST
Find some present for me to give her. *off*

MEPHISTOPHELES
Presents? Already? That'll do the trick. I know some good spots with hidden treasure in them. I'll have to scout around a bit.

scene 8

Evening. A tidy, little room

GRETCHEN *plaiting and binding up her hair*
I'd give something to know who the gentleman was today. He certainly seemed all right, and he must be well-born. You could tell that from the look of him. And he wouldn't have acted so free, if he wasn't. *off*

MEPHISTOPHELES
Come in, come in, quietly now.
FAUST *after an interval*
Please leave me here by myself.
MEPHISTOPHELES *poking around*
Not all the girls are as clean and tidy as this one. *off*
FAUST *looking round*
Welcome, sweet twilight, flooding this holy place. Now let the pangs of love that live and languish on the dew of hope lay hold of me. Here where everything breathes quietude, order, contentment. So rich is this poverty, so blissful this confinement.
He sits down in the leather armchair by the bed
Let me sit here where so many have sat in joy or in sorrow in days gone by, where children time and time again have gathered round their old grandfather. Perhaps my sweetheart, yet a child, once kissed his aged hand in piety and in gratitude for her Christmas gift. O girl, I feel your spirit of order and of comfort whispering in the air about me, the spirit that lovingly teaches you day by day to spread the clean cloth and sprinkle the sand on the floor with that dear hand of yours, making this lowly dwelling a heaven indeed. And here.
He lifts a bed-curtain
This makes me tremble with delight. I could linger here for hours. Here is where she has slept her tender sleep, dreaming nature's dreams and slowly growing into the angel she was born to be.

But me? What brings me here? What do I want here? Why am I so oppressed, so moved? Poor Faust, I hardly know you.

Is there some spell at work? I was out to gratify my lust and I find myself lost in a love-dream. Are we a prey to every breeze that blows?

And if she came in this minute, I should pay dearly for my offence. How small I should feel, prostrate at her feet.
MEPHISTOPHELES *entering*
Quick. I see her coming down below.
FAUST
Away. I'll never come here again.
MEPHISTOPHELES
Here's a jewel-box I got somewhere. Stick it in her cupboard. It'll turn her head, you'll see. It's fairly heavy. I put a few things in that were meant for someone else. But, after all, one girl's as good as another, and it's all in the game.
FAUST
I don't know whether I ought.
MEPHISTOPHELES
A silly question. Perhaps you want to keep the box for yourself. Are you a miser by any chance? If you are, waste no more time and save me further trouble. Here I am, scratching my head and rubbing my hands –
He puts the box in the cupboard and closes it   *page* 45

Now quick, we must be off. – Trying to bring the little girl round to where you want her. And you stand there looking as if you were going to give a lecture, with the grey ghosts of physics and metaphysics staring at you. Come on. *off*

GRETCHEN *with a lamp*

It's so close here, so stuffy. *She opens the window*

And yet it's fresh enough outside. I feel so queer. I wish mother was home. I'm all of a tremble. What a foolish, frightened girl I am. *She sings while undressing*

> There was a King in Thule once, he was faithful to the very end. His lover on her death-bed gave him a gold cup.
>
> He prized it above everything, he emptied it at every feast. And when he put it to his lips, the tears always came into his eyes.
>
> When his turn came to die, he went over his possessions and left them all to his heir. But not the gold cup.
>
> He sat at the royal banquet with his retainers round him in the high ancestral hall of his castle by the sea.
>
> Then the old fellow rose, drained the cup for the last time, and threw it into the water.
>
> He saw it fall and fill and sink deep into the sea. His eyes closed. He never drank again.

She opens the cupboard to put her clothes away and sees the box

How did this lovely box get in here? I know I locked the cupboard. It's strange. I wonder what's inside. Perhaps someone left it in pawn with mother. And there's the key on a ribbon. I've a good mind to open it. What's this? I never saw anything like it. Jewels. Jewels that a great lady could wear on special holidays. I wonder how I should look in the necklace. Who can all these splendours belong to?

She puts it on and stands before the mirror

I wish the earrings were mine. You look so different with them at once. Ah poor me, a pretty face doesn't help. It's all very well, but no one heeds. Or they praise me and pity me. It's money they're after, money does everything. And we're just the poor.

scene 9 ON A WALK

Faust in thought pacing up and down. Mephistopheles joins him

MEPHISTOPHELES

By unrequited love. By all the fires of hell. I wish there was something worse that I could swear by.

FAUST

What's got you? What's eating you? I never saw such a face in all my life.

MEPHISTOPHELES

If I wasn't the devil myself, I'd say devil take me.

FAUST

Have you got a tile loose? It's funny to see you behaving like a lunatic.

MEPHISTOPHELES

Just think. The jewels I got for Gretchen, the priest has swiped them. Her mother saw them and got cold feet right away. She has a sensitive nose. She's always sniffling in her prayer-book and knows by the smell whether a thing is sacred or profane. She knew at once there was something wrong with the jewels. Child, she said, unlawful property snares the soul and dries the blood. We'll give them to the Virgin and she'll reward us with manna from heaven. Gretchen pulled a long face and said to herself they needn't have looked her gift-horse so in the mouth, and surely it can't have been a wicked man that gave her it. Her mother sent for the priest and told him what had happened and he liked what he saw. You did right, he said, to resist temptation, it always pays. The church has a good stomach, it has gobbled up whole countries and never overeaten. The church alone, good women, can digest unlawful property.

FAUST

This is the way it goes, they all do it.

MEPHISTOPHELES

Whereupon he pocketed the lot – bracelets, rings, chains like so many trifles, a mere bagatelle, and barely thanked them. Told them they'd get their reward in heaven and left them all uplifted.

FAUST

And Gretchen?

MEPHISTOPHELES

She's restless, doesn't know what to do, doesn't know what she wants. Thinks about the jewels day and night and thinks still more about who gave her them.

FAUST

This distresses me. Get her some more jewels. There wasn't much to the first batch.

MEPHISTOPHELES

Oh yes, sir, all child's play to you.

FAUST

Hurry up and do as I wish. Get hold of her neighbour. Don't be such a pudding-head. And don't forget the new jewels.

MEPHISTOPHELES

Yes, sir, yes. Happy to oblige.

Faust off

These foolish lovers would blow up the whole works – sun, moon, and stars – to please their women.

scene 10 A NEIGHBOUR'S HOUSE

MARTHE *alone*

God forgive that husband of mine. He didn't treat me right. Went off, disappeared, and left me in the lurch. I never gave him any trouble. God knows I was fond of him. (*She weeps*) Perhaps he's dead. Oh dear. If only I had a death certificate.

GRETCHEN
Frau Marthe!

MARTHE
O Gretchen, what is it?

GRETCHEN
My knees are shaking. I've just found another of those boxes in my cupboard, an ebony one, lovely things in it, much better than the first.

MARTHE
Don't let your mother know. She'd take it to the priest again.

GRETCHEN
Oh look. Just look.

MARTHE *adorning her*
You lucky, lucky thing.

GRETCHEN
But I can't be seen in the street with them, nor in church either.

MARTHE
Come to see me whenever you like, and put them on, just for you and me. Walk about in them for an hour or so in front of the mirror. And some day, some holiday, there'll be a chance to let people see you in them, bit by bit. A necklace to begin with, and then an earring. Your mother won't notice and if she does we'll bluff her.

GRETCHEN
Whoever could have brought these jewel-boxes? There's something wrong about it. (*a knock*) Heavens. Can that be mother?

MARTHE *looking through the curtain*
It's a strange man. Come in.

Enter Mephistopheles

MEPHISTOPHELES
Forgive me, ladies, for butting in like this. *to Gretchen, very respectfully*
I'm looking for Frau Marthe Schwerdtlein.

MARTHE
That's me. What is it, sir?

MEPHISTOPHELES *whispering to her*
No more for the present, now I know you. You have a lady visiting you. Forgive me for disturbing you. I'll come back this afternoon.

MARTHE *aloud*
Think of it, lass, he takes you for a lady.

GRETCHEN
The gentleman is very kind. But I'm just a poor girl. The jewels aren't mine.

MEPHISTOPHELES
It isn't only the jewels, it's herself, her eyes so clear. How nice that I don't have to leave immediately.

MARTHE

What brings you here? I'm curious to know.

MEPHISTOPHELES
I wish I had better news. Please don't blame me for it. Your husband's dead.
He sends you his best.

MARTHE
Dead. The good man dead. Oh, I can't bear it.

GRETCHEN
Please don't take it too hard.

MEPHISTOPHELES
Let me tell you the sad story.

GRETCHEN
I don't want ever to love anyone. Losing him would be so cruel.

MEPHISTOPHELES
Joy needs sorrow, sorrow needs joy.

MARTHE
Tell me how he died.

MEPHISTOPHELES
He's buried in Padua, near to St Anthony, sleeping peacefully in consecrated
ground.

MARTHE
Is that all?

MEPHISTOPHELES
I bring a request from him. He wants you to have three hundred masses
sung for him. For the rest, I haven't a penny in my pocket.

MARTHE
What! Not a keepsake? Not a piece of jewellery? Not what every journeyman
carries at the bottom of his wallet as a souvenir. And would sooner go
hungry, sooner beg, than lose it.

MEPHISTOPHELES
Madam, I'm very sorry. He didn't squander his money. He regretted his
weaknesses and he lamented his misfortune.

GRETCHEN
Why must there be so much unhappiness? I'll say plenty of requiems for
him.

MEPHISTOPHELES
You're a nice girl, just right for marrying.

GRETCHEN
It's early for that.

MEPHISTOPHELES
Well, if not a husband, why not a lover meanwhile? What can compare with
having a girl like you in your arms?

GRETCHEN
It isn't the custom in these parts.

MEPHISTOPHELES
Custom or not. It's done.

MARTHE
Tell me.

MEPHISTOPHELES
I was with him when he died. On a foul bed of straw. But he died as a   *page* 49

Christian and knew he deserved worse. Oh how I hate myself, he said, running away like that from my trade and my wife. Dreadful to think of. If only she would forgive me.

MARTHE *weeping*
The dear man. I forgave him long ago.

MEPHISTOPHELES
But, God knows, she was more to blame than me.

MARTHE
It's a lie! What! Lie like that on the brink of the grave!

MEPHISTOPHELES
True, he was wandering in his mind at the last, if I know anything. I never had any fun, he said, what with children and then feeding them all, feeding them in more ways than one. I hardly had a chance to eat in peace myself.

MARTHE
How could he forget how I toiled for him day and night and loved him and was true?

MEPHISTOPHELES
You're wrong there. He didn't forget. Far from it. He said: When we set out from Malta I prayed for my wife and children fervently. Then we ran into luck and captured a Turkish vessel laden with treasure of the Sultan's. Courage had its reward and I got my full share.

MARTHE
Oh dear. Oh dear. Do you think he buried it?

MEPHISTOPHELES
Who knows where in the world it's gone. A pretty lady took up with him, when he was going about in Naples all alone. She was kind to him, so very kind, that he felt it to the end of his days.

MARTHE
The wretch. Robbing his own children. And going on living that wicked life for all his troubles.

MEPHISTOPHELES
Well. He's dead now. That's the other side of the story. If I were you, I'd put in a decent year's mourning and then look about for someone else.

MARTHE
Oh dear. It won't be easy for me to find another as good as my first. He was such fun he was hard to beat. Only he was too restless, always after women, and wine, and gambling.

MEPHISTOPHELES
Come now, that wasn't so bad, provided he was as indulgent with you. On those terms I wouldn't mind taking you on myself.

MARTHE
Oh sir, what a joker you are.

MEPHISTOPHELES *aside*
Now I must get away. She'd take even the devil at his word.
To Gretchen What about your love-affairs?

GRETCHEN
What do you mean?

MEPHISTOPHELES *aside*
You poor little innocent.
Aloud Goodbye.
GRETCHEN
Goodbye.
MARTHE
Tell me quick. Can I get a certificate to say where and when and how my man died and where he's buried? I like things done the right way and I want to see his death printed in the paper.
MEPHISTOPHELES
Yes, my good woman. The truth calls for two witnesses. I have a friend, a gentleman. I'll get him to swear before the notary and I'll bring him to see you.
MARTHE
Oh, please do that.
MEPHISTOPHELES
And will your young friend be here? He's a nice man, travelled a lot, very courteous to ladies.
GRETCHEN
He'd put me to shame.
MEPHISTOPHELES
No king on earth has the right to do that.
MARTHE
Well, we'll expect you both tonight in my garden at the back.

scene 11 STREET

Faust. Mephistopheles

FAUST
What about it? Are things moving? Will it be long?
MEPHISTOPHELES
Bravo. I see you're all primed. Well, Gretchen will soon be yours. You'll see her tonight in Marthe's garden. There's a woman simply cut out for pandering and such.
FAUST
Excellent.
MEPHISTOPHELES
But we have to do something on our part.
FAUST
One good turn deserves another.
MEPHISTOPHELES
We have to testify that her husband's bones are resting in Padua in consecrated ground.
FAUST
That's a bright idea. We'll have to make the trip.

MEPHISTOPHELES

You silly fellow. We don't have to. Just testify out of the blue.

FAUST

If this is best you can do, our scheme's a failure.

MEPHISTOPHELES

That's just like you, you goody-goody. Is it the first time in your life you've borne false witness? Haven't you held forth mightily, impudently, impiously about God and the world and all that moves in the world, and about man, the heart of man and the head? And, when you come down to brass tacks, you have to confess you knew no more than you do about Schwerdtlein's death.

FAUST

You're a liar and a sophist, and you always were.

MEPHISTOPHELES

You're telling me! Aren't you going to turn poor Gretchen's head tomorrow and swear you love her, and feel virtuous about it?

FAUST

Yes, and with all my heart.

MEPHISTOPHELES

Wonderful. And the talk will be all about faithful unto death and desire irresistible. Will that come from the heart too?

FAUST

Stop. It will. When I feel deeply and find no name for the throng of my emotions and ransack the universe for words to express it and I call the fire that consumes me infinite, eternal, is that only a pack of devil's lies?

MEPHISTOPHELES

But I know.

FAUST

Mark this, please, and spare my breath. Have it your own way, if that's the way you want it. But come now. I'm sick of arguing. I have no choice. I give in.

scene 12 GARDEN

Gretchen arm in arm with Faust. Marthe with Mephistopheles. They stroll up and down

GRETCHEN

I can tell you're just being nice to me, sir, because I'm not in your class. When you're on a journey you make the best of things, good-naturedly. I'm sure there's not much a poor girl like me can say to a man that's seen all you have.

FAUST

A look from you, a word from you, is more to me than all the wisdom in the world. *He kisses her hand*

GRETCHEN

Don't put yourself out. How can you kiss it? It's so horrid, so rough. After all the work I've had to do. And mother's so particular. *They pass*

MARTHE

And you, sir, travel a lot, don't you?

MEPHISTOPHELES
In my business I have to. It's not easy. It hurts to leave places you like. And you just have to push on.

MARTHE
It's all very well to travel up and down the world when you're young and equal to it. But you can't keep it up for ever and, when the end comes in sight, who wants to be a bachelor?

MEPHISTOPHELES
I shiver at the thought of what's ahead.

MARTHE
Then, sir, don't wait too long. *They pass*

GRETCHEN
Yes, out of sight, out of mind. You know how to flatter a girl. But you must have lots of friends, much cleverer than me.

FAUST
What you call clever, my dear, is mostly vanity, all on the surface.

GRETCHEN
How do you mean?

FAUST
Oh to think that the innocent never appreciate themselves at their true worth. Modesty, lowliness, the best of nature's gifts ...

GRETCHEN
You may spare a moment to think of me. I shall have plenty of time to think of you.

FAUST
Are you often alone?

GRETCHEN
Yes, there's not much housekeeping, but it has to be done. We have no help. I have to cook and sweep and knit and sew and run errands early and late and mother is so close about everything. Not that she hasn't enough. We could spread ourselves better than many. Father left a nice little bit of money and a cottage and garden outside. But I'm living quietly these days. My brother's a soldier, my little sister's dead. I had a lot of trouble with her, but I loved her so, I'd do it all again and gladly.

FAUST
A lovely child, if she was like you.

GRETCHEN
I looked after her and she was fond of me. She was born after father died. We gave mother up for lost; she was so low and she only got better very, very slowly. So she couldn't think of nursing the little one. I brought her up myself on milk and water. She was my baby. It was in my arms, on my lap, she kicked and smiled and grew.

FAUST
It must have made you very happy.

GRETCHEN
Yes, but it was often hard on me too. Her cradle stood by my bed at night. I was wide awake, if she so much as stirred. I either had to feed her or take her in bed with me and, if she wouldn't be quiet, dance up and down the room with her and be at the washtub early next morning, then do the shop-

ping and the cooking, and so on one day after another. You don't always feel light-hearted, but you like your food and your sleep. *They pass*

MARTHE

It's hard on us poor women. Bachelors are so hard to get.

MEPHISTOPHELES

If women were all like you, it might be easy.

MARTHE

But honest, sir, are you still free? Haven't you lost your heart to anyone?

MEPHISTOPHELES

The proverb says: A place of your own and a good wife are beyond price.

MARTHE

I mean, have you never been tempted?

MEPHISTOPHELES

People have always been polite to me, very polite.

MARTHE

What I mean is did you never feel drawn?

MEPHISTOPHELES

You can't ever take women lightly.

MARTHE

Oh, you don't understand.

MEPHISTOPHELES

Sorry. You're very kind, I do understand that. *They pass*

FAUST

So you knew me again the moment I came into the garden.

GRETCHEN

Didn't you see? I dropped my eyes.

FAUST

And you forgive me for being so free, so bold, when you came out of church?

GRETCHEN

I was taken aback, no one had ever done that to me. No one could say any-thing bad about me. I wondered did I do something vulgar, something not nice. It seemed to come all over him as if he could do business right away. But I confess, something drew me to you. Whatever it was, I was cross with myself for not being crosser with you. But I couldn't help it.

FAUST

Oh, you dear thing.

GRETCHEN

Don't. *She plucks a daisy and pulls at the petals one by one*

FAUST

What's this? A posy?

GRETCHEN

No, it's just play.

FAUST

How do you mean, play?

GRETCHEN

Don't look. You'll laugh at me. *pulls the petals and mutters to herself*

FAUST

What are you saying?

GRETCHEN *inaudibly*
He loves me – loves me not.
FAUST
You angel.
GRETCHEN *continuing*
Loves me – loves me not – loves me – loves me not –
Plucks the last petal, jubilantly
He loves me.
FAUST
Yes, dear. Let the flower's word be final. He loves you. Do you know what it means? He loves you. *He takes her hands*
GRETCHEN
I'm trembling.
FAUST
Don't be afraid. Let my face, let my hands tell you what words can't say. This surrender, this delight must be for ever. Or I despair. No, it must be for ever.

Gretchen presses his hands, frees herself, and runs away. He pauses a moment in thought, then follows her

MARTHE *coming up*
It's getting dark.
MEPHISTOPHELES
Yes, and we have to be going.
MARTHE
I'd ask you to stay longer. But people here aren't nice. You'd think they had nothing to do but watch their neighbours' every move. They gossip about you, whatever you do. And what about the other two?
MEPHISTOPHELES
They ran up the path there.
MARTHE
He seems to like her.
MEPHISTOPHELES
And she him. That's the way of the world.

scene 13 A SUMMER HOUSE

Gretchen runs in, hides behind the door, puts her finger to her lips, and peeps through the crack

GRETCHEN
He's coming.
FAUST *entering*
Oh, you tease. Have I got you now? *kisses her*
GRETCHEN *returning the kiss*
Oh, I love you.

FAUST *stamping his foot*
Who's there?
MEPHISTOPHELES
A friend.
FAUST
A beast.
MEPHISTOPHELES
It's time we were off.
MARTHE
Yes, sir, it's late.
FAUST
May I accompany you?
GRETCHEN
Mother would ... Goodbye.
FAUST
Must we part? Goodbye.
MARTHE
Bye, bye.
GRETCHEN
See you again soon.

Faust and Mephistopheles leave

GRETCHEN
What thoughts a man like that must have. It puts me to shame. I say yes to everything. I'm a poor ignorant girl. I don't know what he sees in me.

scene 14 FOREST CAVERN

FAUST *alone*
You sublime spirit, you gave me all I asked for, gave me everything. It was not for nothing that you showed your face to me, blazing with fire. You gave me nature for my kingdom, nature in its splendour, and gave me the power to feel and enjoy it, not just coldly at a distance, but like a friend who takes me to his heart. You pass the whole range of living things before my eyes and teach me to know my brothers, my kindred, in the quiet woods, in the air and in the water. And when the storm-wind rages and crashes through the forest, bringing down the giant pine that in its fall ruins the neighbouring trees and makes the hillside boom back with hollow noise, then you guide me to the sheltering cave, you reveal me to myself, and the mysteries that reside in me unfold. And, when as now I see the pure and gentle moon go up the sky, the silvery forms and figures of the early world come hovering out of the rock-steeps and the dripping bushes and temper the austere joy of contemplation.

Oh but now I realise that nothing perfect ever comes. Along with this rapture, bringing me closer and closer to the gods, I am given a companion, who with his cold and withering words humiliates me continually and turns your gifts to nothingness with a whisper. Yet I cannot do without him. He fans in me a burning passion for that fair woman's form, making me go blindly from desire to the fulfilment of desire and in the fulfilment making me yearn again for the desire.

Enter Mephistopheles

MEPHISTOPHELES
Haven't you had enough of it yet, carrying on this way? There can't be much fun in it in the long run. It's all right to try a thing once, but then you want a change.

FAUST
I wish you had something more to do than torment me when I'm feeling better.

MEPHISTOPHELES
Well, I'll let you alone. Only you mustn't say these things to me. I don't get much out of having you for a companion. You're so harsh, so crazy, I have my hands full from morning to night. Impossible to guess what you want and what you don't want.

FAUST
That's the right note to strike. You'd like me to thank you for boring me.

MEPHISTOPHELES
How would you, you poor mortal, ever have managed your life without me? Haven't I cured you finally of your fantastic muddled way of thinking? If it wasn't for me, you'd have shuffled off this mortal coil already. Why do you want to go hiding in cracks and crevices like a screech-owl? Feeding like a toad on these wet rocks and clumps of moss. A nice way to spend your time. You haven't got the professor out of your system yet.

FAUST
Have you any idea what renewed energy I get from this sojourn in the wilds? If you have, you're devil enough to begrudge me my good fortune.

MEPHISTOPHELES
A queer sort of pleasure, almost unearthly. Lying about among the hills in the dark and in the wet, rapturously embracing earth and heaven, puffing yourself up until you think you're a god, permeating the marrow of the earth with your vague anticipations, experiencing the six days of creation in your own heart, extracting I don't know what satisfaction from feeling so high and mighty, merging amorously into the universe and forgetting your mortality altogether, and then – (*with a gesture*) terminating your deep insight I won't say how.

FAUST
Shame on you.

MEPHISTOPHELES
This doesn't suit you, it seems. But what right have you to throw your superior 'Shame on you' at me? Chaste ears can't bear to hear what chaste hearts can't do without. In short, I don't mind if you delude yourself a little now and then. But you won't be able to keep it up. You're worn out again already

and before long you'll be dead with fright or go clean off your head. Enough. Your sweetheart's sitting at home, all shut in and sad. She can't get you out of her mind. She's desperately in love with you. Your passion swept her off her feet like a river that overflows its banks when the snow melts. You've won her heart, and now the flood has receded. It seems to me that instead of presiding in the forest as if you were somebody you ought to reward the silly young thing for her affection. Time is dragging terribly for her. She stands at the window and watches the clouds passing over the old town-wall. Oh for the wings of a dove. That's the song she sings all day long and half the night. Sometimes she's up, mostly she's down. She cries her heart out and then she's quiet. And she's lovesick all the time.

FAUST

You serpent.

MEPHISTOPHELES *aside*

I'll get you yet.

FAUST

Monster. Away with you. Don't speak of her to me. Don't revive in me the desire for her sweet and lovely body. I'm half insane with it already.

MEPHISTOPHELES

What else are we to do? She thinks you've run away and you nearly have.

FAUST

I'm close to her, no matter how far from her I go. I can never forget her. I even envy the sacred host when her lips touch it.

MEPHISTOPHELES

Right you are, my friend. I've often envied you the twins that feed among the lilies.

FAUST

Get out of my sight. You pander.

MEPHISTOPHELES

Wonderful. This abuse from you makes me smile. The god who created boys and girls at once saw the virtue of opportunity-making. Off with you. It's a disgrace. It isn't death that awaits you, it's your girl's bedroom.

FAUST

Suppose I do delight in her embrace and warm myself in her bosom. Do I not feel her plight just the same? Do I not remain the homeless fugitive, an inhuman creature lacking any peace or purpose, roaring down from rock to rock like a cataract in my greed and fury? There she was in her childlike half-awakened state, living in her sequestered little alpine cottage, knowing nothing of life beyond the little round. And I, the accursed of God, was not satisfied with shattering the rocks to ruins. I had to destroy her peace of mind. This is the sacrifice that hell demanded. Help me, you devil, to speed these anxious days. Let what must happen, happen now. Let her fate come down on me and let us both perish together.

MEPHISTOPHELES

There you are again, all froth and fire. You fathead, go in and comfort her. Where your sort can't see the way out, you think the end has come. Long live the bold of heart. Aren't you bedevilled enough already? I can't think

of anything more ridiculous than a devil in despair.

scene 15 GRETCHEN'S ROOM

GRETCHEN *alone, at the spinning-wheel*

My heart is heavy, my peace is gone. I shall never find my peace again.

When he's not there, it's like the grave. The whole world, all of it, is soured.

My poor head is quite unhinged, my thoughts are broken pieces.

My heart is heavy, my peace is gone. I shall never find my peace again.

If I go to the window, I'm looking for him. I'm looking for him, when I leave the house.

His tall figure, his walk, his smile, his piercing gaze.

His magic words, the feel of his hands. And, oh, when he kisses me.

My heart is heavy, my peace is gone. I shall never find my peace again.

My body, yes, my body wants him. Oh just to take him and just to hold him.

And kiss and kiss him the way I'd like, though I die of the kissing.

scene 16 MARTHE'S GARDEN

Gretchen. Faust

GRETCHEN
Tell me truly.

FAUST
If I can.

GRETCHEN
Tell me. What about your religion? You're a good, kind man. But I don't believe religion matters to you.

FAUST
Let it go. You know I like you. I'd die for those I love. I let people feel and worship as they choose.

GRETCHEN
That's not enough. You have to believe.

FAUST
Do you have to?

GRETCHEN
Oh. How I wish you cared about what I think. You don't respect the sacraments.

FAUST
I do respect them.

GRETCHEN
But you don't want them. You haven't gone to mass, you haven't confessed for a long time. Don't you believe in God?

FAUST
Sweetheart, who can say I believe in him? Ask the priests and the philosophers and the answer they give sounds like mockery.

GRETCHEN
So you don't believe in him?

FAUST

Don't misunderstand me, darling. Who can name him and say: I believe in him? Who with honesty can make bold to say: I don't believe in him? He who sustains and embraces all things, does he not sustain and embrace you and me and himself? Isn't the earth firm beneath our feet? Doesn't the sky arch above us? Don't the friendly stars rise aloft? Don't you and I behold one another face to face? Isn't there something filling your heart and mind, something eternally mysterious working visibly, invisibly in the world about you? Fill your heart with it as full as it will hold and when you're filled with it, serenely filled with it, call it what you like: happiness, heart, love, God. I have no words for it. Feeling is everything. Words are just sound and smoke, bedimming the light of heaven.

GRETCHEN

This sounds all right. It's almost what the parson says, but not quite the same way.

FAUST

It's what all men say under the sun, each in his own language. Why shouldn't I say it in mine?

GRETCHEN

When you hear it said, it may seem good enough. But it isn't right. Because you aren't a Christian.

FAUST

Oh, my dear child.

GRETCHEN

It's been distressing me for a long time to see you with that man.

FAUST

How do you mean?

GRETCHEN

That man that's always with you, he revolts me. Nothing ever gave me such a start as the sight of his horrible face.

FAUST

Little girl, don't worry about him.

GRETCHEN

My blood mounts when I'm where he is. Mostly I like people. But while I long to see you, I have a secret horror of him. And I don't trust him either. God forgive me, if I'm unfair to him.

FAUST

There are people like him, so what?

GRETCHEN

I wouldn't care to live with any of them. When he puts his head round the door, he always has that sneering, half infuriated look. You can see he has no feeling for anything. It's written all over his face that he couldn't possibly love anyone. I'm so happy with you, so easy, so relaxed, so snug. But when he comes, it gripes me.

FAUST

You with your fears, you little angel.

GRETCHEN

It overcomes me so, when he joins us, I almost stop loving you. I couldn't say a prayer with him there. I nearly die. Aren't you the same?

FAUST
It's just your prejudice.

GRETCHEN
I have to go now.

FAUST
Shall I never have a quiet hour with you, the two of us, heart to heart?

GRETCHEN
Oh if only I slept by myself, I'd draw the bolt for you tonight. But mother's a light sleeper and if she caught us, it'd be the death of me.

FAUST
Don't worry about that, dear. Here's a bottle. Put three drops in what she drinks and she'll sleep deep and happy.

GRETCHEN
What wouldn't I do for your sake? I hope it isn't dangerous.

FAUST
Would I give you it, if it was?

GRETCHEN
When I look you in the face, I have to agree somehow. I've done so much for you already, there's hardly anything left for me to do. *off*

Enter Mephistopheles

MEPHISTOPHELES
Has she gone, the little minx?

FAUST
Spying again, were you?

MEPHISTOPHELES
I heard everything, professor. She put you through your catechism. I hope it does you good. The girls always want to find out whether a man keeps the old faith or not. They say to themselves, if he does what he's told there, he'll do what we tell him.

FAUST
You dreadful creature, you don't comprehend how this dear soul, so full of her faith, is tormented by the thought that her lover is damned.

MEPHISTOPHELES
What a queer lover you are, down to earth and up in the sky. This slip of a girl is leading you by the nose.

FAUST
You abortion of filth and hell-fire.

MEPHISTOPHELES
And she has physiognomy down cold. When she sees me, it comes all over her. This phiz of mine has a deep meaning. She knows that. She's sure I'm a man of genius, she wonders whether I'm the devil himself. And now, tonight ... ?

FAUST
What business is it of yours?

MEPHISTOPHELES
I get my fun out of it too.

scene 17 AT THE WELL

Gretchen and Lieschen with jugs

LIESCHEN
Have you heard about Barbara?

GRETCHEN
Not a word. I'm not going out much.

LIESCHEN
There's no doubt about it. Sybil told me today. She's landed herself now. This is what comes of putting on airs.

GRETCHEN
How do you mean?

LIESCHEN
You can smell it a mile off. At mealtimes now she's feeding two.

GRETCHEN
Oh.

LIESCHEN
It serves her right. She's been running after that fellow for so long. Taking her out walking, taking her out to the village and dancing with her. She had to be first wherever she went. Making up to her with cakes and wine. So conceited she was about her beauty. She had the cheek to accept presents from him. Fondling and licking one another. And now she's got it.

GRETCHEN
Poor girl.

LIESCHEN
You don't mean to say you're sorry for her. When you and me had to work at the spinning-wheel and mother wouldn't let us out at night, there she was, standing outside with her boy in the dark passage or sitting on the bench, she didn't mind how long. Now she has to take her medicine, do penance at church in the smock.

GRETCHEN
Surely he'll marry her.

LIESCHEN
A fool he'd be. A smart lad like him. He can have fun with others. Besides, he's gone away.

GRETCHEN
That was bad of him.

LIESCHEN
Even if she gets him, she won't like it. The boys'll spoil her wreath of flowers for her and we'll scatter chaff in the doorway. *off*

GRETCHEN
Going home
I used to rail so myself like the best of them when a poor girl went wrong. Couldn't find words enough for other people's sins. Black as they were, I made them blacker, and never made them black enough to suit me. Prided myself and paraded it and now it's me that's the sinner. Yet, everything that drove me to it was sweet and dear, God only knows.

scene 18 BY THE TOWN WALL

Set in the wall is an image of the Mater Dolorosa. Flower pots in front of it

GRETCHEN *putting fresh flowers in the pots*
You who have suffered so, mistress of suffering, turn your face to me in my trouble and be kind.

With the sword in your heart and pains beyond number you gaze at your son dying.

You look at the father and your sighs go up for his ordeal and yours.

But who is there to feel with me the pangs that thrill me and the dread in my heart? Only you know its trembling, its desire, only you.

Wherever I go, this anguish goes with me. No sooner am I alone, than I weep and weep. My heart is breaking.

This morning I plucked these flowers for you in the pots at my window. I watered them with my tears.

The sun came early into my room, to find me already upright in my bed in utter misery.

Help me, save me from shame, save me from death. You who have suffered so, mistress of suffering, turn your face to me in my trouble and be kind.

scene 19 NIGHT. STREET AT GRETCHEN'S DOOR

VALENTIN *a soldier, brother of Gretchen*
It used to be that I could sit at a banquet, with everyone blowing his horn and the boys singing the praises of the girls they liked and emptying their glasses to them, and all I had to do was to sit quietly with my elbows on the table and, when they'd finshed their boasting, smile and stroke my beard and raise my glass and say: Every man to his taste, but is there a girl in the country to touch my Gretchen, is there any girl that can hold a candle to her? Round went the toasts, clink, clank, and some of them would yell: He's right, she's the pick of the lot, the pick of womanhood, and the others hadn't a word to say. But now it's enough to make you pull your hair out in tufts or climb up the wall. Now any Tom, Dick, or Harry can turn up his nose at me and make his snide remarks and I have to sit there, like a culprit, breaking into a sweat at any chance word. I'm fit to smash their heads, all of them, but I can't call them liars.

But who's this slinking along? I believe there's two of them. If it's him, I'll collar him, he won't leave here alive.

Faust. Mephistopheles

FAUST
See how the light from the ever-burning lamp in the little chapel shines up through the window and spreads, getting weaker and weaker till the surrounding darkness quenches it. I feel just like that inside, dark, nocturnal.

MEPHISTOPHELES

And I'm all aching for something, like an alley cat creeping past the fire-escapes and then hugging the wall. I don't feel exactly wicked about it, just a little bit thievish, a little bit lecherous. It's the Walpurgis Night getting into my system. It's due the day after tomorrow. Wonderful. That's when you know what it is to be alive.

FAUST

Is it the light from a hidden treasure that I see flickering over there?

MEPHISTOPHELES

Yes, you'll soon have the pleasure of lifting it yourself. I peeped at it the other day, saw some lovely coins in it.

FAUST

Wasn't there a ring or a piece of jewellery for my girl to wear?

MEPHISTOPHELES

I did see something of the sort. Maybe a string of pearls.

FAUST

Good. It hurts me to go to see her without any presents.

MEPHISTOPHELES

I don't see why you should mind having your pleasure for nothing occasionally. And now, with the sky full of stars, I'll let you hear a song, a real work of art. It's a moral song, just the sort that'll fool her. *He sings to the zither*

What are you after, here at your lover's door, at daybreak, Cathy? Don't do it. He'll let you in as a virgin. You won't be one when you come out.

Take care, once it's done, then good night, you poor things. If you care for one another, give nothing away for love, unless with the ring on your finger.

VALENTIN *steps forward*

Who are you enticing here, you cursed ratcatcher? To hell first with your instrument. And then to hell with the singer.

MEPHISTOPHELES

You've split the zither. It's no good now.

VALENTIN

Now we'll split heads.

MEPHISTOPHELES *to Faust*

Hold your ground, professor. Quick now. I'll lead. Stick close to me. Out with your sword. At him. I'll parry.

VALENTIN

Parry this one.

MEPHISTOPHELES

Why not?

VALENTIN

And this.

MEPHISTOPHELES

Certainly.

VALENTIN

I believe the devil's fighting me. What's this? My hand's gone lame.

MEPHISTOPHELES *to Faust*

Let him have it.

Oh.

MEPHISTOPHELES

That's settled him, the lout. But now we must be off, we must disappear.
There'll be a hue-and-cry in no time. I'm on good terms with the police, but
when it comes to murder, there's not much I can do.

MARTHE *at the window*

Help. Help.

GRETCHEN *at the window*

Bring a light.

MARTHE *as above*

They're scrapping, shouting, yelling, and fighting.

CROWD

One of them's killed.

MARTHE *coming out*

Have the murderers got away?

GRETCHEN *coming out*

Who lies here?

CROWD

The son of your mother.

GRETCHEN

Almighty God. This is fearful.

VALENTIN

I'm dying. It's soon said, and sooner done. What are you women standing
around for, weeping and wailing? Come here and listen to me.

They all come closer

Gretchen, you're young still, young and foolish. You've made a mess of
things. I'll tell you. Between you and me, you're just a plain whore. So be
a real one.

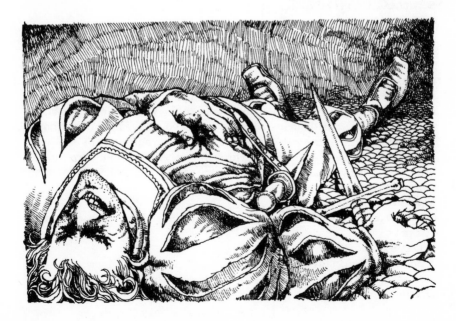

GRETCHEN
My brother. O God. What will you say next?

VALENTIN
You leave God out of it. What's done can't be undone. So on you go. You
started off with one, secretly. There'll be others soon. When a round dozen
have had you, the whole town'll have you.

When shamefulness is born, it's born in secret. You pull the veil of night
over its head. You're ready to strangle it. But if it grows, if it gets bigger, it
goes about by day, though it isn't any better to look at. The uglier it is, the
more it seeks the light.

I see the time coming when decent folk will keep away from you,
shun you, you wanton, as if you were a putrid corpse. When they look you
in the face, your heart will quail. No more gold necklaces then. No more
standing at the altar. No more fun at the dance in a lace collar. You'll have
to hide in dark corners with beggars and cripples. God may forgive you, but
on earth you'll be accurst.

MARTHE
Commend your soul to God. Do you want to die a blasphemer?

VALENTIN
If I could only get at your scraggy body, you foul go-between, I might hope
to find forgiveness – yes, and to spare – for all my sins.

GRETCHEN
Oh my brother. Oh what agony.

VALENTIN
I tell you, stop your blubbering. When you disgraced yourself, you dealt me
the worst blow. I was a soldier, a good soldier, and now I must sleep the sleep
of death and find my God. *He dies*

scene 20 CATHEDRAL

*Service, organ, singing. Gretchen in a crowded congregation. The evil spirit
behind her*

EVIL SPIRIT
How different it used to be, Gretchen, when in your childhood innocence you
came to the altar and lisped your prayers from the worn little prayer-book,
God mingled in your thoughts with the games you played. How is it now?
With what sin in your heart? Are you praying for your mother's soul who
passed in sleep to endless torment? Through you? At your door whose blood
is it? And inside you can't you feel it yet, the something stirring, threatening
you both, always with you?

GRETCHEN
Oh, oh, oh, to be rid of these thoughts that shuttle to and fro, reproaching me.

CHOIR
Dies irae, dies illa
Solvet saeclum in favilla.

Organ

The wrath of heaven seizes you. The trumpets sound. The graves are quaking. And your heart, roused from its ashes to suffer the flames, leaps in agony.

GRETCHEN

Oh to be out of here. These organ tones suffocate me. The chanting breaks me utterly.

CHOIR

Judex ergo cum sedebit,
Quidquid latet ad parebit,
Nil inultum remanebit.

GRETCHEN

I can't move. The pillars imprison me. The great vault crushes me. I'm stifling.

EVIL SPIRIT

Hide yourself, would you? Sin and shame cannot be hidden. You want air? You want light? No.

CHOIR

Quid sum miser tunc dicturus?
Quem patronum rogaturus,
Cum vix justus sit securus?

EVIL SPIRIT

Angels turn their faces from you. The pure shudder at the thought of touching you.

CHOIR

Quid sum miser tunc dicturus?

GRETCHEN

Neighbour. Your smelling-bottle. *She swoons*

scene 21 WALPURGIS NIGHT

Harz mountains. Neighbourhood of Schierke and Elend
Faust. Mephistopheles

MEPHISTOPHELES

Don't you wish you had a broomstick to ride on? The thing for me would be a tough old billy-goat. We've a good way to go yet by this route.

FAUST

As long as my legs hold out, this cudgel of a walking-stick will do for me. What's the point of shortening our route? Having to find our way through a tangle of valleys and then climb these rocks with the everlasting waterfalls splashing down is just what spices a trip of this sort. Spring's already got into the birch trees and even the pines are beginning to feel it. Why shouldn't we feel it too?

MEPHISTOPHELES

Myself, I don't notice it. I'm all wintry. I wish the snow was here. Look at this melancholy red moon rising so late, what there is of it, and not giving enough light to keep us from bumping into the trees or stumbling over a   *page 67* rock. Excuse me if I engage a will-o'-the-wisp. I see one there, shining merrily. Hello, my friend, will you join us? No use wasting your light. Give us the benefit of it like a good fellow. Here's where we're going up.

WILL-O'-THE-WISP

Perhaps my respect for you will enable me to control my frivolous nature. I usually go in a zigzag.

MEPHISTOPHELES

Listen to this. He's trying to imitate mankind. Go straight, damn it all, or I'll blow you and your flimsy light out altogether.

WILL-O'-THE-WISP

I see, sir, that you're the boss and I'll do my best to oblige. But please don't forget that the mountain tonight is bewitched and, if a will-o'-the-wisp is to guide you, you mustn't be too particular.

FAUST, MEPHISTOPHELES, WILL-O'-THE-WISP *singing in turn*

It seems we have entered the realm of dreams and magic. Now do your best and lead us forward in the big barren spaces.

Look at the trees, trees behind trees, whizzing past and the cliffs reaching out over us and the long-nosed rocks blowing and snoring.

And little streams, tiny streams, speeding through the rocks, through the grass. I hear a rustling. Is it song? Is it love's sweet lament, voices from those heavenly days, voices of love, of hope? And there comes the echo like a tale of days gone by.

And hark at the screech-owl, the night-owl, the plover, the jay, coming nearer and nearer. Have they all stayed awake? Is it lizards in the shrubs, long legs, fat bellies? And see the gnarled roots, twisting snake-like out of the rocks, out of the sand, to frighten us, to catch us, stretching their fibrous tentacles at the passer-by. And the mice, hordes of mice, of every colour, running through the moss, the heather, and glow-worms flying in swarms, leading us off the trail.

And tell me, are we standing still or moving? Everything's spinning round, the rocks and the trees pulling faces at us. And will-o'-the-wisps, more and more of them, puffing themselves out.

MEPHISTOPHELES

Take a good hold of my coat-tails. This is one of the middle-sized peaks, where you can see something that will surprise you – the whole mountain made luminous by Mammon, the lord of wealth.

FAUST

What a curious dim light there is in the lower regions, like the red sky at dawn. And feeling its way into the very deepest chasms. Mist rising here, stretches of it there, the glow shining through, creeping along in threads, breaking out like a cascade, reaching down the valley in countless veins, and a patch of it in a nook there all by itself. Look at those sparks flying close by like golden sand scattered in the air. And see, the whole rocky cliff's lit up from top to bottom.

MEPHISTOPHELES

Yes, doesn't Mammon do a good job of illuminating his palace for the festival? You're lucky to have seen it. And now I can hear the unruly guests arriving.

My, what a raging gale. Hitting me, slamming me, in the back of the neck.

MEPHISTOPHELES

You must hang on to these ribs of rock, or down you'll go into the depths. The mist makes it darker than ever. Do you hear the cracking in the trees, flinging up the startled owls? Do you hear the columns of the ancient green palaces splintering, the branches creaking and snapping, the roots grinding, gaping, the tree trunks thundering down, falling on one another in dreadful confusion, with the wind howling in the chasms they cover? Can you hear voices in the air, some near, some far off? Yes, the mad, magic singing is streaming across the hillside.

CHORUS OF WITCHES

The witches are heading for the Brocken. The stubble is yellow, the crop is green. That's where they all gather, with Urian presiding. So on we go over stump and stone. The billy-goat stinks, the witch takes it.

VOICE

Mother Baubo's coming by herself, riding on a sow.

CHORUS

Let Mother Baubo take the lead, the place of honour is hers. With those two in front the rest of the witches will follow.

VOICE

Which way did you come?

VOICE

I came by Ilsenstein. I peeped into an owl's nest. Oh, how it stared.

VOICE

To hell with you, why ride so fast?

VOICE

She's scraped me, look at my wounds.

CHORUS OF WITCHES

The road is broad, the road is long. What a mad throng this is. The hayfork pricks, the broom scratches, the child chokes, the mother bursts.

HALF-CHORUS OF WITCHMASTERS

We're crawling like snails. The women are all in the lead. When it's a visit to the devil, the women are a thousand paces ahead.

THE OTHER HALF

We don't worry about that. The woman does it in a thousand paces. But, however fast she goes, the man does it in one big jump.

VOICE *from above*

Come with us, come up from the rocky lake.

VOICE *from below*

We'd like to come up. We're all washed and clean, but we shall never bear.

BOTH CHORUSES

The wind has dropped, the stars are gone. The moon likes to hide too. The magic chorus, roaring along, is scattering thousands of sparks.

VOICE *from below*

Stop. Stop.

VOICE *from above*

Who's calling out of the cleft?

VOICE *from below*

Take me with you. Take me with you. I've been climbing for three hundred years and I can't reach the summit, where I belong.

BOTH CHORUSES

You can ride a broom, ride a stick, ride a hayfork, ride a goat. If you can't get a move on today, you're lost.

HALF-WITCH *from below*

I've been trotting behind for ages. The others are so far ahead. I have no peace at home and can't find any here.

CHORUS OF WITCHES

The salve makes witches bold. A rag will do for a sail. Any tub will do for a boat. Fly in the air today or you never will.

BOTH CHORUSES

And when we reach the summit spread out and cover the whole ground with witches.

They settle

MEPHISTOPHELES

They crowd and push and rush and rattle. They hiss and twirl and tug and babble. They shine and crackle, and stink and burn. There's witches for you. Now stick close to me or we'll lose one another in a minute. Where are you?

FAUST *at a distance*

Here.

MEPHISTOPHELES

Have they carried you that far? I'll have to use my authority. Make way, Voland, the devil, is coming. Make way, good people, make way. Here, professor, grab hold of me and, in one dash, we'll get out of the crowd. It's too much even for me. There's a queer light shining yonder. I feel drawn to those bushes. Come on, we'll slip over there.

FAUST

You spirit of contradiction. But anyway, lead on. I begin to think you managed it well. We came to the Brocken on Walpurgis Night and then, having arrived, we go off into a corner.

MEPHISTOPHELES

See there, what a nice bonfire. It's a merry club-meeting. We shall feel more at home in a small circle.

FAUST

But I'd rather be up on top. I can see the lights and the smoke whirling. The crowd is streaming up to the evil one. We'd be solving some riddles there.

MEPHISTOPHELES

Yes, and setting up some new ones. You just let the great world wag. We'll have a quiet time here. We'll make a little world inside the big one. It's often done. I see some young witches there, all naked, and some old ones who know what to cover up. Be nice to them for my sake. No effort and lots of fun. I can hear music playing. A cursed noise. You have to get used to it.

Come along, you can't back out now. I'll lead the way and introduce you,

find you some new friends. What do you say? It isn't so small a place. Look. scene 21
You can hardly see the end. There's a hundred bonfires burning in a row,
people dancing, chatting, cooking, drinking, making love. Tell me now
where you'd find anything better.

FAUST

Are you going to play the devil here or the magician?

MEPHISTOPHELES

I usually travel incognito. I'm very careful about it, as you know. But on
gala days you can be seen wearing your orders. I can't boast of a garter,
but the horse hoof commands respect. Do you see the snail there, crawling
towards me, feeling its way with its face? It's smelt me out already. No use
trying to conceal myself here. Come along. We'll go from fire to fire. I'll be
the wooer and you'll be the lover.

To a few, sitting by a dying fire

Well, old gentlemen, what are you doing here? I'd think better of you if I
found you in the midst of things, in all the youthful revels. We're alone
enough when we're at home.

GENERAL

You can't trust nations. However much you do for them, the young are
always first. It's the same with nations as with women.

MINISTER

We've strayed too far off the right track. Give me the good people we once
had. When we were on top, that was the golden age.

PARVENU

We weren't such fools, yet we often did what we shouldn't. But now everything's gone topsy-turvy and just when we wanted to hang on to it.

AUTHOR

Who today wants to read a book of even moderate intelligence? As for the
younger generation, they're cheekier than ever.

MEPHISTOPHELES *who suddenly appears very old*

On this my last ascent of the witches' mountain I feel that the people are
ready for the Judgment Day. My sands are running out and so the world
is on the way out too.

HUCKSTER-WITCH

Gentlemen, don't hurry past, don't miss this opportunity. Look at my wares.
I have all sorts of things in my store, but nothing that hasn't done serious
harm. Not a dagger but has drawn blood, not a cup but has poured burning
poison into a healthy body, not a jewel but has seduced a good woman, not
a sword but has played false, maybe run its opponent through the back.

MEPHISTOPHELES

My old friend, you're behind the times. What's done is done with. Go in
for novelties, novelties is what we want now.

FAUST

What a riot it all is. I almost lose my identity.

MEPHISTOPHELES

They're all streaming up to the summit. You think you're pushing and
you're being pushed.

FAUST

Who's that? page 71

MEPHISTOPHELES
Take a close look at her. It's Lilith.

FAUST
Who?

MEPHISTOPHELES
Adam's first wife. Beware of her lovely locks, unique in their beauty. When she catches a young man with them, she doesn't soon let go.

FAUST
There's two there, an old witch and a young one. They've hopped about plenty already.

MEPHISTOPHELES
There's no rest for anyone today. Here's another dance starting. Come on, we'll help ourselves.

FAUST *dancing with the young one*
Once I had a lovely dream. I saw an apple tree with two shining apples on it. I climbed up after them.

THE PRETTY ONE
You've always liked apples, ever since paradise. It pleases me to think that my garden bears them.

MEPHISTOPHELES *with the old one*
Once I had a lurid dream. I saw a cleft tree. It had a hole in it. Big as it was, I liked it.

THE OLD WITCH
My compliments to the knight of the hoof. Hold ready you know what, unless you funk it.

PROKTOPHANTASMIST
You cursed people. What presumption. Haven't we proved it to you long ago that a spirit has no feet to stand on, and here you are, dancing like ordinary mortals.

THE PRETTY ONE *dancing*
What's he doing at our ball?

FAUST *dancing*
Oh, he goes everywhere. Others dance and he judges them. If he can't discuss every step, it's as if it was never taken. What annoys him most is when we progress. If you would just go round in a circle, as he does in that old mill of his, he might approve, especially if you praised him for it.

PROKTOPHANTASMIST
Are you still there? This is an outrage. Off you go. Haven't we had the age of reason? These devil folk, they won't obey the rules. We're so bright now and yet there still are ghosts in Tegel. I've worked so long against superstition, yet we never get rid of it. It's an outrage.

THE PRETTY ONE
Will you just stop making yourself a nuisance.

PROKTOPHANTASMIST
I tell you spirits to your face, I won't have this tyranny of the spirits. I have no spirit for it.

They go on dancing
Today I see is one of my bad days, but I don't mind taking a journey and
I trust before I finish I shall exorcise both devils and poets.

MEPHISTOPHELES

He'll go now and sit in a puddle. That's his way of relieving himself. If leeches settle on his arse, he'll be cured of spirit and spirits too.

To Faust who has withdrawn from the dance

Why did you let the pretty girl go? She sang so beautifully when she was dancing.

FAUST

While she was singing, a red mouse jumped out of her mouth.

MEPHISTOPHELES

That's all right. You mustn't be too fussy. At least the mouse wasn't gray. Who cares anyway in a flirtation?

FAUST

Then I saw ...

MEPHISTOPHELES

What?

FAUST

Mephisto, look there. A lovely girl, so pale, standing off by herself. She's sliding slowly away, as if her feet were bound together. I confess she looks to me like my dear Gretchen.

MEPHISTOPHELES

Keep away from her. She's no good to anyone. She's a phantom, an image, not living. She's not safe. That fixed stare of hers congeals your blood and nearly turns you into stone. You've heard of the Medusa, haven't you?

FAUST

Yes, I see, it's the eyes of the dead, not closed by a loving hand. This is the breast that Gretchen offered me, the sweet body that I enjoyed.

MEPHISTOPHELES

All magic, you simpleton. She looks like his sweetheart to every man.

FAUST

What joy, what suffering. I can't take my eyes off her. Strange how the red line round her lovely neck suits her. Not wider than the back of a knife.

MEPHISTOPHELES

You're right, I can see it too. She can carry her head under her arm as well. Perseus cut it off. Can't you get over this love of illusions? Come along up this little hill. It's as merry here as in the Prater. And, unless I'm mistaken, there's a theatre there. What are they doing?

SERVIBILIS

They're just beginning again. A new piece, the last of seven. It's usual here to do seven. A dilettante wrote it and dilettantes act it. Excuse me, sirs, if I leave you. I have a dilettante impulse to draw up the curtain.

MEPHISTOPHELES

It's right and proper that I should find you on the Brocken. This is where you belong.

scene 22 WALPURGIS NIGHT'S DREAM OR
OBERON AND TITANIA'S GOLDEN WEDDING
INTERMEZZO

PROPERTY MASTER
We stagehands have an easy day today. This old mountain and the misty valley are all the scenery needed.

HERALD
It takes fifty years to make a golden wedding. But if the quarrel is over, that's the golden wedding for me.

OBERON
Any spirits that are near, show yourselves now. The king and queen are one again.

PUCK
Here comes Puck and does a spin and trails his foot. Hundreds follow him in the merry dance.

ARIEL
Ariel leads the song in tones divinely pure. Many crude natures are attracted, but the refined are drawn to it too.

OBERON
Wives and husbands, learn from us how to get along. Go apart and love will bring you together again.

TITANIA
Yes, if he sulks and she mopes, take him off to the far north and take her to the south.

ORCHESTRA *fortissimo*
A fly's snout and a midge's nose, and all their relatives. Frog in the leaves and cricket in the grass. These are the musicians.

SOLO
Here comes the bagpipes. He's only a soap-bubble. Can you hear him go clickety-clack with his pug-nose?

MIND IN THE MAKING
Give him a spider's foot, a toad's belly, and give him wings. He won't come alive unless in verse.

A COUPLE
A tiny step and then a jump in the honeysweet air. You trip along nicely, but we don't take off.

INQUISITIVE TRAVELLER
This must be a carnival joke. I can hardly trust my eyes. Oberon, the handsome god, on view here even at this late day.

ORTHODOX
He may have neither claws nor tail, but there's no doubt. He's just as much a devil as the gods of Greece.

NORTHERN ARTIST
Anything I undertake today is just sketchy. But I am preparing betimes for my Italian journey.

A PURIST
Oh, it's my bad luck that brought me here where all is snares and tempta-

tion. And out of all this crowd of witches only two are powdered. scene 22

YOUNG WITCH

Let those that are old and gray powder themselves and wear a skirt. Me, I sit naked on my billy-goat and show my husky body.

MATRON

We're too polite to quarrel with you here, you young and tender things. All we say is: 'May you rot in your tracks.'

CONDUCTOR

Fly's snout and midge's nose, don't buzz around this naked beauty. Frog in the leaves and cricket in the grass, see that you keep time.

WEATHERCOCK *pointing one way*

You couldn't wish for better company. Would you believe it, nothing but brides and bachelors, all brimming with hope.

WEATHERCOCK *pointing the other way*

If the earth doesn't gape to swallow them, I'll go straight to hell on the high run.

EPIGRAMS

Here we come as insects with sharp little claws to honour Papa Satan as he deserves.

EDITOR

Look at the crowd of them there, naively chatting and joking. Next thing, they'll claim to be kind-hearted.

LEADER OF THE MUSES

I love to lose myself among all these witches. I'd find them easier to lead than the Muses.

QUONDAM JOURNAL

It pays to get among the right people. Hang on to my coat-tails. The Brocken is like the German Parnassus – there's plenty of room at the top.

INQUISITIVE TRAVELLER

Who's that striding along so stiff and haughty? He's sniffing and sniffing for all he's worth. 'He's hunting for Jesuits.'

CRANE

I like to fish in clear waters, I like to fish in muddy. This is why you find me, pious as I am, consorting with devils.

PAGAN

Believe me, these men of piety can function anywhere. They often hold their conventions on the Brocken.

DANCER

That must be a new gang arriving. I can hear their distant drums. Don't worry. It's the bitterns *unisono* in the reeds.

DANCING-MASTER

See how each of them picks his way, as best he can. The crooked ones jump, the heavy ones hop. They don't care how they look.

FIDDLER

These low people hate one another, murderously. The bagpipes unite them, as Orpheus with his lyre tamed the beasts.

DOGMATIST

You can't shake me with your noisy doubts and objections. The devil must page 75 be somebody, else why should there be devils at all?

IDEALIST

Imagination in my sense has gone too far this time. Truly, if I'm a part of all that, I'm off my nut.

REALIST

These goings-on are a torment, they're more than I can take. For the first time I don't know where I stand.

SUPERNATURALIST

I'm happy to be here and enjoy this company. I can reason from devils to good spirits.

SCEPTIC

They're tracking out the little flames and think they're near the treasure. Doubt goes with devil, d with d. This suits me entirely.

CONDUCTOR

Frog in the leaves and cricket in the grass. You cursed dilettantes. Fly's snout and midge's nose, what musicians!

OPPORTUNISTS

This host of merry creatures is called sans-souci. We can't walk any longer on our feet, so we walk on our heads.

THE NE'ER-DO-WELLS

We've scrounged many a meal so far, but now God help us. We've danced right through our shoes and we're down to our bare feet.

WILL-O'-THE-WISPS

We come from the swamp where we were born. But here we rate at once as shining gallants.

SHOOTING STAR

I came from high up in the starry light. Now I lie sprawling in the grass. Who'll help me on to my feet?

THE CRUDE ONES

Make way, make way. We tread down the grass. Spirits can be heavy-footed too.

PUCK

Don't stamp so, like baby elephants. Let Puck be the heaviest of us.

ARIEL

If nature or the spirit gave you wings, follow my light tracks to the rosy hill-top.

ORCHESTRA *pianissimo*

Clouds and mist are lit from above. A breeze in the trees and wind in the reeds, and everything vanishes.

scene 23 DULL DAY. A FIELD

Faust. Mephistopheles

FAUST

An outcast, driven to despair. Wretchedly wandering the wide earth and now at long last a prisoner, a condemned criminal, locked in a dungeon, exposed to the cruellest torture, the dear girl and so ill-fated. Had it to come to this? And you kept it from me, you vile, you treacherous spirit. Yes, you can stand there and roll your devil's eyes in fury. Stand and defy me with your intolerable presence. A prisoner. In hopeless misery. At the mercy of evil spirits and the unsparing censure of mankind. And meanwhile you distract me with your vulgar entertainments, keep her desperate plight from me, and leave her to meet her end alone.

MEPHISTOPHELES

She's not the first.

FAUST

You beast. You foul monster. O infinite spirit, turn this reptile back into its canine form, the dog, that used to run ahead of me on my evening walks, roll at the feet of unsuspecting strangers and jump on their shoulders when they tripped over him. Turn him back into the shape that suited him so that he may crawl again in the sand at my feet and let me spurn him, him the lowest of the low. Not the first! Oh the shame of it, beyond human power to comprehend, that more than one of us mortals reached this depth of misery, that the death-agony of the first was not enough to clear all the others in the eyes of the great forgiver. The suffering of this single one racks me, marrow and bones. But you pass over the fate of thousands with a grin, unmoved.

MEPHISTOPHELES

Here we are again at the far edge of our intelligence. A step more and you people go stark mad. Why do you have dealings with us if you can't go through with it? You want to fly and you're afraid your head'll swim. Did we force ourselves on you or you on us?

FAUST

Don't gnash your savage teeth at me that way. It revolts me. You mighty spirit who deigned to appear before me, you know me heart and soul. Why did you tie me to this abominable creature who feeds on mischief and destruction and rejoices in it?

MEPHISTOPHELES

Have you finished now?

FAUST

Save her, or it'll be worse for you. It'll be curse on you, the direst curse, for centuries to come.

MEPHISTOPHELES

I'm powerless to loose the avenger's chains or to draw his bolts. You say 'Save her.' Who was it that brought her to ruin? Was it me or was it you?

Faust looks about him wildly

MEPHISTOPHELES

You're looking for a thunderbolt. It's good that thunderbolts weren't given to wretches like you. This is the way of tyrants, when they're in a jam, to free themselves by shattering their innocent opponents.

FAUST

Take me there. She must be free.

MEPHISTOPHELES

Think of the risks you're running. Remember there's blood on the town, blood that you shed. Avenging spirits are hovering over the place where

the victim fell and waiting for the murderer to return.
FAUST
Must I hear this from you? May a whole world of death and destruction come down on you, you monster. Take me there, I tell you, and set her free.
MEPHISTOPHELES
I'll take you there and now I'll tell you what I can do. Do you think I have unlimited power in earth and heaven? I'll cloud the mind of the jailer. You grab the keys and lead her out by a mortal hand. I'll keep watch. The magic horses are ready. I'll abduct you. This I can do.
FAUST
Up and away.

scene 24 NIGHT. OPEN FIELD

Faust, Mephistopheles, galloping past on black horses

FAUST
What's going on there at the raven-stone?
MEPHISTOPHELES
I can't say what they're brewing and doing.
FAUST
They go up and then down. They're bending and bowing.
MEPHISTOPHELES
A meeting of witches.
FAUST
They're scattering something, blessing something.
MEPHISTOPHELES
Come on, come on.

scene 25 PRISON

FAUST *with a bunch of keys and a lamp, at an iron door*
I shudder so. I thought I had forgotten how. The whole misery of mankind comes over me. Here she is behind these dripping walls. And her sole offence came of a harmless wish. You hesitate to go to her? You dread seeing her again? Folly. If I delay I only bring death nearer. *He takes hold of the lock.*

Singing within
  My mother, the whore,
  She murdered me.
  My father, the rascal,
  He ate me up.
  My little sister
  Gathered my bones
  In a cool place;
  I turned into a song-bird.
Fly away, fly away.

She doesn't dream her lover's listening and can hear the chains rattling, the straw rustling. *He goes in*

GRETCHEN *trying to hide on her pallet*

Oh, oh, they're coming. Oh death, oh bitter death.

FAUST *quietly*

Quiet now. Quiet. I've come to rescue you.

GRETCHEN *writhing at his feet*

Are you human? Then share my suffering.

FAUST

You'll wake the guards. *He takes hold of the chains to unlock them*

GRETCHEN *on her knees*

Headsman, who gave you this power over me? You've come for me at midnight. Wouldn't tomorrow morning do? Have pity on me. Let me live a little longer.

Standing up

I'm so young, so young. Too young to die. I was pretty too, and that was my ruin. My lover was close, now he's far away. My wreath of flowers torn and scattered. Don't take hold of me so roughly. Spare me. I never hurt you. I never saw you before. Are all my pleas in vain?

FAUST

This is fearful. This is too much.

GRETCHEN

I'm in your hands. I'm at your mercy. Let me nurse my baby first. I cuddled it all night. They took it from me, just to be unkind. And now they say I killed it. I shall never be happy again. They sing songs about me. It's horrid of them. An old tale ends this way. Why tell it of me?

FAUST *throwing himself down*

This is your lover, your lover at your feet, ready to take you out of this miserable bondage.

GRETCHEN *throwing herself down beside him*

Oh let us kneel down together and pray to the saints. See, under these steps, under this door, hell is blazing, the evil one raging, shouting in his fury.

FAUST *louder*

Gretchen. Gretchen.

GRETCHEN *paying heed*

That was my sweetheart's voice.

She jumps up, the chains fall off her

Where is he? I heard him call. I'm free. No one can stop me. I'll cling to his neck. I'll lie in his arms. He called Gretchen. He was standing at the door. I heard his voice, that dear, dear voice of his, right through the howling and the chattering, and the cruel mockery of hell.

FAUST

Yes, it's me, me.

GRETCHEN

It's you. Oh say it again.

Taking hold of him

It's him. It's him. Where is all the agony now? Where is the prison, the chains, the fear and torment of it all? It's you. You've come to save me. I'm   *page 79* saved. Now I can see the street where I first saw you, and the happy garden and me and Marthe waiting for you.

FAUST *trying to pull her away*

Come along. Come along.

GRETCHEN

Oh stay. I so like to be around where you are. *fondling him*

FAUST

Hurry, hurry. If you don't hurry, we'll pay for it in the worst way.

GRETCHEN

What, can't you kiss me any more? Oh my love, you've been away so short a time and you've forgotten how to kiss. I have your arms round me and I'm so frightened. It used to be like heaven when you looked at me and said things and kissed me fit to choke me to death. Kiss me now or I'll kiss you. *She embraces him*

Oh, oh, your lips are cold. You don't say a word. You don't love me. Where's your love gone? Who took it away? *She turns from him*

FAUST

Come. Follow me. Sweetheart, be brave. I'll hug you with my heart on fire. Only follow me. Just follow me. That's all.

GRETCHEN *turning to him*

Is it really you? Are you sure?

FAUST

Yes, it's me. Come now.

GRETCHEN

You've taken the chains off. You've taken me on your lap. How come you aren't afraid of me? Do you know who it is you're setting free?

FAUST

Come, come. It'll soon be daylight.

GRETCHEN

I killed my mother. I drowned my baby. Wasn't it my baby and yours? Yours too? It's you. I can hardly believe it. Give me your hand. Yes, it's not a dream. It's your hand, your dear, dear hand. But it's wet. I think there's blood on it. Wipe it. Oh God, what have you done? Put up your sword. Please, please.

FAUST

Forget the past. You're killing me.

GRETCHEN

No. You must live. I'll tell you about the graves. You must see to them tomorrow. Give mother the best place and put my brother beside her, and me a little distance away, not far. And put the baby to my right breast. Else I shall lie there alone. It was lovely, lovely to snuggle up to you. But I can't do it any more. It seems I have to force myself on you and you're pushing me away. And yet it's you. And you look so good and kind.

FAUST

Come on then, if you're sure it's me.

GRETCHEN

What, out there?

FAUST

Yes, out into the open.

GRETCHEN

If the grave's out there and death waiting, come with me. From here to my last rest and not a step further. Are you going? Oh, I wish I could go too.

FAUST

You can. If you want. The door's open.

GRETCHEN

I can't go. There's no hope for me. What's the good of running away? They'll watch out for me. It's wretched to have to beg, and with a bad conscience too. It's wretched to roam about in strange places. And they'll get me anyway.

FAUST

I'll stick with you.

GRETCHEN

Quick, quick, save your poor child. Off you go. Up the path by the brook. Over the little bridge. Into the wood where the board fence is. In the pond. Get hold of it. It's trying to rise. It's struggling. Save it. Save it.

FAUST

Think. Only think. One step and you're free.

GRETCHEN

If only we were past the hill. Mother's sitting there on a rock, wagging her head. It gives me the shivers. She doesn't nod, she doesn't wave. Her head's heavy. She's slept so long she'll never wake. She slept so we could have fun. Those were happy days.

FAUST

It's no use talking any more. I'll have to carry you off.

GRETCHEN

Leave me alone. I won't have violence. Loose your grasp. I always did what you wanted before.

FAUST

Day's coming. Darling. Darling.

GRETCHEN

Yes, day. The last day. It was to have been my wedding day. Don't tell anyone you were at Gretchen's. Oh my flowers. Well, it's done. We'll meet again, but not at the dance. The crowd's gathering. You can't hear them. The streets, the square won't hold them. The bell calls. The staff is broken. They're seizing hold of me, binding me, dragging me to the block. Everyone feels at his neck the axe blade that's meant for me. The world is silent as the grave.

FAUST

I wish I'd never been born.

MEPHISTOPHELES *appearing outside*

Up. Or you're lost. This delay, this chattering's useless. My horses are shivering. It'll soon be light.

GRETCHEN

Who is that rising out of the ground? Send him away. What's he doing here in this holy place? He's after me.

FAUST

I want you to live.

GRETCHEN
God's judgment. I submit to it.
MEPHISTOPHELES *to Faust*
Come, or I'll leave the two of you.
GRETCHEN
Heavenly father, I'm yours. Save me. Angelic hosts, surround me, preserve me. Faust, I shudder at you.
MEPHISTOPHELES
She is doomed.
VOICE *from above*
She is saved.
MEPHISTOPHELES *to Faust*
Come here. *He disappears with Faust*
VOICE *dying away*
Faust, Faust.

scene 26

A pleasant landscape. Faust couched on flowery grass,
tired, restless, trying to sleep

DAWN

Chorus of Spirits, pleasant little creatures, hovering in the air

ARIEL *singing, accompanied by Aeolian harps*
Now when the spring blossoms are floating down on the world and everywhere green crops catch the eye with their promise, we little elf-spirits eagerly give what help we can. We grieve for a man in misfortune, no matter who he is, a saint or a sinner.

You elves, circling above him, behave as good elves should. Ease the dire conflict in the man's heart, pluck out the bitter, burning arrows of reproach, purge his soul of horror. Take charge of the four watches of the night and make them cheerful. Lay his head down on a cool pillow, then bathe him in Lethe's dew. As he sleeps and gathers strength to meet the new day, his limbs will relax. Perform the fairest of elfin services. Return him to the sacred light.

CHORUS *singly, in pairs, or full chorus, in turn*
With gentler breezes fanning this woodland plot, twilight lets fall its veil of mist and its sweet scents, whispering peace, lulling the heart like a child's, closing the day's door for these weary eyes.

Night has fallen. The holy stars come one by one. Great lights and little lights, shining afar, glittering near, glittering in the lake, shining aloft in the clear night. The full moon, presiding in its splendour, sets its seal on rest, rest perfect and profound.

The hours are spent. Pain and joy have vanished. You will be strong and well again. Let yourself feel it coming. Trust the new daylight. See, the

valleys are turning green, the little hills are swelling, showing their trees and shade, and in waves of swaying silver the season's crop advances.

To get your wish, your every wish, turn your eyes to the light. Your bonds are fragile. Sleep is a husk, throw it off. Lose no time, be bold, let others doubt and linger. A real man can achieve anything if he takes hold intelligently and doesn't delay.

A tremendous noise announces the approach of the sun

ARIEL

Listen. Listen to the tempest of the hours. The new day is being born, the spirit's ears can hear it. Rock-portals grind and rumble. Phoebus's wheels are rattling along. What noise comes with the coming of the light. A drumming, a trumpeting. Dazzling the eyes, and staggering the ears with more than they can hear. Slip away into the flower-cups, into the leaves, into the rocks, deeper, deeper, out of hearing, or you'll never hear again.

FAUST

Life's pulse in me is beating strong again, ready to hail and welcome this ethereal dawn. And you too, earth at my feet, have been constant through the night and are breathing now with new vigour, surrounding me with delights and rousing my ambition to strive and strive to reach the summit of existence. The world lies revealed in the half-light. The forest has come alive and rings with a thousand voices. Valleys up and down are streaked with mist, but the clear light of heaven reaches the depths. And twigs and branches there revive and spring out of the dimness they were sleeping in. Colour too upon colour comes out clear against the ground where leaf and flower are trembling with dew-drops. Whichever way I turn, I see a paradise.

Look up. The mighty mountain peaks are announcing the solemn hour. Already they're enjoying the eternal sunlight, which later creeps down to us. Meanwhile the upper meadows stand out clear and brilliant in their greenness. And now step by step it approaches. There. The sun has risen. But ah, it dazzles me, hurts me, and I have to turn aside.

This is what happens, when you hope and yearn for something and work your way towards realising it and believe you are near. You find the great gates of fulfilment flung wide open to receive you. But now, from the eternal sources beyond, a flame bursts on you, an excess of flame, a conflagration. We are taken aback. We wanted to light life's torch, and we find ourselves instead engulfed in a fiery ocean. Oh what fire! Is it love? Is it hate? that wraps its flames about us, pain alternating stupendously with joy, so that we are driven back to earth again and try to hide ourselves in earth's most youthful veils.

Very well, let me turn my face from the sun and have it at my back. This waterfall, noising down the crags – the more I look at it, the more I delight in seeing it plunge thousandfold from level to level, throwing its spray high, so high, in the air, scattering cool showers round about. And then, rising gloriously out of the commotion, comes the arch of the changing-unchanging rainbow, now sharply drawn, now blurred and lost. This is the mirror of our human endeavour. Ponder it and you will see: The many-coloured life we know is life reflected too.

scene 27 IMPERIAL PALACE

Throne Room. State Council awaiting the emperor. Trumpets. Courtiers of every kind, richly dressed, step forward. The emperor ascends the throne, the astrologer at his right hand

EMPEROR
I greet you all, you faithful ones, assembled from near and far. I have the philosopher at my side, but whatever has happened to the fool?

NOBLEMAN
He collapsed on the stairway right behind you. They carried him off in his fat. Dead or drunk, they don't know yet.

SECOND NOBLEMAN
But immediately, instantaneously, another offered himself. Amusingly dressed, but weird-looking. The watch is holding him at the door with crossed spears. There he is, the brazen fool.

MEPHISTOPHELES
Kneeling before the throne
What is accursed and always welcome? What is desired and then dismissed? What is for ever being protected? What is first censured, then accused? Whom mustn't you summon? Whose name does everyone like to hear? Who is approaching your throne? Who has banished himself?

EMPEROR
Spare your words. This is no place for riddles. I leave it to these gentlemen. Here you, you answer. I'd be curious to hear what you'd say. I'm afraid my old fool has gone for good. Take his place and come beside me.

Mephistopheles mounts the steps and stands on the left

A new fool – New trouble – Where does he come from? How did he get in? –
The old fool collapsed – He's done – First it was a barrel – Now it's a shaving.
EMPEROR

And so, my faithful ones, welcome from near and far. You have come together at a favourable moment. Good fortune is promised us from above.
But tell me why in these days when we were intending to forget our troubles,
put on our masks for the carnival, and altogether have a good time, tell me
why we should torment ourselves with a council meeting. However, you said
it had to be, and we've called one, so let us proceed.
CHANCELLOR

Justice, the highest of the virtues, rests on the emperor's head like a halo.
He alone can execute it. What all men love, demand, desire, and sorely
need – it is for him to grant it to them, as his people. But what use are
intelligence, kindness, readiness to head, heart, and hand when the body
politic is in a raging fever and a single evil breeds a host of evils? If you
cast your eye over the vast empire from this high chamber, it's like a
nightmare, where one rank disorder operates through another, lawlessness
becomes law and has its way, and a whole world of wrong is the result.

One man helps himself to a herd of livestock, another to somebody's
wife, and a third steals cup, cross, and candlestick from the altar and they
boast about what they've done for years after and get away with it without so much as a scratch. The courthouse is thronged with plaintiffs and
there sits the judge in all his upholstery; meanwhile the angry mob outside
is swelling and seething in waves of revolt. It's easy to parade your crimes
and your sins when you can count on accomplices who have a worse
record than you. Where innocence is its own defence, you'll hear a verdict
of guilty every time. And so, you see, the whole world is breaking up,
destroying all decency and propriety. How in such case is the state of mind
to develop that alone can give us direction? Things have gone so far that
a worthy man has to compromise with the unworthy, with flatterers and
corrupters. A judge who has lost his judge's power joins forces with the
criminal. I've drawn a black picture. I only wish I could make it blacker.
A pause

Decisions will have to be made. When everyone suffers and everyone is
harmful, the throne itself is threatened.
MINISTER OF WAR

What madness is abroad in these disordered days. There isn't anyone that
isn't either killing or being killed. And the word of command falls on deaf
ears. The townsman behind his town walls, the knight perched in his rock-
bound castle have put their heads together and decided to hold their resources and stick it out. Our mercenaries are getting impatient and shouting for their pay. They'd take off altogether if we didn't owe them money.
Let them all want a thing and it's like putting your head in a wasp's nest
to forbid it. They're supposed to guard the empire, and the empire's been
pillaged and devastated from end to end, violently. We do nothing to stop
it. Half the world's wrecked already. And our neighbouring kingdoms
think it's no concern of theirs.

LORD TREASURER

You can't count on allies. The subsidies they promise us are like tapwater that doesn't run. Besides, in your vast empire, sir, who owns the property? Wherever you go, you find a newcomer settled in, and he wants his independence. All you can do is to look on. We've surrendered so many privileges, we haven't one left. And as for parties, as they're called, you can't trust them either nowadays. Whether they like us or don't like us, praise us or blame us, it makes no difference. Both the Guelphs and the Ghibellines have gone into hiding and are taking a rest. Who in these times wants to help his neighbour? Every man has to look after himself. There's no gold to be had, the gates are barred. Everyone is scratching and scraping and hoarding. And the treasury's empty.

COURT STEWARD

And what misfortunes beset me too. We try day by day to save and day by day we need more. And every day brings new troubles. The cooks have nothing to complain about. Boars, venison, hares, turkeys, chickens, geese, ducks – all these come in pretty regularly as payments in kind. But we're short of wine. We used to have barrel on barrel in the cellar, the best vineyards, the best years. But the endless boozing of these noble gentlemen has consumed our last drop. The city hall has had to tap its supplies. They come with bowls and basins, and next thing they're all under the table. Now I have to pay wages, foot bills, and take out loans that set me years back. We can't wait to fatten the pigs. Everything's on borrowed money, the beds we sleep in and the bread we eat.

EMPEROR *to Mephistopheles after some reflection*

Tell me, fool, haven't you any complaints?

MEPHISTOPHELES

Not me. When I see you and your retainers in all this splendour. How could confidence be lacking, when your majesty is obeyed unqestioningly; the army is ready to scatter its enemies; goodwill, shrewd practical goodwill, is at your service, and activity of every kind? Under these circumstances how could evil forces gather against you? When such stars as these are shining, how could there be darkness?

VOICES

He's a scamp – He knows the game – Bluffs his way in – For as long as it lasts – I can tell you now – I know what's behind it – What is it then? – Some new proposal.

MEPHISTOPHELES

Wherever you go in this world there's always a shortage of something. It might be this, it might be that. Here it's money we're short of. Now you can't just pick up money from the floor. But there's nothing sunk so deep we can't get hold of it, if we use our wits. There's gold, coined or uncoined, under old walls or in the belly of the hills. And if you ask me who is to unearth it: An intelligent man using the brains that nature gave him.

CHANCELLOR

Nature! Brains! You can't talk this way to Christians. We burn atheists for that, because such talk is most dangerous. Nature is sinful, brains are of the devil. Between them they breed doubt. A misshapen bastard. Don't

talk that way to us. In our ancient domains two powers have arisen to support the throne, the clergy and the nobility. They beat off all attacks and they take church and state as their reward. If a rebellion breaks out in the confused mind of the mob, who's behind it? The heretics and witch-masters. They're the ruin of the country, and this fool's one of them. He's trying now with his smart talk to smuggle them into this high company. Don't trust them, they're treacherous.

MEPHISTOPHELES

Just like you learned gentlemen. If you can't touch a thing, it doesn't exist. If you can't grasp it, it's miles away. If you can't put it into figures, it's not true. If you can't weigh it, it has no weight. If you can't coin it, you say it's false.

EMPEROR

This won't solve our problems. What's the good of your lenten sermon? I'm sick of all this arguing. We're short of money, get us some.

MEPHISTOPHELES

I'll get you what you want and get you more. It's easy enough, but easy isn't easy. The stuff's there, but the trick is how to get it. Who knows? But just consider. In those terrible times when human floods swamped the land and the people how many a one in his fear and dread hid away what was dearest to him in some place or other. They did it in the days of the Romans, they did it yesterday, they're doing it now. It's all lying buried in the ground. The ground belongs to the emperor. Let him have it.

LORD TREASURER

For a fool he isn't doing badly. What he claims is the law.

LORD CHANCELLOR

There's something wrong about this. Satan's laying his golden snares.

COURT STEWARD

I don't mind being a bit in the wrong, if he gives the court something it likes.

MINISTER OF WAR

The fool is wise, he promises benefits to all. A military man doesn't ask where they come from.

MEPHISTOPHELES

And if you don't trust me, there's a man here, the astrologer, ask him. He knows his way about in the heavens, circle upon circle. Tell us how it looks there.

VOICES

A pair of rogues – They're in cahoots – A fool and a dreamer – So near the throne – An old, old song – We're tired of it – The fool prompts – The sage speaks.

ASTROLOGER speaks

Mephistopheles prompts

The sun is all gold. Mercury is running errands for pay. Venus is putting it over all of you, eyeing you sweetly, early and late. The moon is chaste and moody. Mars is either striking or threatening. Jupiter is the handsome one. Saturn is large, but looks small so far away. Not greatly valued as metal, but heavy. Yes, when sun and moon accord, gold with silver, then all is well in the world. Everything else can be had, palaces, gardens, women's breasts, red cheeks. We can't do it ourselves, but this learned man can procure them for you.

EMPEROR

Everything he says I hear double, but still it doesn't convince me.

VOICES

What does this mean? – A worn out joke – An old wives' tale – A phony science – I've often heard it – Been fooled before – Just let him come – He's a swindler.

MEPHISTOPHELES

There they are, standing around and gaping. They don't believe in the great find. One of them's babbling about mandrakes. Another's seen the black dog. It won't help them, this talking clever, this charge of witchcraft, when suddenly the soles of their feet begin to prickle and they find themselves stumbling about.

You can all feel the secret working of nature. The living trace finds its way up from the lowest regions. When you're plagued in every limb and the place seems creepy, don't lose a minute, start digging for all you're worth. That's the lucky spot.

VOICES

My foot's like lead – Can it be the gout? – My big toe's tickling – I've cramps in my arm – My back aches all the way down – To go by these indications – This must be a wonderful place for treasure.

EMPEROR

Be quick then. You can't slip away now. Give us the proof of your vapourings, and show us these noble regions at once. I'll put sword and sceptre aside, dig with my own imperial hands, and finish the job, if you are to be trusted. If not, I'll consign you to hell.

MEPHISTOPHELES

Well, I could find the way there all right. – But I can't overstate it about the

wealth that's lying around everywhere, waiting to be picked up. The farmer, ploughing his furrow, turns up a gold jug. He tries to scratch saltpetre from some clay pot and with trembling joy finds his poor hand filled with gold. What vaults there are to open, what clefts, what passages the treasure-hunter must enter to join the company of the underworld. In old cellars he'll find rows and rows of plate, ruby goblets, and, if he's so minded, there's casks of old wine to hand. But – would you believe it – the wooden staves have rotted away and the inner crust holds. Wines seek the night not less than gold and jewels. A wise man searches undismayed. It's easy to work in daylight, but mysteries belong to the dark.

EMPEROR

I leave mysteries to you. What good is gloom? If a thing's worth having, it should be brought into the daylight. You can't tell a thief in the dark, when all the cows are black and all the cats are gray. These gold-filled pots of yours, plough them up, let us see them.

MEPHISTOPHELES

Take pick and spade and dig yourself. This peasant labour will make you strong. And a herd of golden calves will rise up from the soil. Then delight is yours. You can adorn yourself and your lady in shining jewels, enhancing beauty and majesty both.

EMPEROR

Only be quick. How long must I wait?

ASTROLOGER *as above*

Sire, curb your eagerness. Let us wait till the carnival is over. When people are distracted, they're useless. We must first compose ourselves penitently. Earn the lesser things by way of the higher. Only a good man can do good. If you want joy, calm yourself. If you want wine, press ripe grapes. If you want miracles, strengthen your faith.

EMPEROR

Very well, let us pass the time in merriment. And then Ash Wednesday, when it comes, will be welcome. Meanwhile we must celebrate the carnival as riotously as we can.

Trumpets. Exeunt

MEPHISTOPHELES

The fools don't realise the connection between reward and merit. Even if they had the philosopher's stone, it would be no use to them.

scene 28 A SPACIOUS HALL WITH SIDEROOMS DECORATED FOR THE CARNIVAL

HERALD

Remember, this is not Germany with its dances of death, devils, and fools. A bright and happy festival is awaiting you. Our sovereign on his visits to Rome has made the journey serve our pleasure as well as his advantage, and he's brought back a merry world with him from beyond the Alps. First at the pope's feet he was given the authority to rule and next he picked up the fool's cap along with the crown. Now we are all as if born again. Any man who knows the world will cheerfully pull the cap over his head and ears, making himself look like a crazy fool, and then use his discretion inside it. I can see them assembling, sorting themselves out and pairing off, one group forcing itself on another, in and out, quite unperturbed. After all, the world with its countless absurdities remains the great big fool that it always was.

FLOWER GIRLS *singing, accompanied by mandolins*
We girls have come from Florence, following the German court. We've dressed up for tonight in the hope of pleasing you.

You see our dusky locks all decked with flowers. Threads and wisps of silk are what we used.

We thought you would approve. Our artificial flowers stay in bloom the whole year round.

We trimmed all sorts of coloured cuttings. You may disapprove of this and that, but the whole is attractive.

We're nice to look at, we flower girls, and stylish too. Artifice sits well on a woman.

HERALD
Show us the lovely baskets that you have on your heads or bulging in your arms. Everyone is free to choose what he likes. Quick, let us turn the walks and alcoves into a garden. These girls are worth looking at, not less than what they offer.

FLOWER GIRLS
Buy away, but on this happy occasion there must be no haggling. Let a few neat words tell each of you what he's getting.

OLIVE BRANCH WITH FRUITS
I don't feel envious of flowers. I avoid all conflict, it's against my nature. I'm the marrow of the earth, a sure token of peace everywhere. Today I hope to be so lucky as to adorn a fair and worthy head.

WREATH OF GOLDEN-RIPE CORN
Ceres' gifts, man's need of needs, are beautiful too. They'll look well on you.

A MIXED WREATH
A surprise. All these flowers that look like mallows, growing out of moss. It isn't quite natural, but fashion can do it.

A MIXED NOSEGAY
Even Theophrastus wouldn't venture to name me. Yet I hope to find favour with some at least, one perhaps who would bind me in her hair or wear me on her heart.

ROSEBUDS *hidden, challenging*
Let these caprices pass as things of fashion, oddly put together, foreign to nature, green stems, golden bells, peeping out of rich hair, but we ...

ROSEBUDS *showing themselves*
We hide away. Lucky those who can find us. When summer comes and roses break into bud, who would not care to see? This promise, this fulfilment in Flora's realm captures the eye, the mind, and the heart.

The flower girls display their wares along the arboured walks

See how the flowers decorate and adorn. The fruits we offer are honest. You must taste them to enjoy them.

Cherries, peaches, plums, all sun-browned. Buy them. Tongue and palate will tell you more than the eye.

Come, feast on our ripe fruits. You can write verse about roses, but apples you have to eat.

Allow us to join your young folk and dispose our ripe offerings among theirs.

In these festoons, in bays and bowers, you'll find everything at once – bud, leaf, flower, and fruit.

Singing in alternate choirs, with guitars and lutes, they continue to bargain and decorate

Mother and Daughter

MOTHER

Daughter, when you were a baby, I put a little hood on you. You were so sweet, so delicate. I saw you at once betrothed, married, and well off. I saw you as a woman.

But now so many years have passed and nothing has happened. The wooers, so gay, so many, quickly flitted by, though you danced with one and nudged another with your elbow.

Whatever parties we planned, they led to nothing. Forfeits and such-like games never worked. The silly men are all on the loose today. Sweetheart, try uncrossing your legs. You might catch one that way.

Other young girls join the party, and there is intimate chatter among them. Fishermen and bird-catchers with nets, fishing-rods, limed sticks, etc. enter and mix with the girls. Attempts on both sides to capture or evade lead to pleasant dialogue

WOODCUTTERS *entering, boisterous and clumsy*

Make way, make way. Give us lots of room. We cut down trees. They fall with a crash. And when we carry them, we're rough and ready. Don't take this wrong. Just say to yourselves: If there were no crude ones like us in the country, how could refined ones be there at all, no matter how clever? Remember this: We have to sweat, to keep you from freezing.

CLOWNS *awkward, almost silly*

Fools you are. Born with your backs bent. We, the clever ones, never carried a load. The things we wear, caps, rags, and jackets, sit light on us. We're always easy, always idle, lightly shod, ready to run through the crowded market, or stay and gape or, hearing a catcall, glide through the throng, slippery as eels, or dance or shout, all of us together. You're free to blame us, you're free to praise us, we don't mind at all.

PARASITES *fawning*

You woodcutters and your fellows, the charcoal-burners, are the men for us. For all our bowing and all our scraping, our yes-yes nodding, and flowery   *page 91* phrases, and blowing cold or blowing hot, to suit the moment, what good would it be? Even fire from heaven would be no use, unless there were logs, and loads of charcoal, to fill the hearth and make a fire, for food to fry on and cook and sizzle. The real gourmand that licks his plate will smell the roast and smell the fish and outdo himself at his patron's table.

DRUNKARD *blind drunk*

Today must go without a hitch. I never felt so grand. Let's have some fun and sing some songs, if I sing the songs myself. So here goes again. We'll drink together. You behind there, come here, come here. When our glasses clink, then all is well.

My wife got mad, she yelled at me, when she saw me strutting in these gay colours. She called me a dummy, a tailor's dummy. But me, I drink with the other dummies. When our glasses clink, then we're all right.

Don't tell me I'm lost. I'm where I want to be. I'm where I'm happy. The landlord chalks it up. If not, his wife'll do it. At a pinch the barmaid will. I just drink, drink with everyone, clink, clink. There you are, that's the way.

I don't mind how I have my fun. I don't mind where I have it. It's all the same to me. Leave me lying where I lie. I'm sick of standing.

CHORUS

Drink, brothers, drink. Clink, brothers, clink. Stay glued to your seats. He's under the table. He's finished.

The herald introduces various poets, poets of nature, court poets, love poets, sweet or passionate. In the pressure of competition none lets the other speak. But one of them gets a word in

SATIRICAL POET

Do you know what would really delight me as a poet? To write and recite what no one wants to hear.

The night and graveyard poets beg to be excused, because they are having a most interesting conversation with a newly arrived vampire, which might lead to a new form of poetry. The herald has no choice but to agree and he fills the gap by calling on Greek mythology which, while in modern costume, remains true to character and retains its appeal

The Graces

AGLAIA

We bring grace into life. Put grace into your giving.

HEGEMONE

Put grace into your getting. It is lovely to get your wish.

EUPHROSYNE

And in the quietness of your days make saying thank you gracious too.

The Fates

ATROPOS

Today they've given me the spinning to do, me the old one. There's much to think about, much to ponder, when you have life's delicate thread before you.

To make the thread supple and soft I had to sort out the finest flax. My skilful fingers will make it smooth and even.

If you're tempted to go too far in your sport and your dancing, remember the thread's limits. Take care, the thread can break.

CLOTHO

Please note that the shears have lately been entrusted to me. They weren't pleased with the way the old one handled them.

Interminably dragging out lives most futile; cutting off others full of hope and promise, and consigning them to the grave.

But I too, young as I am, have made many mistakes, so tonight, to keep myself in check, I've put the shears away.

I'm happy to do this and I look on with a friendly eye. Make the most of the opportunity and have your fun.

LACHESIS

They left the winding to me, the only sensible one. My distaff never stops, never hurries.

Threads come, I wind the threads and guide each one, never letting any slip, always keeping them in place.

If ever I forgot myself, I should fear for the world. Hours add up, years add up, and the weaver takes the skein.

HERALD

You won't recognise the next batch, no matter how learned you are. To look at them, you'd never dream what mischief they've done. You'd say they were welcome guests.

You'd never believe that these were the Furies. They're so pretty, such good figures, friendly, and not old at all. But you just have dealings with them and you'll soon see what serpents they are, for all their harmless look.

They're malicious, sure enough. But today, when every fool boasts of his failings, they don't want to pose as angels either. They confess they're the plague of town and country.

The Furies

ALECTO

He's warned you, but you'll trust us just the same, we're so young, so pretty, and such flatterers. If one of you has a sweetheart, we'll scratch him behind the ears.

And tell him face to face that she's going after one or two others, and she's stupid anyway and doesn't stand straight and has a limp and, if he's thinking of marrying her, she's a poor choice.

And we'll get after the girl too and say to her that not long ago he was running her down to that other girl. Some of this'll stick, even if they make it up again.

MEGAERA

That's nothing. Let them once get joined together and I take over. I know how to sour their happiness for them and never miss. There's always a weak point or a weak moment, if you watch out.

And no one ever attains his heart's desire and clasps it to him, but he tires of it after a while and foolishly starts longing for something else. He runs away from the sun and tries to warm an iceberg.

I know how to manage all this, and at the right time I introduce my faithful Asmodeus and let him scatter the seeds of calamity. In this way, couple by couple, I bring mankind to ruin.

TISIPHONE

No whispering and slandering for me. I mix poison for all traitors, I sharpen daggers. If you go after other girls you'll come to grief sooner or later, I promise you.

Your sweetest ecstasy will turn to gall. You won't get a hearing. You'll pay the price in full for what you did.

Don't babble to me about forgiveness. I make my charge to the rocky cliff and the echo says revenge. The unfaithful lover must perish.

HERALD

Would you please draw to one side. Something is coming now that is different. Look, there's a whole mountain approaching, its loins proudly draped with gay carpets. It has a tusked head, and a squirming trunk – very mysterious, but I'll give you the key. Seated on its neck and driving neatly with a slender staff you see a dainty slip of a woman. And standing behind her another most imposing, most exalted, with a dazzling light playing round her. On either side two noblewomen chained, the one fearing for her freedom, the other happily assured of it. Let each of the two tell us who she is.

FEAR

Smoky torches, lamps, and lights half-illuminate the festive throng. And here I am with no escape, chained, among these phantoms.

Off with you, you and your grinning and giggling. Who would trust you? All my enemies must be after me tonight.

There, a friend's become a foe. I can see through his disguise. Another here would murder me. I've found him out and now he's slinking off.

What would I give to run away no matter where in the world. But everywhere destruction threatens me. I'm caught among these misty horrors.

HOPE

Greetings, dear sisters. You may have revelled in your disguises for these two days, but I know for certain that you will leave them off tomorrow. And if you weren't altogether at ease in this torchlight, we shall soon walk happily again at our own sweet will, alone or not alone, in the lovely open country, and rest when we choose, or busy ourselves, in a life free from care, never going short of anything or failing in our endeavour, knowing too that whatever house we enter we shall be welcome. Surely, the best of life is waiting for us somewhere.

PRUDENCE

I'm protecting this company from two of mankind's greatest enemies, Fear and Hope, whom you see here in chains. Make way and let them pass. You're safe.

I'm in charge of this living colossus with its towered back. It makes its way unperturbed, step by step, on steep paths.

But up there on top you can see a goddess with quivering wings outstretched, ready to move, for gain, in any direction.

The glitter, the splendour, that encircles her can be seen shining on every
side from far away. Her name is Victoria and she is the activity goddess.

ZOILO-THERSITES

Ha, ha. I've come just at the right moment, to tell you all you're no good.
But Victoria up there's my real target. With those white wings of hers she
must think she's an eagle, thinks everything is hers wherever she goes. But
when anything worthy or praiseworthy happens, that's when I get angry.
Make low high and high low, crooked straight and straight crooked. That's
the only way for me. It's the way I want things everywhere.

HERALD

Then let my good staff work its trick on you, you dirty dog. Now you may
twist and turn. See how the creature, doubly dwarfed, rolls up into a horrid
lump. But what a thing. The horrid lump has turned into an egg. And see,
the egg has swelled up and burst and given birth to twins, an adder and a
bat. The one's crawling off in the dust and the other's flying to the ceiling.
They mean to meet outside. I wouldn't care to join them.

VOICES

Quick, they're dancing over there – Oh, I wish I was out of here – Can't you
feel these weird creatures all round us? – I can feel something in my hair –
I've got it in the foot – None of us are hurt – But we all got a fright – The
fun's over – That's what they wanted, the vermin.

HERALD

Being your appointed herald on such occasions, I'm keeping watch carefully
at the door and I never leave it lest anything should intrude that would mar
our merriment. But I'm sorry to say that some ghostly creatures are coming
in through the window and I can do nothing with ghosts or with magic. I was
dubious about that dwarf. But now there's something more powerful thrusting in from the back. I would explain these intruders if I could, but you can't
explain what you don't understand. You must help me. Do you see it coming?
It's a gorgeous carriage and four, passing through the crowd, but not dividing it. There's no disturbance anywhere. I can see coloured lights away off
and stars floating round. It's like a magic lantern. Now the thing comes
snorting up. Give it room. It's frightening.

BOY CHARIOTEER

Whoa. Horses, check your flight. Answer the rein as usual. Slow down at
my command. Put on speed when I incite you. But let us do honour to these
halls. See the revellers gathering round us, more and more of them, in ad-
miration. But come, herald, do your job before we leave. Name us, describe
us. It shouldn't be hard. You can see we're allegorical.

HERALD

I can't name you. I might be able to describe you.

BOY CHARIOTEER

Come on then.

HERALD

Well, to begin with, I must admit you're young and handsome. You're only
a boy half-grown, but one that the other sex will want to see when you're
bigger. A budding ladies' man; in fact, a born seducer.

BOY CHARIOTEER

Good. Go on. Solve the riddle.

HERALD

Dark, flashing eyes, thick dark hair, a jewelled headband, a pretty robe hanging down to your feet with purple hem and tinsel. Nearly like a girl, but, for better or for worse, one that the girls would already appreciate. They'd teach you your letters.

BOY CHARIOTEER

But what do you say to this one, throned so splendidly in my chariot?

HERALD

He looks like a king most rich and kind. Happy the man who enjoys his favour. He has nothing to seek for himself. He's quick to see where there's a need. The sheer joy of giving means more to him than possessions or good fortune.

BOY CHARIOTEER

You can't stop there. You must describe him.

HERALD

Dignity can't be described. But I see a healthy face, round as the full moon, a generous mouth, fresh cheeks, a handsome turban, flowing robes that sit easy. What can I say of his noble bearing? As a ruler of men I believe I know him.

BOY CHARIOTEER

He is Plutus, whom they call the god of wealth, travelling in splendour on his way to the Emperor who urgently wishes to see him.

HERALD

But now you. Tell me who you are.

BOY CHARIOTEER

I am poetry, the spendthrift, the poet who fulfils himself by throwing away what is intimately his. I too am wealthy, as infinitely wealthy as Plutus, whose festivities I enrich and enliven, supplying the things he lacks.

HERALD

Your boasting sits well on you. But show us your tricks.

BOY CHARIOTEER

See here. I just snap my fingers and at once there's a shine and a glitter all round the chariot. There comes a string of pearls.

He goes on snapping his fingers here, there, and everywhere

Here's golden clasps for neck or ear, brooches, crowns, jewelled rings. Sometimes I scatter flames too and watch them set things on fire.

HERALD

See the dear folk grabbing and snatching, crowding him, almost jolting him. They're snatching away all over the hall. And he's snapping out his treasures as if in a dream. But now comes a new trick. For all their efforts they get little in return. The gifts fly away. The pearl necklace has turned into so many beetles in a man's hand. He's thrown them away, poor fellow, and now they're buzzing round his head. Others, expecting something solid, are finding they've only captured silly butterflies. What a rogue he is, promising so much and only giving what glitters but isn't gold.

BOY CHARIOTEER

I see you know how to interpret costumes, but it isn't your official business as herald to go to the heart of the matter. This calls for a sharper vision. But I won't quarrel with you. I'll turn to you, my master, and ask you (*turning to Plutus*). Did you not entrust your whirlwind chariot to me? Haven't I driven it well and taken you where you said? Didn't I with bold flight win the palm of victory for you? When I fought for you, did I ever fail? If laurels deck your brow, wasn't it me that thoughtfully twined them?

PLUTUS

If I have to give you a testimonial, I am happy to say you are spirit of my spirit. You always act in my sense. You're richer than I am. I value the green branch I reward you with above all the crowns I wear. I can declare frankly to everyone: My beloved son, in thee I am well pleased.

BOY CHARIOTEER *to the crowd*

I've scattered my finest gifts among you. There's a head here and there with a little fire burning in it that I started. It jumps from one to another, it stays with this one and leaves that. Sometimes, but not often, it flares up in a quick blaze, but in many cases it goes out altogether, unnoticed.

WOMEN CHATTERING

That's a charlatan for sure, up on top of the chariot. And crouching behind him the clown, all starved and shrunken. We've never seen him like that before. You might pinch him now, he'd never feel it.

THE SCRAGGY ONE

Keep away from me, you disgusting women. I know I'm not wanted. In the days when women ran the house, my name was Lady Avarice, and all went well. A lot came in and not much went out. I kept a jealous eye on chests and cupboards. It gave me a bad name. But now that women have stopped being economical and are bad with money and care more for desires than dollars, the menfolk have a great deal to put up with, debts confronting them, whichever way they turn. What cash the women can scrape together they spend on their finery or on their lovers. They eat better and drink more in their wretched company. All this makes me greedy for gold. I'm male, not female any more. Call me the miser.

LEADER OF THE WOMEN

Let the old dragon stick to his dragons. The whole thing's a hoax. He's come to stir up the men and they're trouble enough already.

CROWD OF WOMEN

A man of straw. Give him a punch. He's thin as a lath, can't frighten us. Paper dragons too. Let's have a go at them.

HERALD

See my staff. Calm yourselves. But I'm not needed. These fierce monsters have got excited. They've quickly cleared a space. They're spreading their double pairs of wings and spitting fire angrily from their scaly jaws. The crowd has scattered. The place is clear.

Plutus dismounts

HERALD

He's stepping off. How like a king. He raises his hand. The dragons at once lift down the treasure chest with the miser sitting on it and set it in front of him. It's a miracle.

PLUTUS *to the charioteer*

Now I release you from your irksome duties. Off you go lightly to where you belong. This is no place for you, beset as we are all round by things garish, confused, ugly, turbulent. You need to be where you can look with a clear eye into the clear, be master of yourself and confident, in a world that cares for the good and the beautiful. Seek an abode in solitude and create your world there.

BOY CHARIOTEER

I shall value myself as your envoy and love you as my nearest of kin. Wherever you go, there is plenty, there is abundance. Where I go, everyone feels himself gloriously the gainer. Men often hesitate in this contrary life: Should they go with you or go with me? If they go with you, they can idle their time away. With me there's always something to be done. I never act in secret. I only have to breathe and I give myself away. Goodbye then. I know you wish me well. But say the word, whisper it, and I'll be back.

PLUTUS

The time has come to release our treasures. I touch the locks with the herald's staff and the chest springs open. And see, red gold rising molten in these bronze vessels, threatening to engulf the treasures – crowns, chains, rings.

SHOUTS FROM THE CROWD

Oh, look, just look, it's welling up in the chest. It's overflowing. – Gold vessels melting away, turning into rolls of coins. – Ducats brand-new bobbing up and down, what a temptation. – See my heart's desire bouncing on the floor. – Don't miss the opportunity, bend your backs and get rich. – Let's grab the whole chest in a flash.

HERALD

You fools, what are you up to? It's only a joke. You'll forget it all by tonight. Do you think the money's real? Counters would be too good for you. Stupidly taking a pretty effect for the truth. The truth would be wasted on you, you snatchers at illusion and obscurity. – Plutus, hero of the masquerade, scatter these people, clear the floor.

PLUTUS

Your staff is handy. Lend me it for a moment. I'll dip it in the brew. Now, you masqueraders, look out. See the flashes, the sparks flying. The staff's catching fire already. If you come near, you'll get singed and no mistake. Now I'll go the round.

SHOUTS FROM THE CROWD

Oh, we're done for. – Escape, if you can. – Get back, you behind there, it's spraying right into my face. – My, that staff's heavy as well as hot. – It's the end for all of us. – Get back, you mummers, back, you idiots. – If I'd wings, I'd fly.

PLUTUS

The crowd has scattered. – They're all pushed back and no one hurt. But I'll draw an invisible line for safety.

HERALD

Splendid work. I'm grateful to you.

PLUTUS

Be patient, good friend. There's plenty of disorder yet to come.

AVARICE

Now, we can take a friendly look at these people, all ranged round in a circle. And why shouldn't we? The women are always to the fore, when there's anything to nibble or to stare at. I'm not so shrivelled up yet that I don't find a pretty woman pretty. And today, seeing that it costs nothing, I'll try my luck among them. But it isn't easy to make yourself heard in all this crowd, so I'll see what I can get across to them with a little pantomime. There are things you can't say with your hands and feet. I'll have to fall back on one of my pranks. I'll treat this lump of gold as wet clay. After all, you can do anything with gold.

HERALD

What's the skinny fool doing? You wouldn't think he had a sense of humour. He's working the gold in his hands like dough, squeezing it, rounding it, but it's still shapeless. And now he's turned to the women and they're all shrieking and shrinking back in disgust. He's a mischief. I'm afraid he's being indecent and liking it. I can't let this pass. Give me my staff and I'll drive him out.

PLUTUS

He has no notion what is about to descend on us. Leave him to his fooling. He'll soon be pushed aside by forces stronger than himself.

RIOTOUS CROWD *singing*

Here we come, from hill and dale, the riotous army of Pan's worshippers, forcing our way into the empty circle. We know something. You don't know what.

PLUTUS

But I know you and your great god Pan. You've taken a bold step. And I know what you know. It is my duty to let you in and I hope your bold adventure will not turn out badly. There's no telling what can happen. They aren't prepared. They don't know what they're in for.

RIOTERS' SONG

Look out, you tinselled, titivated people,we're coming on the run, coming in great jumps. We're a rough crowd.

FAUNS

We fauns are dancing a merry dance, with oakleaves in our curly hair and pointed ears peeping out, a broad face and a blunt little nose. This doesn't hurt with women. When a faun offers his paw, no woman, even the fairest, would care to say no.

SATYR

The satyr comes hopping with his goat's foot and his scraggy, sinewy legs, the kind of legs he needs. He loves to survey the world like the chamois from a mountain-top and, thus refreshed, mock the human kin, young and old, down in the stuffy valleys, so smug and contented, when all the time he's the only one who really lives, in the freedom of the heights.

GNOMES

We little gnomes don't like to stay in pairs, we flit about all over the place in mossy jackets with our little lamps, thronging like ants, always busy, each by himself.

We belong to the good-fellow family, well-known as rock-surgeons. We cup the veins of the high mountains and pour the metals down with the miners' cheery hail. We mean it well. We are the friends of man. But the gold we turn out only furthers theft and lechery. The iron is wanted by those who in their pride invented wholesale murder. If you ignore these three commandments, you won't respect the others. This isn't our fault. We are patient. You must be patient too.

GIANTS

We are the so-called wild men, well-known in the Harz mountains, giants in our naked strength, with pine trunks in our right hands and thick, rough girdles of leaves and branches slung round our loins. The pope himself has no such body-guard.

CHORUS OF NYMPHS *encircling Pan*

Here he comes, the great god Pan, the god of the universe. You happy ones, enclose him in a lively dance. He's grave, but kindly too, he wants us to be merry. He's stayed awake all the time under his blue roof, but the brooks murmur to him and the breezes soothe him and when he sleeps at noon not a leaf stirs, the balmy scent of plants fills the air, all is silent and still. The nymph daren't stay awake, she falls asleep where she stands. But if suddenly his mighty voice is heard like a peal of thunder or the sea roaring, then everyone is in a panic, armies scatter in the field, heroes tremble in their midst. So, do homage where it is due, hail him who has brought us here.

DEPUTATION OF GNOMES *addressing Pan*

When the shining precious metal streaks through chasms so hidden that only the divining-rod can trace its windings, there in the gloom we delve our dwelling, all for you to apportion the treasures we bring in the clear daylight. But now we have discovered close by a source of treasure exceeding our expectation, and easy to reach. From here on you, sir, please take charge. We shall all get the benefit of any treasure that is in your hands.

PLUTUS *to the herald*

We must now most solemnly compose ourselves and let what happens happen. You've always shown yourself a man of courage. Now something most

horrible is about to come. People will deny it, stubbornly. But you must set it down faithfully in your minute-book.

HERALD *taking hold of the staff which Plutus keeps in his hand*

The dwarfs are conducting great Pan to the fire. It boils up from deep down and then falls back, leaving the dark mouth gaping. Then it foams up hot again. Pan is standing undisturbed, enjoying the strangeness, while pearly drops are scattered right and left. Why is he so unsuspecting? He bends over to look down inside and his beard has fallen in. Whose can that smooth chin be? He's put his hand over it and we can't see. And now comes a catastrophe. His beard has caught fire and flown back on, setting his wreath and his head and his breast alight. Our pleasure has turned into pain. The crowd has run up to put the blaze out, but none of them escape it themselves, and the more they beat about them the more the flames grow. A whole group of masqueraders are involved in them and consumed.

But what are they announcing now, passing the word from mouth to mouth, ear to ear. O unhappy night, ever unhappy, what suffering you have brought on us. Tomorrow the unwelcome news will be heard on every hand: It is the emperor who was burned. Oh that this should be the truth. The emperor is burned and those with him. Cursed be the company that led him astray, dressing up in resinous twigs and coming here yelling their heads off and bringing everyone to grief. O young people, when will you learn to keep your merry-making within bounds? O majesty, when will you learn to combine power with reason?

The whole wood has gone up in flames, with sharp tongues that are licking the timbered roof and threatening to burn the palace down. What grief. It is too much. Who can save us? All this imperial splendour reduced to ashes in a single night.

PLUTUS

We have had shocks enough. Now relief is needed. You sacred staff, strike the floor till it shakes and rings again. And you, circumambient air, fill with freshness. Come, you mists and pregnant lines of cloud, spread out and cover this raging fire. Rustle, roll, sprinkle, moisten, quench. Turn the silly flames into summer lightning. When spirits threaten us, magic must step in.

scene 29 PARK

A sunny morning. The Emperor, Courtiers. Faust and Mephistopheles in conventional dress, not conspicuous, both kneeling

FAUST

Has your majesty forgiven us for putting on that magic fire-show?

EMPEROR *beckoning to them to stand up*

I could do with many such entertainments. I saw myself suddenly transported into a glowing region, almost as if I was Pluto. It was a rocky valley, dark and smouldering, with deep pits in it and here and there flames whirling out of them, arching and closing overhead in a flickering vault that came and went incessantly. Through twisted columns of fire I saw far off ranks of people approaching in a wide sweep and doing homage to me as usual. I recognised a courtier or two among them. I felt as if I was lord of countless salamanders.

MEPHISTOPHELES

And so you are, sir, because each of the elements recognises your majesty as supreme. You've tested the fiery element and found it obedient. Now throw yourself into the sea where it is roughest and you'll at once find you're treading a pearly floor, beautifully enclosed in shifting light-green waves edged with purple, a lovely place to dwell in, and yourself at the centre of it. When you move, step by step the palaces move with you. The walls themselves are alive with things thronging, darting swiftly this way and that. Sea monsters crowd towards the strange, soft light, they come with a rush, but they can't enter where you are. You'll see richly coloured dragons with gold scales, sharks with open jaws; you can look right down their throats. You may be delighted with all your court round you, but you never saw such a throng as this. And you won't lack what is sweetest. Nereids will come, all curious to see this new dwelling-place in the watery world, the young ones like fishes timid and lustful, those behind them more experienced. Thetis will hear the news and offer her hand and her lips to a second Peleus. And now for your seat on Olympus ...

EMPEROR

You can keep Olympus and the airy spaces. That's a throne we shall mount only too soon.

MEPHISTOPHELES

And, as your majesty knows, you already own the earth.

EMPEROR

What a stroke of luck it was that brought you here straight out of the Arabian Nights. If you are as inexhaustible as Scheherazade you may be assured of my highest favour. Stand ready to oblige when the daily world disgusts me, as it often does.

MARSHAL *in a hurry*

Your highness, I never dreamed in all my life that I should have such a piece of good fortune to announce. I'm delighted and doubly so in your presence. We've paid off all our debts and got out of the usurer's clutches. Those hellish worries are over. I couldn't be happier if I was in heaven.

MINISTER OF WAR *also in a hurry*

We've issued an instalment of pay and the whole army's loyal again. The men are in good spirits. The pubs are full and the girls are busy.

EMPEROR

To think how you ran to tell me. And you're breathing freely again and your faces are all smoothed out and smiling.

LORD TREASURER *entering*

Enquire of these two. They did the job.

FAUST

It is for the chancellor to explain.

CHANCELLOR *approaching slowly*

Feeling great happiness in my old age on account of all this. – Hear me then and look at this momentous piece of paper, which has turned all our woe to weal. *He reads* 'To whom it may concern, this paper here is worth a thousand

crowns, its collateral lying safely in the wealth of buried treasure within our
borders. Steps have been taken for this treasure to be raised without delay
so as to redeem the pledge.'

EMPEROR

This, I suspect, is criminal, a gigantic fraud. Who forged the emperor's
signature? Has this offence gone unpunished?

LORD TREASURER

Don't you remember? You signed yourself only last night. The chancellor
came up and said to you in our presence: Allow yourself the high pleasure
on this festive occasion of ensuring your people's welfare with a few strokes
of the pen. You signed, and our conjurors, the printers, quickly ran off a
thousand copies. We stamped them at once to let everyone share the benefit
without delay. Tens, thirties, fifties, and hundreds are all ready. You can't
imagine how happy the people are. Look at your city. It was rotting and half
dead, and now it's alive again with pleasure-seekers. Your name has always
spelt happiness, but never before has it looked so benign. We don't need
the rest of the alphabet now. Your signature's enough to make them all as
happy as lords.

EMPEROR

Do you mean to say they take it for good money? The army's satisfied with
it, the court? It looks queer to me, but I must let it pass.

COURT STEWARD

It was impossible to hold them back. They scattered in the twinkling of an
eye. The money-changers have their doors wide open, cashing all the bills
in gold and silver – at a discount, of course. And from there, people go to
the butchers and bakers or to the pubs. Half the world has no thought of
anything but eating, the other half's strutting about in new clothes. The
drapers are cutting out, the tailors are busy sewing. In the wine-cellars
they're toasting the emperor in torrents. The frying-pans are sizzling, the
plates are clattering.

MEPHISTOPHELES

If you stroll along the terraces by yourself, you'll soon spot a pretty lady,
gorgeously decked out, smirking at you and peeping with one eye from
behind her peacock fan to see if you'll produce one of these bills, and quicker
than by any smart talk or rhetoric it will procure you the best that love can
offer. You don't have to bother with a purse or a satchel. You can carry a
bill easily in your bosom alongside of a love-letter. The priest can carry it
piously in his prayer-book, and the soldier can take the weight off his legs
and move more freely. Your majesty must pardon me if I seem to be making
light of this great achievement by going into these details.

FAUST

The unlimited treasures lying buried in your territory are not being used. A
wealth exceeding the farthest range of thought. Let your imagination strain
to the limit, it will still fall short. But deep-seeing minds have infinite confidence in the infinite.

MEPHISTOPHELES

Compared with gold and pearls a paper like this is so convenient, and you
know what you've got, no bargaining over it, no exchange needed, nothing
to stop you taking your fill of love and wine. If you want cash for it, you

can have it. Otherwise you do a little digging. You can auction your valuables, your cups or chains, and the bills you get can be redeemed at once, thus putting all the doubters and mockers to shame. You become quite used to this and don't want it otherwise. There'll always be treasure, gold, and paper enough anywhere in the empire.

EMPEROR

The emperor has to thank you both for this great benefit. I propose to make the reward as nearly as possible equal to the service. I put our underground territory in your charge and I appoint you custodians of its treasures. You're well informed about them. All digging must be under your control. Join your forces, you masters of our treasures, and enjoy the dignity of your office, in which the underworld and the upper world will work harmoniously together.

LORD TREASURER

I welcome the magician as my colleague. There will be no friction between us whatsoever. *off, with Faust*

EMPEROR

I am now going to give each one of you a present, but you must tell me what you will do with it.

PAGE *receiving*

I shall be merry, light-hearted, content.

ANOTHER *likewise*

I shall buy rings and chains for my sweetheart.

CHAMBERLAIN

From now on I shall treat myself to choicer wines.

ANOTHER

The dice are already itching in my pocket.

BANNERET *deliberately*

I shall clear the encumbrances on my property.

ANOTHER

It's valuable; I'll put it away with the rest of my valuables.

EMPEROR

I hoped to hear talk of new activities, but anyone who knows you can soon see through you. With all your wealth, you'll just remain what you were.

FOOL *entering*

You're giving presents. Give me one.

EMPEROR

You'll only spend it on drink.

FOOL

These magic pieces of paper. I can't figure it out.

EMPEROR

I can believe that. You make such poor use of them.

FOOL

There's more of them falling on the floor. What shall I do?

EMPEROR

Pick them up. They're meant for you. *off*

FOOL

Five thousand crowns. Can these be mine?

MEPHISTOPHELES
You guzzler, have you come back to life again?
FOOL
I've done it many times, but this is the best yet.
MEPHISTOPHELES
You're so delighted you're all in a sweat.
FOOL
Look here, is this worth real money?
MEPHISTOPHELES
Yes, you can eat and drink your fill with it.
FOOL
Can I buy land with it, a house and livestock?
MEPHISTOPHELES
Of course. Bid and you'll get it.
FOOL
And a castle, a forest to hunt in, a trout stream?
MEPHISTOPHELES
I must say I'd like to see you as lord of the manor.
FOOL
I'll be a landowner this very night. *off*
MEPHISTOPHELES *alone*
Who'll say now that our fool's a fool?

scene 30 A DARK GALLERY

Faust and Mephistopheles

MEPHISTOPHELES
What are you dragging me off into these dark passage-ways for? Isn't there fun enough in there, all the opportunities you want for your tricks and pranks, among that mixed crowd of courtiers?
FAUST
Don't say that to me. You've talked that way too many times before. This running about now is just to avoid speaking with me. But I'm in a fix and don't know what to do. Both the marshal and the steward are after me. The emperor wants to see Helen and Paris right away. It has to be a clear picture of them. The ideal man and the ideal woman. So get to work at once. I've given my word and I must keep it.
MEPHISTOPHELES
Silly of you to promise so casually.
FAUST
You didn't consider where your arts would lead us. We've made him wealthy. Now he expects us to amuse him.
MEPHISTOPHELES
It can't be done in a minute. Don't fool yourself. This is unfamiliar ground, most unfamiliar. It's a stiffer climb altogether. You'll end by getting wickedly involved again. You think it's as easy to call up Helen as to call

up those ghosts of paper money. Now if it was witches you wanted, dwarf deformities, or spooky spectres, I could supply them. But the devil's girls, though not to be despised, can't pose as classical heroines.

FAUST

There you are again, grinding out the same old tune. With you I never know where I am. You make difficulties at every turn, new demands all the time. You only need to mutter a few words and it's done. I know that. They'd be here before you could say Jack Robinson.

MEPHISTOPHELES

Those pagans are no concern of mine. They have a hell of their own. But there is a means.

FAUST

Out with it then and don't prevaricate.

MEPHISTOPHELES

I dislike letting out one of the higher secrets. There are goddesses throned in solitude, outside of place, outside of time. It makes me uneasy even to talk about them. They are the Mothers.

FAUST *startled*

The Mothers.

MEPHISTOPHELES

Does it give you the shivers?

FAUST

The Mothers. The Mothers. It sounds so queer.

MEPHISTOPHELES

Queer it is. Goddesses unknown to mortal men, hardly to be named by them. You'll need to dig deep to reach them. It's your fault if we have to do it.

FAUST

Show me the way.

MEPHISTOPHELES

There is no way. You'll enter the untrodden, the untreadable, the unpermitted, the impermissible. Are you ready? There'll be no locks or bolts. You'll be pushed about from one emptiness to another. Have you any notion what emptiness is? Barrenness?

FAUST

I should have thought you'd spare me this jargon. It all smacks of the witch's kitchen to me and the long, long ago when I had to mix with others, learn meaningless things and teach them too. If I talked good sense as I saw it, I was contradicted more than ever. There were disagreeable incidents. I had to run off into the wilds and be alone. And finally, lacking all other company, I was driven to joining up with the devil.

MEPHISTOPHELES

And even if you'd swum across the ocean and seen its infinitude and feared you were done for, you'd at least have seen something. You'd have seen waves following waves and when the sea was quiet you'd have seen dolphins gliding through the green water. You'd have seen sun, moon, and stars, and clouds passing. But here you'll see nothing in all the empty distances. You won't hear the tread of your own feet. You'll find nowhere to
rest your head.

FAUST

You talk like the biggest mystagogue that ever fooled his simple pupils.
Only you're in reverse. You're sending me into nothingness, where I'm
supposed to improve myself in my art. You're making me pull the chestnuts
out of the fire for you like the cat in the fable. Well, here goes. We'll see
what's at the bottom of it all. In this nothing of yours I hope to find the
everything.

MEPHISTOPHELES

I see you understand the devil and I'll give you a word of approval before
you go. Here, take this key.

FAUST

That little thing.

MEPHISTOPHELES

Take hold of it and don't underrate it.

FAUST

It's growing in my hand. It's shining, flashing.

MEPHISTOPHELES

Now you're beginning to see what it's worth. This key will nose out the
way for you. Follow its lead. It'll conduct you to the Mothers.

FAUST *shuddering*

The Mothers. It hits me every time. What is this word that I can't bear to
hear?

MEPHISTOPHELES

Why let a new word disturb you? Are you as narrow-minded as that? Do
you only want to hear what you've heard before? Don't let anything bother
you, whatever comes. You're well used now to the strangest happenings.

FAUST

To slacken and come to a stop will never suit me. The thrill of awe, of won-

derment, is the best we have. The world may make us pay heavily for our feelings, but when the tremendous thing comes we know how to respond.

MEPHISTOPHELES
Down you go, then. I might equally say: Up you go. It's all the same. Escape the created world and enter the world of forms. Take your pleasure in what has long ceased to exist. You'll see it all as drifting clouds. Swing your key and keep it from you.

FAUST *enthusiastically*
Good. I feel a new access of strength as soon as I grip it firmly. My chest expands. On to the great task.

MEPHISTOPHELES
When you come to a glowing tripod you'll know you're as far down as you can go. By the light it throws you'll see the Mothers. Some sitting, some standing or walking about. It just depends. Formation, transformation, the eternal mind eternally communing with itself, surrounded by the forms of all creation. They won't see you. They only see ghosts. You'll be in great danger and you'll need a stout heart. Go straight up to the tripod and touch it with your key.

Faust strikes a commanding attitude with the key

MEPHISTOPHELES *looking at him*
That's the way. It'll connect and follow you as your servant. Now you'll calmly ascend. Your good fortune will hoist you. And before they notice, you'll be here with it. And once you have it here you can call up hero and heroine from the shades. You'll be the first to pull it off. It'll be done and you'll have done it. The clouds of incense will turn into gods as part of the magic process and so remain.

FAUST
And what do I do now?

MEPHISTOPHELES
Let your nature will your descent. Stamp your foot and you'll go down. Stamp again and you'll come up.

Faust stamps his foot and disappears

MEPHISTOPHELES
I hope that key works. I'll be curious to know if he ever gets back.

scene 31 HALLS BRIGHTLY LIT

Emperor and princes. Courtiers moving about

COURT STEWARD *to Mephistopheles*
You haven't yet put on the ghost scene you promised. Get to work. The emperor's impatient.

MARSHAL
His majesty has just been enquiring. Make haste. You mustn't let him down.

MEPHISTOPHELES
It's this very business that's taken my partner away. He knows what to do and he's working quietly. It requires a very special effort. When you're evoking that precious thing called the beautiful, you need the highest of the arts, you need the philosopher's magic.

MARSHAL
It's all the same to me what arts you need. The emperor wants results.

BLONDE
A word with you, sir. You can see that I have a clear complexion. But in summer, I'm sorry to say, I get freckles by the hundred all over my white skin. Give me a remedy.

MEPHISTOPHELES
Too bad. To think of a handsome girl like you all spotted in maytime like a leopard. Take some frogs' eggs and mix them with toads' tongues. Distil carefully in the full moonlight and apply to your skin when the moon is waning. When spring comes, you'll find your freckles have disappeared.

BRUNETTE
People are beginning to crowd round you. Please tell me what to do. I have a game leg. It makes me limp when I walk or try to dance or even make a bow.

MEPHISTOPHELES
May I put my foot on yours?

BRUNETTE
Well, that's what lovers do.

MEPHISTOPHELES
The touch of my foot means more than that. Like to like is the thing for all ailments. Foot cures foot. It's the same with the other parts. Come here and watch out. Don't respond.

BRUNETTE *shrieking*
Ouch. It burns. That was a hard tread you gave me. It felt like a horse's hoof.

MEPHISTOPHELES
But it's cured you. You can dance all you want now. Touch feet under the table with your sweetheart.

LADY *pressing forward*
Let me through. I'm in great trouble. It makes me boil with rage. I was his dream until yesterday. And now he's dropped me and gone after her.

MEPHISTOPHELES
Difficult. But listen to me. Take this piece of charcoal, sidle up to him, and mark him with it as best you can on his sleeve, shoulder, and cloak. He'll feel a pang of remorse. But you must eat the charcoal at once and touch neither wine nor water. He'll be sighing at your door before the day's over.

LADY
Pressing forward
I trust it's not poisonous.

MEPHISTOPHELES *enraged*
Madam, do you wish to insult me? This is no ordinary piece of charcoal. It comes from far away, from a funeral pyre that we used to work harder.

PAGE
I'm in love, but they don't believe I'm old enough.

MEPHISTOPHELES *aside*

I don't know which way to turn. (*to the page*) Don't set your heart on the youngest of them. The older ones will appreciate you better.

Others press him

More coming. What a tussle I'm having. I'll have to start telling the truth. That's the poorest way out. But what can you do in a crisis like this. O you Mothers, do let go of Faust.

Looking around

The lights in the hall are burning low. The courtiers are all moving off, passing quietly down long corridors, distant galleries, and assembling in the old baronial hall, big but hardly big enough to hold them. Tapestries hanging on the walls. Armour in every nook and corner. No magic words needed here, I should think. The ghosts will come of themselves.

scene 32 BARONIAL HALL

Dimly illuminated. Emperor and Courtiers already assembled

HERALD

It is my longstanding duty to announce the play, but there are supernatural forces at work which make it difficult. It's impossible to find any rational explanation of the confusion that prevails. The seating arrangements have been completed, the emperor facing the wall where he can enjoy the tapestries recording the great battles. Here they are then, emperor and courtiers, all ranged round with the crowded benches behind them where lovers can sit close together in the uncanny twilight. And so, since all are now seated, we are ready, the spirits may come.

Trumpets

ASTROLOGER

Let the play begin. The emperor so commands. Open up, you walls. It's plain sailing now, with magic at our disposal. See, the carpets are disappearing as if curled up in fire. The wall divides and reverses. To all appearance we now have a deep stage before us, and there's a mysterious light coming from somewhere. I'll go up on the proscenium.

MEPHISTOPHELES *sticking his head out of the prompter's box*

I hope you'll all approve of me in my present capacity. Prompting is the devil's rhetoric.

To the astrologer You know the rhythm of the stars. You'll understand my whisperings perfectly.

ASTROLOGER

Here, revealed by the power of magic, is an ancient temple, massive as you see. The row of pillars makes us think of the giant Atlas who once held up the sky. They're certainly equal to the weight of stone they have to bear. Any two of them would suffice for a big building.

ARCHITECT

You call that classical? I don't like it. I call it crass and overloaded. If a thing's crude, they say it's noble. Clumsy, they say it's great. What I love is slender columns, soaring up into the infinite, pointed arches that uplift the spirit. There's the style that truly edifies.

ASTROLOGER

Accept this heaven-sent occasion with reverence due. Let magic words suspend your rational thinking and, instead, let fantasy, the rich and free, come from far away and rule us. Look now on the scene you so boldly demanded. It's quite impossible and for that very reason worthy of belief.

Faust mounts the proscenium from the other side

ASTROLOGER

See the wonder-worker in priestly robes with a wreath on his head, fulfilling the task he so confidently undertook. A tripod has risen with him from below and he is about to consummate his achievement. If I'm not mistaken, I can smell the incense from the bowl. Things can't go wrong now.

FAUST *impressively*

In your name, O Mothers, enthroned in the illimitable, always alone, yet not unsociable. The forms of life revolve around you, mobile, but lifeless. All that once was in all its spendour is in motion there, seeking to be made eternal. You supreme powers part them in two, assigning some to the tent of day, to be drawn into life's sweet course, others to the vault of night where the magician seeks them out. Whatever wonders are desired, he has in full measure the power to reveal them.

ASTROLOGER

No sooner does the red-hot key touch the bowl than a mist gradually fills the scene, rolling in clouds that spread or shrink or cross or part or join. And now comes a masterpiece of magic. The clouds, as they drift, make music, airy notes like nothing that ever was. Everything, even the columns, the triglyph, is turning into melody. I verily believe the whole temple is singing. Now the mist is dropping and through the thin veil a handsome youth comes forward with measured step. And here I must pause. I don't need to name him. Who could fail to see that this is Paris.

Paris steps forward

LADY

Oh what a picture of youth in its bloom and its strength.

SECOND LADY

Fresh and juicy as a peach.

THIRD LADY

And those lips, so delicately drawn, and yet so sweet and full.

FOURTH LADY

A sip from that cup is what you'd like.

FIFTH LADY

He's very pretty, but not exactly refined.

SIXTH LADY
I do wish he was a little less awkward.

KNIGHT
He still bears the marks of a shepherd boy, I feel. Nothing princely about him, no courtly manners.

SECOND KNIGHT
No doubt he's good-looking when he's half naked. But how would he be in a coat of mail?

LADY
He's seating himself in an attractively feminine way.

KNIGHT
I daresay you wouldn't mind sitting on his lap.

ANOTHER LADY
He's putting his arm behind his head so gracefully.

COURT STEWARD
How vulgar. It shouldn't be allowed.

LADY
You gentlemen find fault with everything.

COURT STEWARD
Stretching out like that in front of the emperor.

LADY
He's only acting. He thinks he's alone.

COURT STEWARD
In this place the play itself ought to be polite.

LADY
The charmer has dropped asleep.

COURT STEWARD
And he's immediately beginning to snore. It's so natural. It's perfect.

YOUNG LADY *delighted*
What is that scent that mingles with the incense and so gladdens my heart?

OLDER LADY
You're right. There's a breath of something that moves me deeply. It comes from him.

STILL OLDER LADY
It's ambrosia, the scent of youth flowering, filling the air about us.

Helen appears

MEPHISTOPHELES
So there she is. She wouldn't bother me. Pretty, no doubt, but not my sort.

ASTROLOGER
To be honest, I must confess I'm helpless here. When beauty comes, tongues of fire are not enough. The praises of beauty have been sung and sung again from the beginning. Those who behold it are swept beyond themselves. Those who ever enjoyed it were rewarded beyond their deserts.

FAUST
Do I see with my eyes? Or is it deep in my inner mind that the source of beauty is thus poured out before me? My fearful journey has brought a

marvellous reward. How futile the world was, before it was opened to me. What is it now after my term of priesthood? Desirable, deep-founded, permanent as never before. May the breath of life leave me if ever I go back on you. The fair form that once delighted me, swept me away, in the magic mirror was mere froth beside this. To you I owe the springs of every action and the quintessence of passion. I devote myself to you in affection, love, worship, yes in madness.

MEPHISTOPHELES *from the prompter's box*
Pull yourself together and remember your part.

OLD LADY
Tall, well-built, but the head rather too small.

YOUNG LADY
Look at her feet. Could they be clumsier?

DIPLOMATIST
I've seen great ladies just like her. It seems to me she's beautiful from top to toe.

COURTIER
She's slowly, cunningly approaching the sleeper.

LADY
How ugly she looks beside his youthful purity.

POET
The light of her beauty is shining on him.

LADY
Just like the painting of Endymion and Luna.

POET
You're right. The goddess seems to be coming down from above. Now she's bending over him to drink his breath. A kiss. The lucky man. It's the limit.

DUENNA
In front of everybody. It's too much.

FAUST
What a terrific favour to this lad.

MEPHISTOPHELES
Be quiet. Let the ghost do what it wants.

COURTIER
She's tripping away stealthily. He's waking up.

LADY
She's looking back. I thought she would.

COURTIER
He's astonished. He thinks it's a miracle.

LADY
What she sees is no miracle to her.

COURTIER
She's turned round and coming back, with great decorum.

LADY
I can see she's taking him in hand. In this situation all men are simpletons. He probably thinks he's the first.

KNIGHT
I won't have a word said against her. She's majestic and most refined.

LADY

The jade. I call that vulgar.

PAGE

I wish I was where he is.

COURTIER

What man wouldn't get entangled with her?

LADY

She's a jewel that's passed through many hands. The gilt's a bit worn.

ANOTHER LADY

She's been no good since she was ten years old.

KNIGHT

Everyone on occasion takes the best. This lovely leftover would do for me.

PEDANT

I can see her all right, but I must confess I doubt if she's the right one. Face to face with her you lose your judgment. For myself I stick to the books and the books say she delighted all the old men of Troy. It seems to me that this holds good now. I'm not young, but I like the look of her.

ASTROLOGER

He's a boy no longer. He's heroic and daring. He's seized hold of her. She's practically defenceless. He's hoisted her up on his mighty arm. Is he going to run off with her?

FAUST

The reckless fool. To be so bold. Can't you hear? Stop. This is too much.

MEPHISTOPHELES

Aren't you the man that's putting it on, this crazy ghost-play?

ASTROLOGER

One word more. To go by what we've seen, I'd call it *The Rape of Helen*.

FAUST

Rape indeed. Do I count for nothing here? Have I not this key in my hand? The key that led me through horrid seas of solitude to a firm landing where I could set down my two feet. These are realities. Standing here, my spirit can hold its own with spirits and master the two realms. She was so far off and now she could hardly be nearer. If I rescue her, she'll be doubly mine. I'll take the risk. O Mothers, grant me this. When you've once set eyes on her, you can't give her up.

ASTROLOGER

Faust, Faust, what are you up to? He's grabbed hold of her. She's beginning to blur. He's turned his key towards the boy and touched him with it. Oh dreadful, dreadful.

Explosion. Faust collapses. The spirits disappear in smoke

MEPHISTOPHELES *throwing Faust over his shoulder*

Now we've got it. Taking up with fools, even the devil's the loser in the long run.

Darkness, confusion

scene 33

A high, narrow, vaulted Gothic chamber, formerly Faust's, unchanged

MEPHISTOPHELES *coming from behind a curtain. He raises the curtain and looks back at Faust lying prostrate on an old-fashioned bed*
Lie there, you luckless man, caught in bonds of love not easy to break. When Helen's knocked you out, you don't get your wits back in a hurry. *looking about him*

If I look round me here, I find everything just as it was, nothing moved, nothing damaged. The stained glass seems a bit darker. More cobwebs. The ink's dried, the paper's yellowed. But everything's in its place. There's even the pen here that Faust signed himself to the devil with. And deep down in the reed a drop of the blood that I coaxed out of him on that occasion. A curiosity, unique, one that any collector might be proud of. And look, there's the old gown on the old hook. Reminds me of the crazy notions I once put into that boy's head. He's probably drawing on them still, now he's a little older. I really feel tempted, with this warm gown on, to play the professor again, very pompous, very sure of himself. Learned men know how to carry it off, but the devil's right out of practice. *He shakes the furry gown and crickets, moths, and beetles fly out of it*

CHORUS OF INSECTS
Welcome, boss, welcome, dad. Here we are again, flying and buzzing. We know you all right – you quietly planted us one at a time, and now we come in hundreds and thousands. The devil may like to hide his thoughts, but we little things soon slip out of the fur.

MEPHISTOPHELES
How this young brood delights me. You just sow the seed and some day you'll reap the harvest. I'll give the old sheepskin another shake. Here's one or two more fluttering out. Off you go now, my dears, and hide in holes and corners. Plenty of them over there among those old boxes, faded parchments, dusty flowerpots, or even in those skulls' eyesockets. In a place as messy and mouldy as this there'll always be some queer notions and things stirring. *He slips into the gown*

Come, drape me again. I'm the head of the firm once more. But what's the use calling myself that? Who recognises me as such? *He pulls the bell which rings with a piercing, shrieking tone, making the halls rock and the doors fly open*

FAMULUS *tottering down the long, dark corridor*
Oh what a frightening, shattering noise. The stairs and walls and windows all quaking. And lightning flashing through the stained glass. The floor's giving way under me and there's mortar and rubble coming down from overhead. By some magic or other the door's burst its bolts. And standing there – how dreadful – a giant wearing Faust's old gown, staring at me and waving his hand. My knees are nearly giving way under me. Shall I run or shall I stay? Oh what will happen next?

MEPHISTOPHELES *with a gesture*
Come here, my friend. Your name is Nicodemus.

FAMULUS

Yes, your honour, it is – Oremus.

MEPHISTOPHELES

You can leave that out.

FAMULUS

I'm so glad you know me.

MEPHISTOPHELES

I know you well enough. Older now and still at college, an old-timer in fact. Even a man of learning goes on studying because he can't stop. Building his little house of cards. But the best among you never finishes. Your professor, though, is smart, that Dr Wagner whom we all know and respect. The leading figure in the world of knowledge, the one man that holds it together, and adds a little every day to the world's wisdom. He's a shining light in the lecture room. People crowd after him to hear him and learn from him. He handles the keys like St Peter, both to the higher world and the lower. He's so brilliant no one can stand up against him. Even Faust's name is over-shadowed. Wagner gets the credit for everything.

FAMULUS

Forgive me, venerable sir, if I make bold to contradict you. It isn't the way you say. He's modest through and through and he can't reconcile himself to Faust's unaccountable disappearance. He prays that the great man may return happily and put his mind at rest. Faust's room here is waiting for him; it's never been touched since he went away. I hardly dared to come in. What can be happening now, at this great moment? The very walls seem terror-struck. The door-posts rocked. The bolts sprang. Otherwise you'd never have got in yourself.

MEPHISTOPHELES

Where's Wagner gone? Take me to him or bring him here.

FAMULUS

I don't see how I can. He's strictly forbidden it. He's been working for months in the utmost seclusion on his great project. He's the gentlest of his kind and he looks like a charcoal-burner, with his face black all over, his eyes red with puffing the flames. He hangs with bated breath on every moment. The mere sound of the tongs is music in his ears.

MEPHISTOPHELES

Is he going to refuse me, when I'm the very man to speed the good work?
Famulus goes out. Mephistopheles solemnly seats himself

No sooner have I got myself in place than I see something moving. Yes, it's a visitor I recognise. But this time he's one of the *avant-garde*. He's sure to go the limit.

BACCALAUREUS *striding down the corridor*

The place is wide open today. It makes you wonder whether this fusty death-in-life mightn't come to an end and life be liveable here at last.

The walls are collapsing. If I don't get out quick, I'll be buried underneath them. I'm not a coward by any means, but this is as far as I'm prepared to go.

But what a thing. Isn't this the spot where years ago I came as a freshman, quaking in my shoes, trusting those old graybeards and feeding on their prattle.

From those ancient books of theirs they dished out the lies they had ready. Had them ready but didn't believe them, and made life miserable for them and me. But what's this? Someone's sitting back there in the study, half in the dark.

And how surprising. When I get nearer, it's him, still sitting there in that fur-lined gown, just as I left him. I thought he was clever then, when I hadn't got his number. It won't work today. So here goes.

Well, old chap, I see your head is bald and bowed, but if Lethe's waters haven't wetted it yet, you may recognise me, your former pupil. I've outgrown the academic drill now and can claim your approval. You look as if you hadn't changed a bit, but me, I've changed a lot.

MEPHISTOPHELES

I'm glad my bell brought you along. I never thought badly of you. The grub, the chrysalis always gives a hint of the bright butterfly that is to come. I remember your childish pleasure in curly hair and a lace collar. I'm sure you never wore a pigtail. Today you have your hair cut short. You look quite sturdy, quite resolute. All very well. But you mustn't be absolute.

BACCALAUREUS

Old man, here we are in the old place. But consider how times have changed and stop this talking two ways at once. We aren't as stupid as we used to be. You made fun of me without much effort when I was young and innocent, but that's all over now.

MEPHISTOPHELES

If you tell young people the honest truth, which they never like to hear, and then years after they arrive at it by their own bitter experience, they flatter themselves it came from them and they haven't a good word for their teachers.

BACCALAUREUS

He's a sly one. Did you ever hear before of a teacher who told you the straight truth face to face? They all know how to ring the changes, soft pedal or loud, grave or gay, according to need.

MEPHISTOPHELES

There's a time for learning, but, as I see, you're ready to start teaching. You've no doubt collected a lot of experience over the months and years.

BACCALAUREUS

Experience – empty stuff. Not comparable with the mind of man. Come now, confess, nothing we've ever known was worth knowing.

MEPHISTOPHELES *after a pause*

I've often wondered. I was a fool. I feel now how superficial, how silly I am.

BACCALAUREUS

Pleased to hear you say so. You're talking sense. The first old buffer to do it that I've met.

MEPHISTOPHELES

I was searching for hidden gold and came back with dust and ashes.

BACCALAUREUS

Tell me, is that bald pate, that skull, of yours any better than those hollow ones?

MEPHISTOPHELES *cheerfully*

You've no idea, my friend, how rude you are.

BACCALAUREUS

In German, if you're polite, you're not being honest.

MEPHISTOPHELES *who has been approaching the front in his wheelchair, addresses the audience*

Up here I can hardly breathe or see. Have you any room for me down there?

BACCALAUREUS

I find it presumptuous, when the game is up, for you to go on pretending to be something when you're nothing at all. Life is in the blood, and where is the blood so active as in a young man, where it's fresh and vigorous and creative too? Never inert, never wasted, rejecting the weak, favouring the strong. And while we've been conquering half the world, what have you done? Nodded, meditated, dreamed, pondered, plan upon plan. There's no doubt about it, old age is an ague, a cold fever, all whims and worries. A man over thirty's as good as finished. Best thing would be to bump you off.

MEPHISTOPHELES

From the devil at this point no comment.

BACCALAUREUS

The devil only exists with my approval.

MEPHISTOPHELES *aside*

The devil will get you yet, you'll see before long.

BACCALAUREUS

This is the glorious mission of the young. There was no world at all till I created it, fetched the sun up out of the sea and set the moon on its changing course. For me, in all my paths, the earth grew green and blossomed and was beautiful. A sign from me on that first night of all and the stars came out in their splendour. Who was it but me that rescued your minds from the clutches of philistinism? For my own part I'm happy and free to follow the promptings of my spirit and my inner light. And so, in raptest joy of self, I speed along my way, the dark behind me and all bright and clear ahead. *off*

MEPHISTOPHELES

On you go in your glory. This lad is priceless. How it would hurt his feelings to know there's nothing wise and nothing foolish that hasn't been thought of long, long ago. But he won't do any harm. A few years from now and he'll be different. The new wine may play its pranks, but it mellows with time. *To the younger members of the audience who have refrained from applauding*

You don't approve of what I say. You're young and I forgive you. Remember, the devil is old. When you're old, you'll understand him better.

scene 34 LABORATORY

Medieval; clumsy, sprawling apparatus, for fantastic ends

WAGNER *at the furnace*

That dreadful bell's ringing, making these sooty walls shake and tremble. It can't be long now before this extreme tension is relieved, and the result known. The dark is lessening, in the innermost bottle there's a glow like live coal, almost like a lovely carbuncle, sending its rays out into the gloom.

And now there comes a clear white light. Oh, I hope it won't go wrong this
time. But there, what's that rattling the door?

MEPHISTOPHELES *entering*

Greetings, a friend.

WAGNER *nervously*

Greetings to you, at this great moment. (*quietly*) But don't say a word, don't
breathe. A grand piece of work is being completed.

MEPHISTOPHELES *more quietly*

Tell me.

WAGNER *still more quietly*

We're making a man.

MEPHISTOPHELES

A man. Did you lock a pair of lovers up the chimney?

WAGNER

God forbid. That old way of doing it is quite out of fashion now. We call it
nonsensical. The tender point of life beginning, the sweet energy forcing
its way out from within, taking and giving, imposing its pattern, appropriat-
ing what is near, then what is less near – all this is discredited. Animals may
still take their pleasure in it, but man with his great gifts must have a higher
origin, a purer one, henceforth. (*turning to the furnace*) See the light there.
Now we can really hope that after duly mixing these hundreds of substances
– it's all a matter of mixing – to make the human substance, and then sealing
it up and thoroughly redistilling it, the work'll prove to be a quiet success
in the end. (*turning again to the furnace*) It's coming now. The mass is
clearing. I feel surer and surer. What we used to acclaim as nature's mystery
we now boldly try to perform with our intelligence. Where nature used to
grow things, we crystallise them out.

MEPHISTOPHELES

A man learns a lot if he lives long enough. Nothing new can happen anywhere for him. I've run into this crystallised sort of people before, on my
travels.

WAGNER *who has kept his eye on the bottle*

It's rising, flashing, mounting. In a jiffy it'll be done. A great project seems
crazy at the beginning, but the day will come when we'll laugh at our luck.
Sooner or later a thinking man will be able to make a thinking brain.
(*looking delightedly at the bottle*) The glass is ringing with amorous force.
It fogs and then clears. It must be coming. I can see a neat little mannikin
gesturing. What do you want? What more would you have? The secret's
out now. Just listen to the sound. It's turning into a voice, it's speaking.

HOMUNCULUS *addressing Wagner from the bottle*

Well, father, how are you? That was no joke. Come, give me a hug, but
gently, gently, or you'll break the glass. This is the way of things. The whole
world's hardly big enough for natural life. But artificial life has to be con-
tained. (*to Mephistopheles*) You here, brother, you rogue. Thank you for
coming, and at the right moment too. Very fortunate. While there's life in
me, I must be up and doing and I want to get to work right away. You're
just the man to help me.

WAGNER

But one word more. I've always been embarrassed. People old and young come at me with problems. For instance, no one can understand how body and soul go so well together, cling as if they would never go apart, and yet are for ever quarrelling. Then ...

MEPHISTOPHELES
Stop. I'd rather enquire why man and wife don't hit it off better. My friend, you'll never get to the bottom of it. But there's a job of work here, the little fellow wants it.

HOMUNCULUS
Direct me.

MEPHISTOPHELES *pointing to a side-door*
Show your talents here.

WAGNER *still staring into the bottle*
You surely are a darling boy.

The side-door opens, showing Faust stretched out on the bed

HOMUNCULUS *astonished*
Important, this. (*The bottle slips out of Wagner's hands, hovers over Faust, and shines a light on him*) A beautiful setting. A clear pool shut in among trees. Women undressing. Delightful women. It's getting better all the time. But one there is outshines the rest in splendour, a woman sprung from a line of heroes, if not from the gods. She dips her foot in the transparent flood, cools her lovely body's flame in the yielding, glittering water. But what a din of swiftly flapping wings. A plunging and splashing that shatters the smooth mirror. The girls run off in fright, but she, the queen, calmly looks on and, with a woman's pride and pleasure, watches the prince of swans nestle at her knees and, gently insistent, stay. He seems to like it there. But suddenly a mist rises and quite blots out this most charming of scenes.

MEPHISTOPHELES
The things you have to tell. You're a little fellow, but my, what an imagination you have. I can't see anything.

HOMUNCULUS
I don't wonder. You that came from the north and grew up in the dark ages, in all that jumble of popery and chivalry. How could you expect to see with a clear eye? You're only at home in the gloom. (*looking round him*) Look at this stonework, brown with age, mouldy, horrid. And pointed arches, twirligigs, so confining. If he wakes up on us, there'll be more trouble. He'll drop dead on the spot. Woodland springs, swans, naked beauties. That was his wishful dream. How could he get used to this? I, the most adaptable of men, can hardly bear it. Away with him.

MEPHISTOPHELES
I'd like to know what you propose.

HOMUNCULUS
Send the soldier into battle, take the girl to the dance, and all will be well. But it suddenly comes into my mind that the Classical Walpurgis Night is on. He'll be in his element there. We couldn't do better than take him to it.

MEPHISTOPHELES
I never heard of anything like that.

How should you? Romantic ghosts is all you know about. Ghosts, to be genuine, have to be classical too.

MEPHISTOPHELES

Well, which way do we go? Classical colleagues, I hate the thought.

HOMUNCULUS

Your stamping-ground, Satan, is north-west, but we fly south-east, to a great plain with the river Peneios ambling through it, fringed with trees and bushes, widening into loops and bays. The plain stretches back to rugged hills and on the slope lies Pharsalus, the old town and the new.

MEPHISTOPHELES

Oh, take it away, forget those wars of tyranny and slavery. They bore me. No sooner is the fighting done than they start all over again. And neither side notices that it's just Asmodeus who's at the back of it all, teasing them. They're supposed to be fighting for freedom, but, when you come to look at it, it's slaves against slaves.

HOMUNCULUS

Don't bother about the contrariness of mankind. Everyone has to stick up for himself from the time he's a boy. In the end it makes a man of him. But our problem is with Faust and how to get him well again. If you have anything to propose, let's try it. If not, leave it to me.

MEPHISTOPHELES

We might try some of the Brocken's tricks. But the heathen gates are bolted against me. Those Greeks were never much good, dazzling you with their free play of the senses, enticing you into happy sinfulness. Our sins, you'll find, are always gloomy. So what now?

HOMUNCULUS

You're not backward as a rule. And if I drop a word about the witches in Thessaly, I presume it registers with you.

MEPHISTOPHELES

Witches in Thessaly. Those are people I've been enquiring about for a long time. I don't know that I care about night after night with them. But I'll try anything once.

HOMUNCULUS

Bring the mantle and put it round him. It'll carry you both as before, and I'll go in front and shine my light.

WAGNER *anxiously*

And what about me?

HOMUNCULUS

Well, you'll have to stay at home and do important work. Unroll your old parchments, collect the elements according to rule and mix them carefully. Consider the what and, still more, consider the how. Meanwhile I'll see a piece of the world and possibly discover the dot on the 'i.' Then my great purpose will be served. The reward is worth the effort. Wealth, honour, fame, health, and long life. And knowledge and virtue as well – who knows? Goodbye.

WAGNER *distressed*

Goodbye. This makes me very sad. I'm afraid I'll never see you again.   *page 121*

MEPHISTOPHELES

Quick now. Off to the Peneios. Our cousin is not to be despised.
To the audience After all, we're bound to be dependent on our own creatures.

scene 35 CLASSICAL WALPURGIS NIGHT

Battlefield of Pharsalia. Darkness

ERICHTHO

The festival of ghosts met here tonight has seen me many times, and now I
come again, Erichtho, the dismal one. Dismal, but not as repulsive as those
wretched poets make me out to be with their endless gibing. Praising or
blaming, they never know when to stop ... The valley in all its length is
paled and whitened with army tents spread like a sea. An after-vision of
that most harrowing, that cruellest of nights. How often it has repeated,
how often will it repeat, year after year after year, for the rest of time.
Neither one yields the empire to the other. Not willingly, least of all when the
other, having taken it with force, rules it with force. Men who cannot master
their inner selves are all too ready in their arrogance to dominate their
neighbours. But here, on this spot, a great issue was fought out. It's the old
story of strength pitted against greater strength, the many-flowered wreath
of freedom torn to shreds and the stiff laurel twisted about the conqueror's
brow. This is where Pompey dreamed his dream of early triumphs come
again, while Caesar there tensely watched the tongue of the balance waver.
The fight is on. We know, the world knows now, which was the winner.

Bonfires are blazing red. The soil exhales the shadow of blood once spilt.
And, drawn by the rare beauty of this shining night, mythical figures of the
Greek world are here in multitude. Fabulous forms of ancient days can be
half seen flitting about the fires, or they sit beside them at their ease ... The
moon is up, not yet at the full, but radiant, shedding its friendly light on
everything. The spectral tents have disappeared. The fires are burning blue.

But now, over my head, a meteor shining. How unexpected. And lighting
up a ball of something. I catch the scent of human life and must not let it
near me, being harmful to it. It would hurt my name and serve no purpose.
Now the meteor's dropping. Discretion bids me keep away. *withdraws*

The Aeronauts aloft

HOMUNCULUS

I'll take another turn over these spooky bonfires. The whole valley bottom
has the weirdest look.

MEPHISTOPHELES

I can make out some appalling ghosts here. It's like looking through the old
window at the horrors of the north.

HOMUNCULUS

Look. There's a lanky one striding past.

MEPHISTOPHELES

It almost looks as if she's had a fright, saw us coming through the air.

HOMUNCULUS

Let her go. Set our gallant friend down and life will immediately come back to him. Here in the world of fable is where he's looking for it.

FAUST *touching the ground*

Where is she?

HOMUNCULUS

Can't quite say. But this is where you'll probably find out. You might, between now and daylight, quickly scout around among the bonfires. A man who's been to the Mothers needn't be afraid of anything.

MEPHISTOPHELES

I have my reasons for being here too. But what better could we do than let each of us go his own way among the fires and have his own fun? Then, when we have to join up again, the little chap can light his glass and make it buzz.

HOMUNCULUS

This is how I'll flash it and ring it. (*The glass lights up and buzzes strongly*) Now off we go in search of more surprises.

FAUST *alone*

Where is she? No need to ask now. If it isn't the soil she trod and the sea-shore she knew, it's the air that spoke her speech. Here, by a miracle, here I am, in Greece. I felt the ground under me at once, warming me with new life after my sleep, making me like some Antaeus of the spirit. And, finding all manner of strange things assembled here in this labyrinth of fire, I'll make a thorough search of it.

Seeking Helen !

scene 36 THE UPPER PENEIOS

every time he falls gets stronger

MEPHISTOPHELES *nosing around*

When I start roaming around among these bonfires, I find myself quite put off. Almost all of them stark naked, and only one here and there with a shift on. The sphinxes utterly indecent, and the griffins brazen too. And then all the rest, winged and hairy, catching your eye from in front or from behind. I don't mean we aren't thoroughly indecent too, but this antique stuff's too vivid altogether. It needs modernizing and plastering over with the newest fashions ... Offensive people. But I shouldn't let this deter me. As a newcomer I must be polite. Greetings to you, fair ladies. And to you too, the knowing grayfins.

GRIFFINS *snarling*

Not grayfins, griffins. Who wants to be called gray? The sound of a word tells you where it comes from: Gray, grave, grating, gruesome. They're all alike, but we don't like them.

MEPHISTOPHELES

But, to stick to the subject, you don't mind being called griffins with a 'grrr.'

GRIFFINS *as above*

Of course not. Griffin goes with grip and grab. It's been proved and proved. Often condemned, but mostly commended. Try grabbing at girls and gold and greatness. Fortune usually favours the grabber.

ANTS *giant variety*

Gold, you say gold. We collected a lot of it and rammed it into caves and holes. Now those arimasps have tracked it down. We don't know where they've taken it. There they are, laughing at us.

GRIFFINS

We'll make them tell.

ARIMASPS

But not tonight. It's a holiday. And by tomorrow we'll have gone through it all. So this time we think we'll score.

MEPHISTOPHELES *who has sat down among the sphinxes*

I find myself so readily at home here. I can understand every one of you.

SPHINX

We utter our ghostly sounds and you folk embody them. And now, for a start, tell us your name.

MEPHISTOPHELES

People have many names for me. Are there any Englishmen here? They generally travel, inspecting battlefields, waterfalls, ruins, dreary classical spots. This would be just the place for them. They identified me as Old Iniquity in one of their early plays.

SPHINX

How did they hit on that?

MEPHISTOPHELES

I can't tell you.

SPHINX

Well now. Do you know how to read the stars? What can you say about the present moment?

MEPHISTOPHELES *looking up*

One shooting star after another. A clipped moon, shining bright. I feel snug here, warming myself against your lion skin. A pity to waste time on the upper regions. Give us some riddles, some charades.

SPHINX

Express yourself and it'll be riddle enough. Try self-analysis. Thus: 'The pious man needs you as much as the wicked. The first needs you as a fencing-jacket for ascetic sword-play. The other as a partner in wild undertakings. And all of it just to amuse the gods.'

FIRST GRIFFIN *snarling*

I don't like him.

SECOND GRIFFIN *snarling louder*

What does he want here?

BOTH TOGETHER

He's nasty. He doesn't belong here.

MEPHISTOPHELES *savagely*

Perhaps you don't think my nails are as sharp as your claws. Try, and we'll see.

SPHINX *gently*

You may stay. You'll soon want to go of your own accord. You may think you're somebody at home, but, if I'm not mistaken, you're not at ease with us.

[handwritten margin notes: "half lion half + eagle", "guarded Gold", "a winged woman", "lion with womans head"]

MEPHISTOPHELES
Your upper half is quite nice. But down below you're beastly, horrible.
SPHINX
You'll pay for this yet, you scamp, because our claws are sound. You with your shrunken hoof don't feel happy in our company.

Sirens practising overhead

MEPHISTOPHELES
What birds are those rocking in the poplars by the river?
SPHINX
Look out for yourself. Their singing has been too much for some of the best.
SIRENS
Why dally with this fabled ugliness? Listen to us. We come in flocks and sing most sweetly, as sirens should.
SPHINXES *mocking them to the same tune*
Make them come down. They're hiding their savage claws in the branches. They'll kill you if you listen to them.
SIRENS
Away with this hate and this envy. We offer the purest delights under heaven, the happiest welcome on land or sea.
MEPHISTOPHELES
There's the new-style playing and singing for you, one note twining around another. Their warbling's wasted on me. It tickles your ear, but it doesn't reach your heart.
SPHINXES
Your heart, indeed. Don't flatter yourself. Your heart's only a shrunken, leather pouch, to go by the look of you.
FAUST *approaching*
How wonderful. The seeing is enough and more than enough. Forbidding, but their features are great and vigorous. All will be well, they seem to say. Where does this solemn sight take me?
Referring to the sphinxes Before these Oedipus once stood.
Referring to the sirens Ulysses writhed before these in hempen bonds.
Referring to the ants These gathered the great treasure.
Referring to the griffins These faithfully guarded it. This freshness of spirit thrills me through and through. The forms are grand. Grand are the memories.
MEPHISTOPHELES
You don't usually tolerate this sort of thing, but today you do. When you're searching for your loved one, even monsters can help.
FAUST *to the sphinxes*
You that are woman-shaped must answer me. Have any of you seen Helen?
SPHINXES
She came after our time. Hercules slew the last of us. But Chiron will be able to tell you. He's galloping about on this ghost-night. If he stops for you, you'll be lucky.
SIRENS
You could find out from us. Ulysses didn't scorn us and hurry past. He stayed with us and he told us many things. We'd pass it all on to you, if

you'd come down to where we live by the sea.
SPHINX

Don't be deceived, good man. Ulysses made them bind him. Let the advice we gave you be binding on you. If you can find Chiron, he'll tell you.

Faust off

MEPHISTOPHELES *vexatiously*

What's that flying past and croaking? So fast, one after another, you can hardly bear to look. Very trying for a hunter.

SPHINX

These are the stymphalids. They have webbed feet and a vulture's beak and they fly like the storm-wind in winter, almost too swiftly for the arrows of Hercules. Their croaking is friendly. They'd like to join our company, as relatives.

MEPHISTOPHELES *as if in fright*

There's something else hissing here.

SPHINX

You needn't be afraid of them. They're the heads of the Lernean dragon, severed from the rump and pleased with themselves. But tell me, what's the matter with you? You're flinging yourself about so. Off you go, where you want. I see that bevy over there has made you crane your neck. Pretty faces. Introduce yourself. They're lamiae, smiling, bold, seductive, favoured by the satyrs. A goat's-foot can let himself go with them.

MEPHISTOPHELES

You'll be staying here, won't you? In case I come back.

SPHINXES

Yes, join the merry crowd. We've been used to sitting enthroned for a thousand years ever since our Egyptian days. Pay us due respect. We sit in front

of the pyramids, regulating the months and years and the fate of nations, *scene 36*
impassively witnessing floods and war and peace.

scene 37 THE LOWER PENEIOS

Stretches of water, nymphs everywhere

PENEIOS

Bestir yourselves, you reeds and rushes, you slender stems of willow, you trembling poplars, breathe ever so lightly, whisper to me in my broken dreams. A strangely disquieting vibration everywhere has shaken me out of my sleepy flow.

FAUST *coming to the river bank*

Can it be human voices I hear coming from these hidden arbours? It almost seems so. The ripples in the water seem to chatter. The little breezes joke and play.

NYMPHS

Lie down here, rest your weary limbs in this cool place, taste the repose you so seldom find. That would be best. And we'll sing to you in a running whisper, a rustling sound.

FAUST

Now I'm awake. Oh, let them have their way with me, the incomparable forms that my eye recovers here. So marvellously am I affected. Is it dreams? Is it memories? Once before I had this joy. Cool water sliding slowly through dense and faintly swaying bushes, sliding so slowly hardly a ripple can be heard. Springs innumerable flowing together from every side to form this clear, clean, evenly shallowed bathing-pool. And healthy young women in it, the liquid mirror making the eye's delight twofold. The women playing gaily together, or boldly swimming or wading timidly, or shrieking and splashing one another. This should be enough for me to feast on, but my thought presses further. And I turn my gaze to where behind that rich green foliage the queen is concealed.

Wonderful. Swans are entering the pool from the outer bays, majestic, poised, tender, but proudly independent in the movement of head and beak. One of them seems to stand out in pride and boldness, sailing through the rest with spreading feathers, like a wave riding on waves, on its way to the queen ... The others move quietly to and fro and then dart at the timid girls to divert them from their duty with concern for their own safety.

NYMPHS

Sisters, put your ears to the ground on the grassy brink. Unless I'm mistaken, I can hear a horse galloping. Who can be bringing news tonight?

FAUST

The ground seems to ring under a horse's tread. Can my good fortune be here, by a miracle? Now I see a man on horseback, a white horse, dazzling white ... and the rider looks like a man of mind and courage. But I know him. It's the famous son of Philyra. Chiron, stop. I've something to say to you ...

CHIRON

What is it?

Chiron — Achilles — Jason

wise and just and learned in medicine educated most famous of Greek heroes

FAUST

Slow down a bit.

CHIRON

I never stop.

FAUST

Then, please, take me with you.

CHIRON

Jump up. Then I can take my time asking. Where are you going? Here you are on the river bank. I'm willing to take you across.

FAUST *mounting*

Wherever you like. I'm eternally indebted to you ... the great man, the noble tutor, who to his glory brought up a race of heroes, the Argonauts, and others who enlarged the world of song.

CHIRON

Forget it. Even Pallas Athene did herself little honour in that role. In the end they carry on just as if they'd never been taught at all.

FAUST

You're the physician who knew his botany well and salved the wounds and cured the sick. I embrace you here in body and in spirit.

CHIRON

If by my side a hero was hurt, I knew what to do. But I finally left all that to the old women and the priests.

FAUST

You're the truly great man who can't bear to be praised. You modestly put it aside and pretend there are others as good as you.

CHIRON

You seem to be one of those clever hypocrites who manage to flatter both the ruler and the ruled.

FAUST

At least you must admit you knew the great ones of your day, you strove to be like the noblest in what you did, and you lived a life worthy of a demi-god. But which of all the heroes did you think the best?

CHIRON

Each of the Argonauts was good in his way and, according to his gifts, could step in where the others were at a loss. The Dioscuri always led in point of youth and beauty. The Boreads, when quick, resolute saving action was needed. As a leader, Jason was strong, thoughtful, accommodating, pleasing to the fair sex. Then there was Orpheus, sensitive, withdrawn, supreme master of the lyre, and keen-eyed Lynceus, who safely piloted their ship through the rocks by day and night. Courage can only be tested in comradeship, when one shows it and the others approve.

FAUST

Have you nothing to say about Hercules?

CHIRON

Oh, don't break my heart ... I'd never seen Phoebus, Ares, Hermes, and the rest. And then I saw a heavenly sight. He was a king among men, marvellously handsome in his youth, subject to his elder brother and to pretty women too. Earth will not see his like again, nor Hebe lead him into heaven.

FAUST

Yes, they may be proud of their works, but they never truly captured him. You've told me about the most beautiful of men. Now tell me about the most beautiful of women.

CHIRON

Beauty in women, there's nothing to it. It's often so rigid, so self-contained. The woman for me must be brimming with life and happiness. And graceful with it. Like Helen when she rode on my back.

FAUST

She rode on your back?

CHIRON

She did.

FAUST

I'm dazed enough already. And now this.

CHIRON

She held my mane, just as you do.

FAUST

Oh, now I'm beside myself. She's my heart's desire. Tell me about it. Where was it? Where did you take her?

CHIRON

I can soon tell you. Her brothers, the Dioscuri, had rescued her from brigands who didn't take a beating lightly. They gave chase. The brothers waded through and I swam. Once across, she dismounted, stroked my dripping mane and thanked me and said nice things. She was so sweet, so assured. And so young and charming too. An old man's joy.

FAUST

And only ten years old.

CHIRON

I see the philologists have fooled you as well as themselves. It's queer about women in mythology. A poet does what he likes with them. They never grow up, they're never old, they're always enticing, they're carried off in youth, courted in old age. Chronology means nothing to a poet.

FAUST

Then let chronology mean nothing to her. Didn't Achilles find her on the island of Pherae, quite outside of time. What a consummation. Love achieved in defiance of fate. And why shouldn't I, with this fierce yearning in me, bring her back to life, this figure the like of which never was? This creature at once so sweet and so sublime and, like the gods, undying. You saw her once. I saw her today. She was as lovely as I imagined her. Now I'm a man possessed. Life without her is impossible.

CHIRON

You strange fellow. Humanly speaking, you're enraptured. But to us spirits you seem nothing short of crazy. However, you're in luck today. Once a year I call on Manto for a few minutes, Aesculapius's daughter. She's praying to her father to enlighten the medical profession at last and make them stop killing people ... Of all the sibyls I like her best. She's not uncouth and restless, she's kind and full of good works. If you stay with her for a while, *page 129* she'll probably be able to cure you completely with her herbs.

FAUST

I don't want to be cured. That would be despicable. My mind is firm.

CHIRON

Don't fail to drink at the healing well. And now jump down. We're there.

FAUST

Where have you brought me through pebbly streams on this weird night?

CHIRON

This is where Greece and Rome fought, Peneios on the right, Olympus on the left. The great empire lost in the sand. The king fled, the citizens won. Look up. There's the eternal temple facing you in the moonlight.

MANTO *dreaming within*

A horse's hoof sounds at my door. Demi-gods arriving.

CHIRON

You're right. Open your eyes.

MANTO *awaking*

Welcome. So you didn't fail me.

CHIRON

Your temple's standing too.

MANTO

Are you always on the move? Do you never tire?

CHIRON

You stay quietly in your sanctuary, while I like to go the round.

MANTO

I wait, and time goes round me. And who's this?

CHIRON

The swirl of this uncanny night has dropped him here. He's mad. He wants Helen and doesn't know where to start. If anyone needs Aesculapian treatment, he does.

MANTO

I like a man who desires the impossible.

Chiron is already far away

MANTO

Come in, adventurer, and rejoice. This dark passage leads to Persephone in the hollow foot of Olympus where she watches for forbidden guests. I once smuggled Orpheus down. Be bold. Make better use of your opportunity. *They go down*

scene 38 THE UPPER PENEIOS

As before

SIRENS

Come, plunge into the Peneios, sport and swim there, and start our songs for the benefit of these unfortunates. There can be no good life away from

the water. If the whole crowd of us went down to the Aegean, every pleasure scene 38
would be ours.

Earthquake

SIRENS

The water came foaming back, but not in its old bed. The ground quaked,
the flood piled up, the shore cracked and smoked. Let's away from here, all
of us. This miracle's no good to anyone.

  Away to the sea-festival all you guests, where the glinting, trembling
waves lightly lap the shore, and the moon shines double and wets us with
its sacred dew. Life there is unconfined, and here – this fearful earthquake.
The place is dreadful. No prudent man would stay.

SEISMOS *making noises under the earth*

Another good shove. Another good heave with my shoulders. Then I'll be
out and they'll all have to scatter.

SPHINXES

What a horrid vibration. What fearful tension in the air. Such a swaying
and tottering and rocking this way and that. It's intolerable, it's monstrous.
But we won't move, though hell itself breaks loose.

  The ground's lifting like a vaulted roof, marvellous. It's the same old man,
the same old greybeard, who made the island of Delos, pushed it up out of
the sea to oblige a woman in travail. Now straining and squeezing away
untiringly with all his might, his arms tensed and his back bent like the
giant Atlas, he's lifting the grass, the soil, the sand, and everything in the
peaceful river-bed, and cutting a gap right across the quiet valley. He's like
a colossal caryatid, still buried below the waist and holding up a huge mass
of rock. But this is where he stops, because we're here.

SEISMOS

I managed this all by myself. You'll have to admit it. And if I hadn't done so
much shoving and shaking, how would it have been with this lovely world?
You'd never have had your mountains towering aloft against the blue sky
in its purity and splendour if I hadn't thrust them up for your pleasure,
showing off in front of our great ancestors, Chaos and Old Night, and in
company with the titans tossing Pelion and Ossa about like playthings. We
carried on this way in youthful exuberance till we got tired of it and
wickedly clapped the two mountains on top of Parnassus as a double nightcap ... Apollo sojourns happily there with his muses. And who was it but
me that planted the throne on high for Jupiter and his thunderbolts? Now
once more I've forced my way with an immense effort out of the bowels of
the earth and call for happy settlers to begin a new life here.

SPHINXES

You'd say this pile was ancient, if we hadn't just seen it forced up from under
the ground. There's a forest spreading across it and more rocks arriving. A
sphinx pays no heed. Our seat is sacred. We refuse to be disturbed.

GRIFFIN

I see gold in the cracks, gold in leaf, gold in sparkles. This is a treasure you
mustn't miss. Off with you, you ants, and pick it out.

CHORUS OF ANTS

Now that the giants have raised it, up the mountain you go as fast as you can, you wrigglers. Go in and out of the crannies. Every grain is worth having, even the smallest. Search every corner, no slackening, no loafing. In with the gold, you throngs upon throngs. Let the rest go.

GRIFFINS

Gold in heaps. In with it. We put our claws on it. No bolts are stronger. The greatest treasure would be safe with us.

PYGMIES

We've really moved in. We don't know how it happened. Don't ask us where we came from. We're just here. Every land lends itself to cheerful living. And if there are cracks in the rocks, the dwarfs soon turn up, not in ones, but in twos, man and wife. They lose no time in getting to work. They're models of their kind. Perhaps it was like this in paradise. But we're glad to be here and we thank our stars. East or west, mother earth is fruitful every-where.

DACTYLS

If she produced these little ones in a single night, she'll produce the littlest too, and they'll find one another.

PIGMY ELDERS

Quick, occupy this good place. Get to work. We're still at peace. Build the forges to make munitions.

   You ants, so nimble, get us the metals. You dactyls, so tiny, so many, fetch us the wood. Make hidden fires for charcoal-burning.

GENERAL

Set out now with your bows and arrows to that pond and shoot the herons nesting there so haughtily and in such numbers. Shoot them all in one go. Then we can wear their feathers in our helmets.

Oh, who will save us? We smelted the iron. They're forging chains. It's too early to revolt. We'll have to lie low.

CRANES OF IBYCUS

Shrieks and moans of murdering and dying. Wings flapping wildly in alarm. What sounds of anguish and agony reach us as we fly. They've all been slaughtered. The lake is red with blood. Foul greed has despoiled them. See their feathers in the helmets of those fat-bellied, bandy-legged dwarfs. You coastal birds, our allies, we call on you in a common cause. Let us swear undying hostility to this brood and take vengeance on them, putting all we have into the attack. *They scatter in the air, shrieking*

MEPHISTOPHELES *in the plain*

Northern witches I've always known how to handle, but these foreign ones bother me. After all, the Brocken's easy-going. You can fit in wherever you happen to be. Frau Ilse's always on the look-out at Ilsenstein. And Heinrich likewise at his place. Elend and the Schnarchers don't hit it off, but, at least, everything stays put for ages. Here you don't know where you are. You don't know whether the ground's going to gape under your feet ... I come strolling down a smooth valley, and suddenly a mountain goes up at my back, well hardly a mountain, but big enough to cut me off from my sphinxes. There's more fires further down, lighting up the scene. That gay crowd's still hovering and tripping in front of me with their tricks, drawing me on, then pulling back. I'd better be careful. I'm so used to nibbling. I can't forgo an opportunity.

LAMIAE *drawing Mephistopheles after them*

Quick, quick, keep moving, keep chatting and then slowing down. It's amusing to make the old sinner come chasing after us and then get punished. He's hobbling and stumbling along with his club-foot, dragging his leg. Trying to catch us. But we won't let him.

MEPHISTOPHELES *coming to a halt*

What cursed luck. Poor Jack gets fooled. Fooled every time, beginning with Adam. We all grow old, but who's the wiser? And to think of the times it's happened before.

   We know this breed is utterly worthless, with their bodies laced and their faces painted. They've nothing sound to offer a man. Rotten in limb, the wretches, wherever you touch them. We know it, we see it plain as day. Yet theirs is the tune we always dance to.

LAMIAE *stopping*

He's hesitating, stopping. Go towards him. Don't let him escape.

MEPHISTOPHELES *advancing*

On with it. Don't get into a tangle of doubts. That's silly. If there were no witches, who the devil would want to be a devil?

LAMIAE *at their most charming*

Let's encircle him. He's sure to take one of us.

MEPHISTOPHELES

In this flickering light I must admit you look pretty. I can't complain about you.

EMPUSA

Nor about me, I hope. So let me join you.   *page 133*

LAMIAE

We don't want her. She always spoils things.

EMPUSA *to Mephistopheles*

Greetings from little Empusa, the lass with the donkey's foot. You only have a horse's. And yet I wish you good-day.

MEPHISTOPHELES

I thought they'd all be strangers. And here I am, landed among relatives. It's an old, old story: from Harz to Hellas cousins all the way.

EMPUSA

I can transform myself in many ways and do it promptly. But today in your honour I've put on my donkey's head.

MEPHISTOPHELES

I see these people set great store by relationship. But, no matter what, this donkey's head is more than I can take.

LAMIAE

Don't bother with that horrid woman. She drives away any thought of charm and beauty. Where she is, charm and beauty don't exist.

MEPHISTOPHELES

These others that look so slender and so tender, I suspect all of them. Their rosy cheeks may hide another metamorphosis.

LAMIAE

Come, try. There's lots of us. Help yourself. With luck you'll catch the best. What's the good of this harping on desire. A nice suitor you are, strutting along and giving yourself airs. – Now he's coming in among us. Drop your masks bit by bit and show what's behind them.

MEPHISTOPHELES

I've picked the prettiest. *embracing her*
Oh what a broomstick, dry as a bone.
Seizing another
And this one? ... What a face.

LAMIAE

Do you think you deserve better? Don't kid yourself.

MEPHISTOPHELES

I'll try the little one ... and a lizard slips through my fingers. Her plaited hair's like a snake. And when I take hold of the tall one ... she's a bacchic wand with a pine-cone on top. Where will it end? ... Here's a fat one that might be fun. I'll make a last attempt. Here goes. She's all flabby and wobbly. Orientals pay high prices for this sort. But ugh, she's burst, a fungus.

LAMIAE

Scatter, flit about like lightning. Flutter round the son of a witch in wavering shuddering circles, black-winged and noiseless like bats. He's getting off too cheap.

MEPHISTOPHELES *shaking himself*

I never seem to learn. It's as ridiculous here as it is in the north. Ghosts just as unpleasant. Poets and people just as crass. A masquerade's a sensual frolic everywhere. I go after a charmer and what I get my hands on gives me the shivers. I wouldn't mind being duped, if it only lasted longer.
Going astray among the rocks

Where am I going? I was on a path and now there's no path. The road was

smooth before, and now I'm faced with rubble. I climb helplessly up and
down. How shall I ever get back to my sphinxes? I never dreamed such things
would happen. A mountain that size in a single night. There's a witches'
ride for you. They bring their Brocken with them.

OREAD *in the older rock*
Come up here. My mountain is old, unchanged from the start, with these
rocky steeps, the last spurs of Pindus. It was imperturbably the same when
Pompey crossed it in his flight. Those illusions, by contrast, vanish at cock-
crow. I've often seen them come and go – go quite suddenly.

MEPHISTOPHELES
All honour to you and veneration, with your mighty forest of oak trees,
where even the brightest moon never enters. – But there's a modest light
moving in the bushes here. How fortunate. It's Homunculus of all people.
Where have you been, little fellow?

HOMUNCULUS
I sort of float about from place to place, wanting to get born the best way
and eager to shatter my glass. I haven't seen anything yet that I'd trust myself to. But, just between you and me, I'm on the track of two philosophers.
I listened to them and they kept saying 'Nature, nature.' I mean to stick to
them. They surely understand the living world and I'll find out from them
where it would be wisest to go.

MEPHISTOPHELES
Act on your own. Where there's ghosts about, the philosopher is welcomed.
He at once creates a dozen new ones, in order to show them his favours.
You have to make mistakes or you'll never learn. If you want to get born,
do it yourself.

HOMUNCULUS
Good advice is not to be despised.

MEPHISTOPHELES
So off you go. We'll see what happens.

They separate

ANAXAGORAS *to Thales*
Will that rigid mind of yours never relent? What more is needed to convince
you?

THALES
Water yields to any wind, but it keeps away from the sharp rock.

ANAXAGORAS
This rock was made by explosion, by fire.

THALES
Life began in the wet.

HOMUNCULUS *between the two*
Let me go with you. I also want to begin.

ANAXAGORAS
Tell me, Thales, did you ever, in one night, make a mountain out of mud?

THALES
Nature, the flow of nature, never depended on hours and days. She lets every
form grow under her control. Even on a big scale there's no violence.

scene 38

ANAXAGORAS

But there was violence here. Cruel, plutonic fire, the tremendous bursting of aeolian vapours, broke through the old flat crust, so that at once a mountain had to arise.

THALES *(handwritten: founder of 1st. Greek school of Philosophy)*

What does it help? What does it lead to? The mountain's there. So far, so good. This sort of argument's a waste of time. It only leads people by the nose, if they let it.

ANAXAGORAS

The mountain's already alive with myrmidons, occupying the cracks. Ants and pygmies and other little busy-bodies.

To Homunculus

You've never aimed high. You've always lived a hermit's life, shut in. If you can adapt yourself to rulership, I'll have you crowned king here.

HOMUNCULUS

What does good Thales say?

THALES

I say don't. Among little people you do little things. Great people make a little man great. Look at that black cloud of cranes. They're threatening the pygmy nation – see how disturbed they are – and they'd threaten the king. They're attacking with beak and claw. Destruction is near. It was criminal to destroy the herons gathered at their quiet pond. But that murderous assault is being savagely avenged. It's aroused the thirst of their kin for the blood of the pygmies. What use to them are shield and spear and helmet now? What use are the herons' plumes? Look at the ants and dactyls trying to hide. Their army's breaking, running. It's collapsed.

ANAXAGORAS *solemnly after a pause*

Till now I've always looked to the powers under the earth, but in this case I turn upwards ... You above, ageless and eternal, triple in form, triple in name, I call on you in my nation's crisis, Diana, Luna, Hecate. You, the heart-inspirer, the philosopher, you so calm-seeming, so passionate, reveal your ancient spell, but without magic. Put on your dread eclipse.

Pause

Has my prayer been granted too soon? Has my appeal to those above upset the order of nature?

See, the goddess's circular throne coming closer and closer, monstrous, fearful to behold. Its blaze is reddening. Come no nearer, you giant disc. You'll destroy the world.

So it's true, is it, that Thessalian witches once, with impious magic, sang you down out of your course and wrung ruinous concessions from you? ... The luminous disc has darkened. Suddenly it's tearing apart and flashing. What a hissing, rattling noise, with wind and thunder crossing it. I cast myself down at the steps of the throne. Forgive me. I evoked all this. *throws himself down on his face*

THALES

The things this man hears and sees. I don't quite know what happened, but I can't go along with him. Let's agree, these are queer times. And there's the moon rocking comfortably in the same place as before.

page 136

Look at where the pygmies settled. The mountain was rounded. Now it's a peak. I felt a tremendous crash. A piece of rock fell out of the moon. It squashed and killed people right and left and asked no questions. But I can't help admiring the skill that created this mountain in a single night, working from above and from below.

THALES

Calm yourself. It wasn't real. Let that horrid brood go their ways. It's just as well you didn't become their king. And now off we go to the happy sea-festival. They expect strange visitors there and honour them. *They withdraw*

MEPHISTOPHELES *climbing on the other side*

Here I am, struggling up the rocks and stumbling over the roots of these old oaks. In my Harz mountains there's a resinous atmosphere with something of pitch in it. A smell I like, next after sulphur ... Here among these Greeks there's no trace of anything of the sort. But I'd be curious to know what they stoke their hell-fires with.

DRYAD

You may have your native wisdom for domestic purposes, but abroad you aren't adaptable enough. You shouldn't be thinking of home at all. You should be paying homage to these sacred oak trees.

MEPHISTOPHELES

You can't help remembering what you've lost. The life you were used to is always like a paradise. But tell me. What is it, crouching in that cavern? The light's bad. There's three of them.

DRYAD

The Phorkyads. Go in and speak to them, if you have the pluck.

MEPHISTOPHELES

Why not? I'm amazed at what I see. I thought I'd seen everything, but I have to climb down and admit I never saw the like of this. They're worse than mandrakes. When you've once set eyes on this three-fold monster, no sin will ever look ugly to you again. No hell of ours, not the cruellest, would let them near its door. And here it is, rooted in beauty's land, the land proudly called antique. They're stirring, they seem to be aware of me, they're whistling, twittering, like vampire bats.

PHORKYAD

Sisters, lend me the eye so that I may see who's coming to our temple.

MEPHISTOPHELES

Revered ones, permit me to approach and receive your threefold blessing. I present myself to you, a stranger, yet, if I'm not mistaken, a remote relative. I've seen ancient gods before, prostrated myself before Ops and Rhea. Even the fates, your sisters, daughters of Chaos, I saw them yesterday, or was it the day before. But I never saw anything like you. I'm delighted and have no more to say.

PHORKYADS

This one seems to have a head on his shoulders.

MEPHISTOPHELES

What surprises me is that no poet has sung your praises. Tell me, how did

Three sisters who share one eye from Jason + the argonauts

this come about? I've never seen statues of you. Yet you are what the sculptor should attempt. Not Juno, Pallas, Venus, and the rest.

PHORKYADS

Sunk, as we are, in deepest darkness and solitude, we never thought of it.

MEPHISTOPHELES

The question never arose. No one ever sees you. You ought to be living in places where art and splendour are enthroned side by side, and every day another new marble statue comes running up at the double-quick. Places where ...

PHORKYADS

Be silent. Don't awaken our desires. What good would it do us to know more? We are born in the night, close to the night, unknown to the world, almost unknown to ourselves.

MEPHISTOPHELES

There's no problem there. All you have to do is to transfer yourselves to someone else. You have one eye and one tooth among you. It might be mythologically possible to compress yourselves from three into two and lend me the third one's figure for a short time.

ONE

What do you think? Could it be done?

THE OTHERS

Let's try – but without the eye and the tooth.

MEPHISTOPHELES

There you're leaving out the best part. The figure'll never look right.

ONE

Close one eye. It's easy. Then show one of your buck-teeth and you'll have our profile exactly like one of the family.

MEPHISTOPHELES

Good. You honour me.

PHORKYADS

Good.

MEPHISTOPHELES *a phorkyad in profile*

There I am. The favourite son of Chaos.

PHORKYADS

And we're certainly his daughters.

MEPHISTOPHELES

But oh the shame of it. They'll say I'm a hermaphrodite.

PHORKYADS

A new trio of sisters. How lovely we are. We have two eyes and two teeth.

MEPHISTOPHELES

Now I'll have to hide myself and then go and terrify all the devils in hell.

scene 39 ROCKY INLETS IN THE AEGEAN SEA

The moon, stationary at the zenith

SIRENS *reclining on the rocks, fluting and singing*
There was a night of terror when witches in Thessaly wantonly drew you down to earth. But tonight is different. Shine peacefully tonight from the circling sky on these trembling, glittering waves. Illuminate the throngs now rising to the surface. O lovely moon, be gracious. We are your servants.

NEREIDS AND TRITONS *as sea-wonders*
Pipe a shriller note, one that will sound across the sea and call up the nations of the deep. We took refuge from engulfing storms in this quiet retreat, drawn by the sweet singing.

See with what delight we put on these gold chains and match crown and jewels with buckle and girdle. All this we owe to you, the demons of our bay. Your singing lured and wrecked the ships laden with these treasures.

SIRENS
We know that fishes like the sea-life so fresh and flitting, so painless, but today, you festive crowds, we'd like to be assured that you are more than fishes.

NEREIDS AND TRITONS
We thought of this before we came. Sisters and brothers, be quick. The shortest of journeys will serve to assure you completely. *They go off*

SIRENS
Off they go in a flash, heading straight for Samothrace. The wind is with them. They're out of sight. What do they expect from their visit to the Kabiri, those curious divinities, self-creating, self-ignorant?

Stay where you are, O gracious moon, lest the night pass and the daylight dispel us.

THALES *on the shore, to Homunculus*
I'd like to take you to Nereus. We're quite close to his cavern. But he's a sour old thing, hard as nails. The whole of the human race can do nothing to please him. But he sees into the future and people respect him for that and honour him. Besides, he's been helpful to many.

HOMUNCULUS
Let's risk it and call on him. It won't cost me my bottle.

NEREUS
Is it human voices I hear? They infuriate me. Always striving to be like the gods and always doomed to stay the same as before. I could have had a fine time for years if I hadn't felt impelled to advise the best of them. When I came to look at what they did, it was exactly as if I'd never spoken.

THALES
And yet, old man of the sea, we trust you. Don't drive us away. See this flame, human-looking I admit, but ready to follow your advice unquestioningly.

NEREUS — *kindly sea deity / can transform himself in various shapes*
Advice. What man ever listened to advice? Wise words always fall on deaf ears. Men may do things that afterwards they bitterly condemn, yet they stay just as obstinate as ever. Wasn't I like a father to Paris and warned him,

before he went after that woman and ensnared her. There he stood on the shore and I told him what my inner vision showed me: the air full of smoke, red flames, burning beams, death and murder underneath. Troy's fearful judgment day, known to the centuries in enduring verse. An old man's words – they meant nothing to him. He went his lustful way and Ilium fell, a giant corpse rigid after long torment, a welcome feast for Pindus's eagles. Ulysses too. Didn't I foretell him the wiles of Circe, the horrors of the Cyclops? His dilly-dallying, the frivolity of his companions. And all the rest. Did it help? No. Till finally, after all his tossing at sea, the waves dropped him on a friendly shore.

THALES

Behaviour of that sort distresses a man of wisdom. But if he's a good man too, he gives it another try. A grain of thanks outweighs a ton of ingratitude and delights the heart. It's no small thing we're asking of you. This boy here wants to get born and needs advice.

NEREUS

Don't put me out of humour on this very happy day. I have quite other things in prospect. I've invited all my daughters, the Dorids, the Graces of the sea. For beauty and daintiness you won't find their equal, not on earth, not on Olympus. You should see how gracefully they spring from their sea-dragons to Neptune's horses. So closely allied are they to the watery element that the very spray seems to lift them. Galatea, the fairest of them all, will come riding in Venus's irised scallop-shell, because Venus deserted us long ago and she inherited her temple-city and chariot-throne and is worshipped in Paphos as a goddess.

Away. In this hour of paternal bliss there must be neither rancour in the heart nor abuse on the lips. Off you go to Proteus, the wonder-man. Ask him to tell you how to get born or get transformed. *He goes off towards the sea*

THALES

We're not a bit better off. Even if we run into Proteus, he'll just dissolve and disappear. Or if he doesn't, he'll only say things that'll startle and confuse us. However, you need the advice, so let's go along and try. *off*

SIRENS *on the higher rocks*

What is this we see far off, coming across the water? It's like white sails, running before the wind. Now it's clear. They're mermaids transfigured. Let's go down. Can you hear their voices?

NEREIDS AND TRITONS

What we're bringing will please you all. Austere forms, riding in Chelone's giant tortoise-shell. They are gods. Sing songs of praise.

SIRENS

Ancient divinities, small but powerful. Savers of the shipwrecked.

NEREIDS AND TRITONS

We're bringing the Kabiri to a peaceful festival. Where they prevail, Neptune will be kind.

SIRENS

We yield to you. When a ship is wrecked, you protect the crew. Your power is irresistible.

NEREIDS AND TRITONS

We've brought three. The fourth wouldn't come. He said he was the right one, who did the thinking for all of them.

SIRENS
One god makes a fool of the other. Honour all the gods. Fear all harm.

NEREIDS AND TRITONS
Strictly there are seven of them.

SIRENS
Where are the other three?

NEREIDS AND TRITONS
We can't tell you. You could find out on Olympus. That's where the eighth
is, whom no one has ever thought of. They're well disposed, but not ready
yet. They always press on, hungry for the unattainable. They're unique.

SIRENS
We worship all the gods, no matter where. It pays.

NEREIDS AND TRITONS
It's our greatest glory to lead this festival.

SIRENS
The heroes of antiquity will suffer in reputation, if they only bring the golden
fleece, while you bring the Kabiri.
Repeated in chorus
If they only bring the golden fleece, while we/you bring the Kabiri.
Nereids and Tritons off

HOMUNCULUS
They're ungainly. Like so many old clay pots. Philosophers bump into them
and crack their skulls.

THALES
That's what's wanted. The value of the coin is in the rust.

PROTEUS *unseen*
This is just the thing for an old fabler like me. The odder it is, the more
acceptable.

THALES
Proteus, where are you?

PROTEUS *ventriloquizing, now near, now far off*
Here, and here.

THALES
Have your old joke, I forgive you. But don't deceive a friend. I know you're
speaking from the wrong place.

PROTEUS *as if far off*
Goodbye.

THALES *whispering to Homunculus*
He's quite near. Turn up your light. He's as inquisitive as a fish. And where-
ever he may be and whatever shape he's in, a flame attracts him.

HOMUNCULUS
Here's my light, plenty of it. But I must be careful not to break the glass.

PROTEUS *in the form of a giant turtle*
What can it be that gives this lovely light?

THALES *concealing Homunculus*
Good. If you want, you can have a better look. Let us see you on your human
pair of legs. You can easily do it. Remember, it's for us to say whether or not
you can look at what I'm hiding here.

PROTEUS *in human form*
You still know all the cunning tricks.
THALES
And you still like to change your shape. *He uncovers Homunculus*
PROTEUS *astonished*
An incandescent little dwarf. I never saw one before.
THALES
He wants advice about how to get born. The way I have it from him, he came into the world only half-born. It's strange. He has plenty of mental attributes, but he's very short on body. So far the bottle is all the weight he has. He longs to be embodied properly.
PROTEUS
A real virgin birth. You're there before you ought to be.
THALES
And there's another difficulty. If I'm not mistaken, he's a hermaphrodite.
PROTEUS
Then all the better. Wherever he lands, he'll fit in. But there's no need to deliberate. You must make your start in the open sea. Begin on a small scale and enjoy swallowing what is smaller. You must grow bit by bit and rise to higher forms.
HOMUNCULUS
The air's so soft here. I love this odour, just like green things growing.
PROTEUS
I believe you, boy. And farther out on this narrow tongue of land the atmosphere is more enjoyable still. You wouldn't believe it. There's the procession coming. It's not far away now. Let's go to meet it.
THALES
I'll come too.

Three strange spirits marching in a row.

Telchines of Rhodes on hippocamps and sea-dragons, wielding Neptune's trident

CHORUS
We forged the trident for Neptune that rules the wildest waves. If the thunder god unleashes his swollen clouds, Neptune retaliates. However fiercely the forked lightning flashes down, wave on wave is thrown up from below. Those who are caught between the two are tossed about and finally swallowed by the deep. This is why he's given us his sceptre for the day. Now we can feel easy and enjoy ourselves.

SIRENS
On the occasion of this moon festival we greet you sun-worshippers, devotees of the happy daylight.

TELCHINES
Dearest goddess, shining aloft, you are happy to hear your brother praised. So lend an ear to Rhodes, where a never-ending paean is sung to him. Whether at the start of his daily course or at the end he looks at us with fiery gaze. Our mountains, cities, shores, waters are lovely and bright. We have no mists. If a mist creeps in – a flash of sun and a little breeze and the island is clear again. The sun god sees himself here in a hundred statues as youth, giant, great, gentle. We were the first to present the gods in human form.

PROTEUS
Let them sing, let them boast, all they want. Dead works of this sort mean nothing to the sun's life-giving rays. They go on persistently with their smelting and moulding and when they have it cast in bronze they think it is really something. What does it come to in the end with these proud images of the gods? An earthquake destroyed them. They were all melted up again.

This earth-life, even at its best, is just a weariness of the flesh. The sea suits life better. Proteus, the dolphin, will carry you out into the eternal waters.

He transforms himself
There, I've done it. Here's the ideal place for you. I'll take you on my back and wed you to the ocean.

THALES
The desire to begin creation at the beginning is most excellent. Surrender to it and be ready for quick action. You'll move in accordance with eternal laws through thousands and thousands of forms. It'll be a long, long time before you're a man.

Homunculus mounts Proteus, the dolphin

PROTEUS
Come with me, what there is of you, into this wet expanse. There you can start living across and along and move about as you choose. Only don't try

to climb the scale. When once you come to man's estate, it'll be all up with you.

THALES

It depends. There's something to be said for being a worthy man in your day.

PROTEUS *to Thales*

Yes, if it's one of your sort. They last for a while. I've seen you for centuries among the pallid ghosts.

SIRENS *on the rocks*

See that splendid ring of clouds round the moon. They're doves aflame with love. Wings as white as the light. Paphos sent them. They are hers. Our festival is now complete, our joy unblemished.

NEREUS

A wanderer in the night might call this an atmospheric phenomenon, but we spirits think differently and we're right. It's doves, accompanying my daughter's ride. A marvellous feat of flying, learned by them in early days.

THALES

I too think it best to trust simple humanity, cherishing a sacred belief in warmth and quietude.

PSYLLI AND MARSI *riding on sea-cows, sea-calves, and sea-rams*

In Cyprus's deep caverns, not swamped by the sea god, not shattered by earthquake, fanned by eternal breezes, we guard Venus's chariot with quiet contentment, as in the earliest days. And in the whispering night-time we bring out our lovely mistress, daughter of Nereus, and ride her here through the woven waves, invisible to the younger generation of men. We busy ourselves quietly, fearing neither eagle nor winged lion, neither cross nor moon, that rule the upper earth, always restlessly changing, banishing, murdering, ruining crops and cities. Meanwhile we bring our dear mistress along.

SIRENS

Come, you sturdy Nereids, primitive and pleasing both. We see you lightly, easily circling the chariot, ring within ring, sometimes snakelike intertwined. And you, tender Dorids, bring your mother Galatea, who is grave like the gods and worthy of immortality, but also graceful and enticing like earthly women.

DORIDS *passing by Nereus in chorus, all on dolphins*

Luna, lend us your light and shade, to show this galaxy of youth, these dear husbands of ours, to our father, with a request. *to Nereus*
We rescued these boys from the raging surf and brought them back to life and warmth on beds of moss. And now with ardent kisses they're faithfully repaying us. Look on them favourably.

NEREUS

A double reward, not to be despised. You're being charitable and you're having fun.

DORIDS

If you approve, father, of what we've done and don't begrudge us our well-earned pleasure, let us keep them and hold them close and stay young forever.

NEREUS

Enjoy your lovely prizes, and bring them from youth to manhood. But I can't grant you what Zeus alone can grant. The sea that rolls and rocks you will not let love last. When your dalliance is over, put them quietly back on land.

DORIDS

You charming boys, we know your worth, but we must part in sadness. We wanted fidelity for ever, but the gods won't have it so.

THE YOUTHS

If you can go on being so kind to us sailor-boys, we ask no better, we never had it better.

Galatea approaches in her shell

NEREUS

There you are, my darling.

GALATEA

O father, what joy. Stay, my dolphins. The sight of him holds me.

NEREUS

They're gone, gone past, in their sweeping motion. What do they care for my feelings. Oh, if only they would take me with them. But a single glimpse is good for a whole year.

THALES

Hail, hail, once again. How I exult, possessed as I am with the true and the beautiful ... Everything came out of the water. Everything is sustained by the water. Ocean, may you hold your sway for ever. If you didn't send your clouds, and brooks in abundance, and streams twisting this way and that, and the great rivers, where would our mountains and plains be, where the world? It is you who keep life at its freshest.

ECHO *all in chorus*

It is you who keep life at its freshest.

NEREUS

They're coming back in wavering course, but not coming back to me. They're all moving, vast in numbers, in extended chains and circles, as part of the festival. But I can see Galatea's scallop again and again, shining through the host like a star, my dear one. Clear and bright, far yet always new and true.

HOMUNCULUS

In all this lovely wetness, wherever I shine my light, everything charms me with its beauty.

PROTEUS

In all this vital wetness, your light shines and rings more splendidly than ever.

NEREUS

What new secret is being revealed to us in the heart of the throng. What is it flames about the scallop, at Galatea's feet, pulsing alternately strong and gentle, as if with pulsations of love.

THALES

It's Homunculus with Proteus in charge. What you see is the symptoms of his imperious desire. Do I not also hear him gasping and droning in anguish? He's going to smash himself against the shining scallop-throne. There, a flame and a flash, and he's spilt himself.

SIRENS

What a luminous miracle transfigures the waves, breaking against one another in fiery sparkles. Everything is lit up, flickering, brightening. All the figures are aglow in the night. Fire is playing over the whole scene. So let Eros prevail. Eros who started everything. Hail to the sea, hail to the waves with the sacred fire over them. Hail to the fire. Hail to the water. Hail to this rare happening.

ALL

Hail to the soft breezes. Hail to the mysterious caves. Hail above all to the four elements.

scene 40

[handwritten: Helen there lived with her husband / Trojan war fought over her]

In front of the palace of Menelaus at Sparta. Enter Helen and a chorus of captive Trojan women, with Panthalis as leader of the chorus

HELEN

[handwritten left margin: carried away by Paris to Troy]

Helen, the much admired, the much maligned, I am that Helen, come now from the beach where our ship landed, still dizzy with the restless rocking of the waves that with Poseidon's favour and the east wind helping brought us on their stiff high backs from the plains of Phrygia into home waters. Down on the shore Menelaus and the pick of his warriors are rejoicing to be back again. But I address myself to this great house and bid it welcome me, the house that after his return Tyndareus, my father, built not far from the slope of Pallas's hill, and fitted out more splendidly than any house in Sparta. So I remember it from childhood when I played here happily with my sister Clytemnestra and with Castor and Pollux too. I greet you now, you brazen double entrance-doors that stood wide open once invitingly on a festive day and Menelaus, my shining bridegroom chosen among many, came in to meet me. Open again for me, that I may deliver an urgent message from the king, as befits the wife. Let me in and let everything stay behind that has raged around me so disastrously till now. From the day I crossed this threshold with a light heart to visit the temple on Cythera, as a sacred duty bade, and that Phrygian brigand seized me, much has happened that people far and wide love to relate, but she of whom the story and the legend grew has little joy to hear.

CHORUS

Do not make light, O noble lady, of the honour, the great good fortune, the supreme gift that is yours. Yours and yours alone. It is beauty, beauty that transcends everything. A hero's name precedes his coming. Hence his pride. But before all-compelling beauty the stubbornest of heroes humbles his mind.

HELEN

Enough. I came here on shipboard with my husband and now am sent to his city ahead of him. But what he intends to do I cannot guess. Coming here, am I his wife? Am I his queen? Or am I to be a sacrifice to his royal grief and the long endured misfortunes of the Greeks? I am a captive. Whether a prisoner or not I cannot say. Truly the immortals gave me a dubious name and a dubious fate as companions of my beauty that even here on this threshold stand, dark and threatening, at my side. In the hollow ship Menelaus seldom glanced at me and never said a heartening word, but sat facing me as if he was planning evil. Then when we were in the mouth of the Eurotas and our front ships' prows had hardly touched the beach he commanded as if god-inspired: Let my men disembark in due order. I will muster them in their ranks along the shore. But you must proceed up the luxuriant banks of the Eurotas, guiding your horses through the lush meadows, until you come to the plain, once rich in crops and beautiful still, where Lacedaemon stands, ringed by solemn mountains. Go into the high-towered palace and inspect the servants I left there and the shrewd old housekeeper. Let her show you the treasures your father handed on, a rich array that I have added to continually in war and peace. You'll find everything in order. It is the ruler's privilege to come back and find the house exactly as he left it, seeing that the servant has no authority to alter anything.

CHORUS

Refresh your eyes and your heart with the sight of these ever-increasing treasures. You'll find them there, beautiful chains and ornate crowns in their pride and their conceit. Go in and challenge them. They'll quickly gather their forces. But I should love to see beauty contesting with gold and pearls.

HELEN

Then there came a further command from our lord and master. When you've gone over everything in proper order, take as many tripods as you think necessary and take such other vessels of one sort or another as are needed in fulfilling the sacred ritual. Kettles, bowls, and shallow basins. Bring tall jugs of the purest water from the sacred spring. Also have ready dry kindling wood that quickly ignites and finally a knife well-sharpened. All the rest I leave to your care. This is what he said, as he hurried me off. But he said nothing of the living thing he means to sacrifice in honour of the Olympians. This has an ominous look, but I pay no heed and leave it on the the lap of the high gods who do what seems good to them, whether men approve of it or disapprove. We mortals, we endure it. Many a time a man has raised his heavy axe over the consecrated beast's neck bowed to earth and could not bring it down, because an enemy came upon him or some god intervened and prevented him.

CHORUS

What is to happen, thinking will never tell you. Proceed, queen, with an easy mind. Good and ill comes to us unexpectedly. Even when foretold, we don't believe it. Didn't Troy burn, were we not faced with death, shameful death? And yet here we are, with you, your joyful servants, seeing the dazzling sun in the sky and you, the fairest thing on earth, our gracious mistress, making us happy.

HELEN

Be that as it may. Whatever awaits us, it is for me now to go up without delay into the palace that I have not seen for years and longed for so much and nearly trifled away. There it is again before my eyes, almost unbelievably. My feet won't carry me up the high steps as confidently as when I skipped up them as a child. *off*

CHORUS

Come sisters, unfortunate captives that you are, throw grief aside and share your mistress's happiness, share Helen's happiness at coming back again to her father's house, more assured in her return, because so long delayed.

Praise the gods who restore such happiness and grant such home-comings. He who is liberated rises as with wings over what is harshest, while the captive yearns and exhausts himself with arms outstretched above his prison's battlements.

But a god took hold of her when she was far away and brought her back from ruined Troy to the old home now newly restored, where after endless joy and pain she can revive her memories of early years.

PANTHALIS *as leader of the chorus*

Sisters, stop your joyful singing now and turn your eyes to the great door. What do I see? Is that not the queen hurrying back in alarm? What is it, queen, what can it be, that has shaken you so in your own precincts where you expect a welcome? You cannot hide it. I see it written on your brow — anger, righteous anger, struggling with surprise.

HELEN *who has left the double door open. She is disturbed*

The common fears of men are not for Zeus's daughter. And terror's fleeting finger never touches her. But the horror that has risen out of primal darkness since the beginning of the world and still comes in many shapes like fiery clouds rolling up from a volcano can daunt the heart even of a hero. And thus the infernal gods have cruelly marked my entry into the house today so that I could gladly turn my back on this longed-for threshold and leave it like a parting guest. But no. I've come out into the daylight. Farther you shall not drive me, you powers, whoever you are. The house must now be purified. Then fire can burn in the hearth and welcome the husband and the wife.

CHORUS

Tell us, lady, what has happened. We're your faithful servants who honour you. Tell us.

HELEN

You shall see with your own eyes what I have seen, unless Old Night has already swallowed its creation back into its dark womb. But to let you know, I'll put it into words: When I went into the palace, thinking dutifully in that grave interior of what was next to do, I was surprised to find the place completely silent. Not a sign or sound of people bustling about doing this and that. No servants, no housekeeper to say the usual word of welcome to a stranger. But when I approached the hearth I saw a tall woman with her head covered, sitting by the dying ashes more in a thinking posture than a sleeping. I ordered her to go back to work, assuming she was the house-keeper my husband had left in charge during his absence. But there she sat, covered and motionless as before. Then when I rebuked her, she raised her right arm as if to dismiss me from the house, whereupon I turned from her in anger and hastened towards the steps leading to the bedchamber and the treasure room beside it. But she sprang quickly to her feet and blocked my way, and now I could see how tall and gaunt she was, with hollow bloodshot eyes and curious build disturbing to behold. I'm talking to the wind. Words always fail to bring a figure back to life. But there she is. She's come out into the light. And here we are the masters, till the king comes. Phoebus, the lover of beauty, drives these fearsome births of darkness back to their

caverns or at least holds them in check.

CHORUS

I've been through much, although these tresses of mine are a young woman's. I've seen terrible things, the misery of warfare and Ilium the night
it was taken.

Through the cloud, the dust, and the din of the fighters I heard the fearful voice of the gods calling. I heard the brazen noise of conflict ringing
across the battle-field, coming towards the walls.

Ilium's walls were still standing, but the blaze leaped from house to house,
spreading with its own storm-wind over the city at night.

As I was escaping, I could see the gods approaching through the smoke
and the heat and the leaping flames, in dreadful anger, marvellous giant
figures, crossing the fiery gloom.

Did I see all this confusion or did I imagine it in my terror? I shall never
know. But I know for sure that I'm seeing this horror before my eyes. I
could touch it with my hands but that for sheer dread I dare not. Which of
Phorkys's daughters are you? You make me think of them. Are you perhaps
one of the Graiae, sharing a single eye and a single tooth?

Do you dare, you horror, to expose yourself to the expert eye of Phoebus
side by side with beauty? But come out. After all, Phoebus doesn't see ugliness, any more than he ever sees a shadow.

But it is the sad fate of us mortals to endure the torture all lovers of beauty
feel at sight of the despicable and the eternally damned.

Listen then. If you defy us, you shall hear curses, threats and curses unlimited, from the lips of those happy ones whom the gods have shaped.

PHORKYAS

It's an old saying, old but as true as ever, that modesty and beauty never
join hands and walk the green world together. There's an old hostility between them so deep-seated that if they ever meet, no matter where, they
turn their backs on one another and hurry away, modesty distressed, but
beauty always bold and impudent till the day when Hades' darkness closes
over her at last, unless old age has tamed her first. You hussies, come from
abroad in all your arrogance, you make me think of a strung-out flock of
cranes passing overhead with shrieking calls that make a quiet traveller
look up at them. But they go their way, he goes his. So it will be with us.

Who are you anyway, to come noising around the king's high palace like
raving maenads or like so many drunk women? Who are you, howling at the
housekeeper like dogs that bay the moon? Do you think I don't know your
kind? You war-begotten, battle-bred young things, you wantons, first
seduced and then seducers in your turn, sapping the strength of soldiers
and civilians both. When I look at the lot of you, you're like a plague of
locusts settling on the green crops. Consumers of others' labour, nibbling
destroyers of good life growing, that's what you are. Spoils of war, bartered
goods, or sold on the market-place.

HELEN

Whoever scolds the servants in the presence of the mistress is interfering
seriously with her domestic rights. It is for her and for no one else to bestow   *page 149*

Bacchus
made them crazy

praise where praise is due and to punish what is reprehensible. Moreover I am well pleased with the service they have rendered me thus far, first at mighty Ilium during the siege and after, and then not less in the vicissitudes of our devious journey where each is apt to think only of himself. I expect the same of them here. The master doesn't ask who his servant is, but only how he serves. Therefore stop grinning at them and hold your tongue. If you've looked after the king's house properly in my absence, it is to your credit. But I am here now. You must step back and not incur reproof after earning our thanks.

PHORKYAS

It is the lady's privilege to be severe with members of the household, and abundantly your privilege, the noble wife of a fortunate leader after so many years of prudent management. Since you, whom I now recognize, are reassuming your old position as queen and mistress, by all means pick up the reins that have long hung slack and rule, take charge of the treasure and take charge of us. But, above all, protect me, who am older, from this gang, who beside the swan of your beauty are nothing more than clumsy geese gaggling.

PANTHALIS

How ugly ugliness is beside the beautiful.

PHORKYAS

How stupid stupidity beside intelligence.

From here on members of the chorus step forward singly and speak

CHORUS 1

Tell us of father Erebus, tell us of Mother Night.

PHORKYAS

Then you must talk about Scylla, your flesh-and-blood cousin.

CHORUS 2

Your family tree has plenty of monsters climbing it.

PHORKYAS

Away you go to Hades to find your ancestors.

CHORUS 3

Those that are living there are all too young for you.

PHORKYAS

Go and make love to old Tiresias.

CHORUS 4

Orion's nurse was your great-great-grand-daughter.

PHORKYAS

You must have been fed by harpies in filth and foulness.

CHORUS 5

How do you nourish that studied skinniness?

PHORKYAS

Not with the blood that you're so greedy for.

CHORUS 6

You're after corpses, revolting corpse yourself.

PHORKYAS

Now I see vampire teeth gleaming in that insolent mouth.

PANTHALIS

It'll close yours if I say who you are.

PHORKYAS

Name yourself first, the riddle will be solved.

HELEN

I have to come between you, not in anger but in sorrow, and put a stop to this brawling. The master of the house has nothing more troublesome to deal with than a secret feud festering among his faithful servants. At such a time his orders are not echoed back harmoniously in prompt obedience. No, the echo blunders about noisily, confusing him and making him complain to no purpose. And there is something else. In your unbridled rage you have evoked unhappy visions that beset me on every side and fill me with terror, as if, in spite of having my feet on home ground, I was being dragged down to Hades. Can it be memory? Or is it some illusion that has taken hold of me? Was I all that? Am I that now? Shall I be that in future? The dream image and the dread image of those destroyers of cities. The girls are alarmed, but you, the old one, are unmoved. Say a sensible word to me.

PHORKYAS

Whoever can look back on long years of varied happiness will think the highest favour of the gods a dream. You more than any, you favoured beyond all measure – your life has been a succession of men desiring you passionately, one after another, all of them ready and eager for any foolhardy adventure. Theseus in his excitement seized you early, a man as strong as Hercules and beautifully built.

HELEN

Carried me off, a slender fawn, a ten-year-old, and kept me in Aphidnus's castle in Attica.

Helen's brothers

PHORKYAS

And when, before long, Castor and Pollux rescued you, you were sought by many heroes, sought by the best of them.

HELEN

But I admit I quietly favoured Patroclus most of all. He was the image of Achilles.

PHORKYAS

But your father insisted on Menelaus, the bold seafarer and man of property too.

HELEN

Yes, he gave away his daughter, gave the kingdom as well. Hermione was born of the marriage.

PHORKYAS

But when he was far away in Crete, securing an inheritance, and you were alone, there came to you too handsome a visitor.

HELEN

But why recall the time I spent half-widowed and all the cruel misfortune that came of it?

PHORKYAS

And that journey of his brought me into captivity and into slavery, long slavery, me a free-born Cretan woman.

HELEN

He sent you here at once as housekeeper, entrusting a great deal to you, the palace and the treasures so boldly acquired.

PHORKYAS

The palace you deserted for the towers of Ilium and the never exhausted joys of love.

HELEN

Speak not of the joys. Upon my head was poured an infinitude of bitter, bitter suffering.

PHORKYAS

But they say you were seen twofold, in Ilium and in Egypt.

HELEN

Don't add confusion to a mind distraught. Even now I don't know which I am.

PHORKYAS

And they say Achilles came up from the underworld and was with you passionately after loving you earlier contrary to fate's decree.

HELEN

I joined him, phantom with phantom. It was a dream, as the words say. I'm losing myself and becoming a phantom again. *She falls into the arms of the half-chorus*

CHORUS

Silence, silence, you ill-favoured, ill-spoken creature. What sounds are these, coming up from that foul gullet, past those loathsome lips and the one tooth.

Malevolence in friendly guise, a wolf in sheep's clothing, is far more to be feared than the jaws of the three-headed hound. Apprehensively we stand and watch and ask: When and where will it strike, this lurking monster of malice.

And now, instead of proffering the few gentle Lethe-giving words of comfort, you stir up all that was worst in the past and little that was good, darkening the bright light of today and the glimmer of hope for the future.

Silence, silence. Let the queen's spirit, now ready to take flight, not lose its hold on the fairest form under the sun. (*Helen has recovered and stands again in the centre*)

PHORKYAS

Come, come clear of fleeting clouds, you sun that lights our day. Lovely enough you were when veiled, but now your brilliance dazzles. How the world unfolds before you you yourself can see. Ugly they say I am, but beauty, beauty I quickly recognize.

HELEN

Coming round from the swoon that seized me, my steps are so shaky, all my bones so utterly weary, rest would be welcome. Suddenly faced with dangers, however, we have to be ready. All men must, but a queen, a queen more than others.

PHORKYAS

Standing there before us now in all your grandeur, your beauty, your look

is commanding. Tell us then, speak, what is your command?

After this impudent altercation amends must be made. Quick then, prepare
a sacrifice, as the king ordered.

PHORKYAS

Everything's there in the house, bowl, tripod, and axe, all that is needed for
sprinkling and purifying. Name only the victim.

HELEN

The king never said.

PHORKYAS

Never said. Oh the pity of it.

HELEN

Why the pity? Why do you care?

PHORKYAS

Queen, he means you.

HELEN

Me?

PHORKYAS

And these here.

CHORUS

Oh misery, misery.

PHORKYAS

The axe is for you.

HELEN

Dreadful for me, but I feared as much.

PHORKYAS

Inevitable, it seems to me.

CHORUS

And what about us?

PHORKYAS

She will die a noble death. But you will twitch and dangle one after another
from the roof-tree, like throstles in a snare.

Helen and Chorus astonished and terrified, in significant grouping

PHORKYAS

You ghosts. There you stand like dummies, dreading to leave the daylight
that isn't yours. Men and ghosts alike are as loth as you to see the last of the
sun in its splendour. But the time comes and there's no stopping it. They all
know it, few of them like it. Enough. You are done for. So now to the work
in hand.

*She claps her hands, whereupon mummied dwarfs appear at the door and
quickly carry out their orders*

Come along, you dingy, podgy creatures. There's mischief here to do, as
much as you could wish. Put the gold-horned altar in its place, lay the shining axe on its silver edge. Fill the water jugs. There'll be black and filthy
blood enough to wash away. Lay the rich carpet here in the sand for the
royal victim to kneel on and then be wrapped in and buried with dignity,
headless though she be.

PANTHALIS

The queen is standing apart and aloof, thinking her thoughts. But the girls are wilting like mown grass in a meadow. Being the oldest of them, I think it my sacred duty to have a word with you, you the ancient one, who are wise and experienced and seemingly well-disposed, notwithstanding the mistaken and brainless way these women received you. Tell me then of any means of escape you know.

PHORKYAS

The answer is easy. It depends on the queen and her alone, whether her life should be saved and your lives too, thrown in as extras. But resolution is called for now and the speediest possible.

CHORUS

Most venerable of the fates, wisest of sibyls, stay your golden shears and save our lives. Already we feel our limbs hanging, swinging wretchedly, when we'd sooner be dancing with them and then resting in our lovers' arms.

HELEN

Leave them to their panic. I feel no fear at all, I feel only the pain. But if you offer a way of escape, you have our gratitude. I know the wise and circumspect can often make the impossible possible. Come, tell us what it is.

CHORUS

Yes, tell us, tell us quickly, how we ever shall elude these nasty snares that threaten us like necklaces that tighten. We can feel it coming now, that breathless, choking feeling only Rhea, the mother-goddess, can protect us from in mercy.

PHORKYAS

Have you the patience to hear my story quietly? There's much to tell. It can't be told in a minute.

CHORUS

Patience, of course, we have. So long as we listen, we live.

PHORKYAS

A man who stays at home and guards his treasures, keeps his palace walls in good repair and roofs it thoroughly against the rain can look forward to prosperity and a long life. But if he carelessly, irresponsibly, takes himself off, he won't find the old place the same when he returns. He may even find it destroyed.

HELEN

What is the point of these sententious sayings now? Stirring unhappy thoughts. Say what you have to say.

PHORKYAS

No reproach is intended. I'm speaking of what has happened. Menelaus roamed the sea from bay to bay as a pirate, raiding island or mainland as he chose, and bringing the booty home that is piled up here indoors. Ten long years he spent at Ilium. How many years on his way home I cannot say. But how is it now with this great house and estate of Tyndareus? How is it up and down his kingdom?

HELEN

Are you so inveterate a faultfinder that you can't open your mouth without showing it?

PHORKYAS

North of Sparta there is hill country that has lain neglected for a long, long time. The Taygetos range stands behind it, where our Eurotas has its source, a merry brook at first and now this broad stream flowing down the valley with its reed-beds and these swans of yours. Back there in the hills a bold race of invaders from the Cimmerian north have quietly settled in and built a stronghold unassailable, and from there they harry the country round about just as they choose.

HELEN

You mean they did all this? It seems impossible.

PHORKYAS

Well, they had time enough. It must be twenty years.

HELEN

Have they a leader? Are they united? Or just robbers?

PHORKYAS

Not robbers. They have a leader. He came down on us once, but I have no quarrel with him. He might have taken all we had, but he was content with little, a few presents. He didn't say they were tribute.

HELEN

What does he look like?

PHORKYAS

Not bad at all. I quite liked him. He's free and easy, a good figure. He has more sense than most of your Greeks. You call them barbarians, but I doubt if any of them are as savage as your men often were at Ilium. I think he's generous. I'd be prepared to trust him. And then the castle he's built. Oh, you should see his castle! A different thing from what your ancestors threw together, rudely piling blocks of stone one on another like cyclops. There everything is vertical and horizontal, and planned. Seen from outside, it soars to heaven, straight, poised, smooth as steel. The thought of scaling it unthinkable. And inside, spacious courtyards, enclosed with buildings of all kinds, for all purposes, pillars and arches big and little, balconies, galleries, interesting inside and out. And coats-of-arms.

CHORUS

What are coats-of-arms?

PHORKYAS

Ajax had a coiled snake on his shield. You all have seen it. The seven against Thebes also had figures on their shields, rich and significant ones. Moon and stars in the night-sky, goddesses and heroes, ladders, swords, torches, and whatever else threatens and assails a beleaguered city. Our heroes have always had the same, dating from long ago, very colourful, lions, eagles, beak and claws, buffalo horns, wings, roses, peacocks' tails, and strips of colour gold and black and silver, blue and red. They have them hanging in their halls, row upon row, halls of endless size, wonderful for you to dance in.

CHORUS

Are there dancers there?

PHORKYAS

The very best, blond and gay, and scented with youth as Paris was scented for Helen.

HELEN

You forget your role completely. Finish what you have to say.

PHORKYAS

It is for you to finish and say a resolute yes. At once I'll take you, transport you, to that castle.

CHORUS

Oh, say the word, the little word, and save us all.

HELEN

What? Have I reason to fear that Menelaus would go the length of treating me cruelly, brutally?

PHORKYAS

Have you forgotten what he did to Deiphobus who after his brother Paris was slain took you himself, risking the consequences, and you were happy together. He cut off his nose and ears and went on mutilating him, stopping at nothing. It was a horror to witness.

HELEN

If he did that, it was on my account he did it.

PHORKYAS

Yes, and it'll be on his account that he'll do it to you. Beauty is indivisible. Whoever has wholly possessed it would sooner destroy it with a curse than share it.

Trumpets are heard. The chorus is startled

Note how the blare of the trumpets tears your ears and tears your very insides. This is how jealousy tears the heart of a man who cannot forget what once was his and now is lost to him.

CHORUS

Can't you hear the horns blowing? Can't you see the flashing arms?

PHORKYAS

Welcome, lord and master, I am ready to give account.

CHORUS

But what about us?

PHORKYAS

You know already. First you'll see her death. Then yours will follow inside. There is no help for it.

Pause

HELEN

My mind is made up now what next I have to do. Something tells me you are not a friendly spirit. I fear that any help from you will prove our loss. No matter, I have decided to go to this castle with you. The rest is my affair. None shall know what the queen is thinking privately, deep in her secret heart. Now lead the way.

CHORUS

Oh how happy we are to go, with tripping foot, leaving death behind us, and coming a second time to a towering impenetrable fortress. Guard it as well as Troy was guarded, which only the basest cunning finally conquered.

Clouds spread, veiling the background and nearer objects too

But, sisters, what is this? Look about you. Wasn't the weather bright? And now mists are streaking up from sacred Eurotas. The beautiful rushy shore is blotted out and the swans too that were swimming together so freely, gently, proudly.

But I can hear them calling. It must be that. Calling a harsh distant call foretelling death, they say. Oh what if instead of the promised rescue it says we shall perish, we with our lovely long white swan-necks and our swan-begotten mistress too.

The mist has covered everything. We can't see one another. Whatever is happening? Are we walking or are we floating, barely touching the ground? Can you see anything? Can that be Hermes hovering in front with his golden staff, bidding us return to Hades, that gray cheerless place filled and overfilled with intangible forms, and eternally empty?

Yes, the mist is suddenly lifting on a gloomy scene, walls dark gray, dark brown, starkly confronting us, blocking the view. Is it a courtyard? Is it a deep pit? Dreadful in any case. Sisters, we are captives again, as captive as ever.

scene 41

Courtyard of a castle, surrounded by rich and fantastic medieval buildings

PANTHALIS
Just like women, this snatching at conclusions foolishly. A prey to the passing moment or any shift of weather. Good luck or bad luck, you can't take either with calmness. One of you always contradicting another, then others contradicting her. Whether in joy or pain you laugh and lament on the selfsame note. But now be quiet and wait to hear the decision our noble mistress comes to for herself and for us.

HELEN
Where are you, Pythoness, or whatever your name is? Come out from behind these gloomy castle vaults. If you went in to tell your wonderful hero of my arrival and ensure me a welcome, thank you. Take me to him without delay. I am weary of wandering. Rest is what I want.

PANTHALIS
There's no one to be seen, lady, not anywhere. That ugly thing has disappeared. She may be still in the mist we came out of so suddenly, somehow, without even taking a step. Or she may be astray in this labyrinth of a castle – it seems like several turned into one – seeking her master to ask him about receiving you. But look, all at once there's a lively commotion of servants flitting about up there in the galleries, at the windows and doorways. It points to a formal reception, welcoming you.

CHORUS
My heart leaps up. Oh look, a procession of young people coming down the stairs, so charming, so decorous, so measured. Who can have ordered it? And assembled it so quickly? What shall I most admire in these handsome boys? Their graceful walk, their locks of hair, their shining brows, their cheeks as red as peaches, and as downy? I'd love to bite them, but dare not when I think in a similar case – oh horror – of the mouth that was filled with

ashes. But here they come, the beauties. What can they be carrying? Steps to a throne, carpet and chair, a canopy embroidered, drawn slowly like wreaths of cloud over the queen who, on invitation, has mounted the throne. Move forward and range yourselves in rows on the steps. Blessed, thrice blessed, be this stately ceremony.

What the chorus says here has been enacted step by step. When the long procession of squires and pages are all down, Faust appears at the top of the stairs, dressed like a medieval courtier, and slowly descends

PANTHALIS *observing him closely*
Unless these are passing gifts, lent by the gods for a brief space only, as is their way, this man's admirable figure, his lofty bearing, and agreeable presence will ensure him success in everything he undertakes, whether in serious battle or in the lighter warfare with fair women. I must say I prefer him to many I have seen that were thought most highly of. Now I see the prince reverently advancing with slow and solemn step. O queen, turn your head.

FAUST *approaching, with a man in chains*
Instead of the solemn words of welcome appropriate to the occasion I bring you this man in chains, who by failing in his duty made me fail in mine. Kneel down here and confess your fault to this greatest of women. Here is a man with a rare gift of seeing, appointed to keep close watch from the tower on sky and land for anything that happens either here or in the valley or the hills beyond, the movement of flocks and herds, it may be, or the approach of an enemy. We protect the one and confront the other. But to-day, what a lapse! You came and he never reported it. We were unable to receive so great a guest with honour due. His life is forfeited. He would have already died the death he deserves save that it is for you, and only you, to punish or pardon at your discretion.

HELEN
This is a great dignity you confer on me, making me both judge and ruler. Perhaps tentatively, but I accept it and exercise the judge's duty to hear the accused. Let him speak.

LYNCEUS, THE WATCHMAN
Let me kneel and let me look, whether death or life awaits me. I am devoted utterly to this woman whom the gods have sent. Watching for the morning light with my eyes fixed on the east, suddenly by a miracle the sun came up in the south. It drew me away from everything else, the heights, the depths, the expanse of earth and sky. I looked only for her. I have eyes as keen as a lynx in a tree-top, but now I found myself fighting my way out of a deep, dark dream. Could I see a thing? No. Not the battlements, the tower, the gate. Such a goddess had come in sight. She dazzled me. I stood there and drank it in, forgetting my watchman's duty, forgetting to blow my horn. If this has aroused her scorn, I still see only her beauty.

HELEN
I cannot punish an offence when I was the cause of it. Oh what a relentless fate pursues me, making me turn men's hearts and heads so that they spare neither themselves nor anything else worth sparing. Abducting, seducing,

fighting, shifting from place to place. Gods and demi-gods, heroes, yes, and
phantoms dragged me about confusedly hither and thither. When there was
only one of me, I caused trouble in the world. More trouble when there were
two. Now that I am threefold, fourfold, it's one calamity after another. Set
this good man free and let him depart. If a divinity turned his head, it's
no disgrace.

FAUST

It amazes me, O queen, to see the sure marksman and the mark attained. I see
the bow that sped the arrow and I see the man it pierced. And now comes
arrow after arrow piercing me. I feel and hear the feathered missiles whir-
ring everywhere around. What am I now? In an instant you make my staun-
chest followers rebellious, you make my very walls unsafe. I fear the army
will now go over to you, the conquering, unconquered heroine. What can I
do but give you myself and all that I vainly thought was mine. I lay myself
at your feet and accept you unreservedly as the ruler who, the moment she
appeared, assumed the throne.

LYNCEUS
Carrying a chest, followed by men also carrying chests
O queen, here I come again, a rich man begging, begging for a look. When
I set eyes on you, I feel both poverty-stricken and fabulously rich. What was
I before? What am I now? What can I now desire or do? What use is my keen
sight when you on your throne defeat it? Out of the east we came. It was
all up with the west. We were a multitude too vast to know how vast it was.
If a man went down, another stepped in. A third was ready, lance in hand.
There was always a hundred to replace one. Thousands might fall. It went
unnoticed. We drove and smashed our way forward, conquering place after
place. Where one day my word was law, the next day it was another's turn,
robbing, plundering, spying in haste, carrying off the prettiest of the women
and the best of the cattle and never leaving a horse behind. But I was on the
look-out for rarities. What satisfied others was worthless to me. I was always
after treasure, trusting my sharp vision, seeing into pockets, seeing through
caskets. I acquired gold in heaps and wonderful jewels. Emeralds alone are
fit for you to wear over your heart. Let oval pearls from the sea-floor hang
from your ears. Your red cheeks would outshine rubies. So here I set these
riches at your feet, the spoils of many a bloody fight. I've brought all these
chests, but I have many more, hooped with iron. Let me be your follower
and I'll fill your treasure vaults, because no sooner did you mount the throne
than everything submitted to you – reason, wealth, power. All this that I
clung to as mine now leaves me and is yours. I thought it valuable. Now it
is no more to me than withered grass. But one happy glance from you will
give it all its value back.

FAUST

Take away this load of yours, so boldly acquired. Be quick about it. No
reward. No reprimand. Everything the castle contains is already hers. Any
particular gift is superfluous. Go and assemble these treasures never seen
before. Put their magnificence on display. Make our vaulted halls as bright
as the sky, a paradise of living lifelessness. Roll flowered carpets everywhere
as a soft flooring for her to tread. Let her eyes, which only the gods can meet,
dwell on a scene of utmost brilliance.

[Handwritten annotations:]
killed Castor
Lyceus and Idas
killed by Pollux
Castor + Pollux

one of the Argonauts

LYNCEUS — able to see through the earth because of his keen eyesight

oxymoron

LYNCEUS

Your orders, sir, are simply fun. They're little sooner said than done. Her beauty is of such command, it makes her mistress of the land. The army is abashed before her. Their hands are limp, their swords are blunted. The sun itself is cold and dull, compared with her. Beside the wonders of her face, all the rest is empty space. *off*

HELEN *to Faust*

I want to speak with you. But come up here. Take the ruler's seat beside me and make mine secure.

FAUST

First, O lady, allow me to do you homage on my knees, then kiss the hand that lifts me up. Confirm me as co-regent of your boundless realm and make me your worshipper, your servant, and your guardian all in one.

HELEN

I keep seeing and hearing things that surprise me, astonish me. And I have many questions to ask. But tell me first why the man's words felt so strange, so strange and at the same time so friendly. One sound seems to fit another. When a word has lodged in the ear, a second word follows and caresses it.

FAUST

If you like the way our people talk, you'll be delighted with their song. It will satisfy your ear and satisfy your mind. But the thing to do is to practise together at once. Conversing will encourage it, draw it out.

HELEN

Well, tell me then how I can speak that way.

FAUST

It's easy. Trust your heart. Your heart will say. And when it is so full you cannot bear it, you cast about and wonder —

HELEN

Who will share it.

FAUST

And now we neither look back nor before. The present is our joy.

HELEN

What need we more?

FAUST

It is our all, our treasure, our domain. And as a pledge —

HELEN

I give my hand again.

CHORUS

Who would hold it against our mistress if she favours the lord of the castle? You mustn't forget we're all captives, as we have been again and again, what with the collapse of Troy and the twists and trials of our endless journey.

Women, used to having men, may be experts, but they can't be choosers. They take what comes and give the freedom of their luxurious bodies alike to a fair-haired shepherd boy or a black and bristly faun.

They're getting closer and closer, leaning on one another, shoulder to shoulder, knee to knee, hand in hand, rocking to and fro on the great cushioned throne, not afraid of displaying their majesty's intimacy before the eyes of the people.

I seem so far away, and yet so near. But here I am and happy to say it.

FAUST

I tremble, I can hardly breathe, hardly speak. It's all a dream, not of this world.

HELEN

I feel both done with and newly made, involved in you, true to the unknown.

FAUST

Don't pry into our unique fate. Our duty is to life now, if only for the moment.

PHORKYAS

Entering in haste

Spelling out your love-story, trifling with it, idling, dawdling, brooding over it. There's no time for that now. Can't you hear a thundering, a trumpeting? Your destruction is near. Menelaus is approaching with his hordes. Prepare for a bitter struggle. If they get hold of you, they'll mutilate you like Deiphobus. You'll pay for your escort. These light girls will tread the air, and the axe newly sharpened is waiting for her at the altar.

FAUST

Outrageous, this intrusion, jarring on my nerves. Even in time of danger I hate precipitancy. The handsomest of messengers looks ugly if his news is bad. You, the ugliest of all, take pleasure in bad news only. But it won't work this time. Go on shaking the air with your empty breath. There is no danger here. If there were, it would be no more than an idle threat.

Signals, explosions in the towers,
trumpets and clarions, martial music.
A powerful army marches past

FAUST

No, indeed. I'll show you at once my heroic generals assembled and united. A man who can't protect his lady to the utmost doesn't deserve her favour. (*to the generals, who detach themselves from their columns and step forward*) You young blossoms from the north, you the strength and flower of the south, meet the enemy with the suppressed fury that will ensure your victory. The army, clad in glittering steel, has shattered empire after empire. It makes the earth shake under its tread. Thunder echoes in its wake. We landed at Pylos. Old Nestor's days were past. The roving army broke up the little kingdoms. Push Menelaus back to the sea at once. There let him roam and lie in wait and plunder, following his destiny and his inclination, as before. The queen of Sparta bids me appoint you dukes. Lay your territories at her feet and reap the benefit from them. You Germans must defend the bays of Corinth. You Goths, Achaia with its hundred gullies. The Frankish army will move to Elis, the Saxons to Messenia, and the Normans will clean up the seas and make Argolis great. Then each of you can settle down, while keeping up a sharp defence. But Sparta, the queen's ancient seat, will preside over you all. She will see you severally enjoying life in a land where nothing lacks. You will look confidently to her for approval and for justice.

Faust comes down. The dukes form a circle round him, awaiting further instructions

CHORUS

Whoever desires to possess the fairest of women, let him be practical above all and see to his armoury. Flattery may have won him earth's topmost prize, but he won't hold it easily. Cunning men will entice her away from him. Brigands will boldly carry her off. Let him give thought to this.

Accordingly I commend our ruler. I rate him higher than others, when I see him boldly making shrewd alliances, getting strong men on his side, ready to obey his orders instantly, each of them acting in his own interest, earning his overlord's thanks, and bringing glory to both.

Who can snatch her away from him now? She is his and he is strong. Let him keep her, as we have good reason to say, seeing that he is protecting us along with her behind his strong walls and with his mighty army in the field.

FAUST

The gifts I have bestowed on these men are great – a rich country for each of them. But let them go now. We hold the central position. They will vie with one another in protecting this all-but-island, linked to Europe's furthest mountains by only a slight chain of hills, and circled by the running waves. The land of lands – may it give happiness to all the tribes – belongs now to my queen, whom it has known from the moment she broke, shining, through her shell among the Eurotas's whispering reeds and dazzled her great mother and her brothers and sisters. This land looks only to you. It offers you its flowering wealth. The whole earth is yours, but surely you put your home country first. And though the jagged summits of the mountain range are barren in the chilly sunlight, the rock is greening in patches and goats there are nibbling scanty nourishment. Springs begin and join with others as they come cascading down. Already the ravines, the slopes, the meadows are green and in the endlessly broken plain flocks of woolly sheep are grazing. Scattered cattle come cautiously to the precipice edge, but there is shelter for all in many rocky caves, where the god Pan protects them. Nature nymphs live in cool moist places in the bushy clefts, and trees crowd trees with their branch-work reaching up aspiringly to higher regions. This is the ancient forest. The mighty oaks stand stiffly, zigzagging in their contours, while the gentle maples, rich in sweet sap, rise clear and carry their weight lightly. In the quiet shade the mother-ewes' warm milk is always there for the lambs and the children. Fruit is not far to seek. Crops ripen in the fields and honey can be found dripping from a hollow trunk. This is where well-being is hereditary, cheeks and lips ever fresh and happy. Each one is immortal in his place. They are healthy. They are contented. And so in perfect days the child grows to manhood. We are amazed. We ask and ask again, whether these are men or gods. When Apollo lived among shepherds he was so like them you couldn't distinguish. Where nature rules unchallenged, all the worlds are interlocked.

Sitting down beside her

This is what we two have achieved. Let us put the past behind us. Remember
you are sprung from the greatest of the gods and in a special sense belong to

the early world. No fortress must enclose you. This Arcadia lies not far from *scene* 41 Sparta in all its eternal youth and vigour for us to dwell in with delight. If you agreed to live on such a heavenly soil you would reach the happiest consummation. Our thrones would turn into arbours. Let us accept this Arcadian joy and freedom.

scene 42

The scene is transformed. A row of rocky caves with closed arbours in front of them. A shady grove of trees extending to the foot of the cliff. Faust and Helen are not on the scene. The chorus are lying around, sleeping

PHORKYAS

How long the girls have been asleep I cannot say. Nor can I say whether they have seen in dreams what I have seen before my eyes. And so I'll wake them and give these young folk a surprise. And you too, you graybeards, sitting down there, waiting to see what comes of all these miracles. Up with you, up. Shake off your sleepiness. Don't blink so. Open your eyes, and listen to me.

CHORUS

Go on then, tell us, tell us what fantastic things have happened. Most of all we'd like to hear what surpasses all believing. Bored to death we are with nothing else but all these rocks to stare at.

PHORKYAS

Bored to death already, are you, when your eyes are hardly opened? Listen then, our lord and lady have withdrawn into these arbours, finding there and in the caves and grottoes a secure retreat, a lovers' idyll.

CHORUS

What, in there?

PHORKYAS

Cut off from the world, making me their sole attendant. No small honour, but I acted as became me, looked away, searched about for roots and mosses, being versed in nature's lore, and left them to themselves.

CHORUS

You talk as if there was a world in there, a world of woods and meadows, brooks and lakes. What rigmarole is this?

PHORKYAS

Certainly there is, you novices. Depths unexplored, halls upon halls, courts upon courts, as I cunningly discovered. But suddenly a burst of laughter echoed through the spacious caverns, and behold, there was a boy there, jumping to and fro between the father and the mother. Such a cooing and caressing, shouts and shrieks of fun and folly. Deafening. I could hardly stand it.

He was naked; like a genius, but wingless; like a faun, but nowise brutish. When he jumped, the ground, reacting, flung him high into the air. He touched the vaulted roof the third time.

His mother, growing anxious, shouted: Jump, jump as often and as freely as you want to, but no flying. Flying is forbidden. And his father warned him likewise, saying: In the earth lies the force that throws you upwards. *page 163*

Touch the earth even with your toe, you'll be strengthened like the son of
earth, Antaeus. The boy hopped up the rock, sprang from one brink to
another like a ball bouncing freely. Suddenly, then, he disappeared in a
crevice, and it seemed as if we'd lost him. His mother grieved, his father
soothed her, anxiously I shrugged my shoulders. But soon he was back again.
And what a surprise! Were there treasures hidden down there? He was now
finely dressed in robes striped and flowered, tassels hanging from his arms
and ribbons on his breast. In his hand a golden lyre, just like a little Phoebus.
He came, all serene, to the rock-edge overhanging us. Wonderful. His
parents embraced in their excitement. Round his head there was a halo.
Where it came from, hard to say. Was it gold he was wearing? Was it mental
energy flaming? Announcing, as he stood there in his boyhood, he was
master-to-be of the beautiful, one through whose limbs the eternal melodies
sounded. This is how you'll see him, this is how you'll hear him, to your
uttermost amazement.

CHORUS

You call this a miracle, you Cretan woman? Have you never heeded the
lesson of the poets, never listened to Ionia's, or Hellas's, wealth of ancient
legends of gods and heroes?

Nothing happens nowadays but is a sorry echo of the glorious ancestral
past. Your story doesn't compare with the lovely fable – a fable more
credible than truth – of the son of Maia.

No sooner born, this neat and healthy child, than his gossipy nurses, little
suspecting, swaddled him in spotless napkins, wound him in precious purple,
but the rogue in his infant strength and skill slily extricated his supple limbs,
leaving the tight swathings where they lay, like the butterfly slipping out
of its stiff chrysalis and spreading its wings to fly at will in the sunny
atmosphere.

This is he who, nimblest of the nimble, quickly showed by his artful de-
vices that he was the spirit-patron of thieves and rogues and all self-seekers.
He lost no time in stealing the sea-god's trident, Ares's sword out of the
sheath, Phoebus's bow and arrow, Hephaestus's tongs. Even Father Zeus's
lightning he would have taken, but for fear of the fire. He tripped and beat
Eros in a wrestling match and filched Venus's girdle while she was fondling
him.

*Charming melodious stringed music is heard in the cavern. They all give
heed to it and are moved by it. The music continues in full till the pause
indicated below*

PHORKYAS

Listen to these sweet sounds. Rid yourselves of fable and let the old gods
go. They have no meaning for us. We demand something better now. What
moves the heart must come from the heart. *She withdraws to the rocks*

CHORUS

If you, monster that you are, respond to these accents, we are moved to tears
by them and revived. When our inner light shines, we can dispense with the
sun, finding in our hearts all that the outer world withholds.

EUPHORION

If you hear children singing, you share the singing with them. If you see me dance in measure, you are my parents and your hearts dance too.

HELEN

When love brings the right pair together, there is human happiness. Make it three and the rapture is divine.

FAUST

Nothing is lacking then, I am yours and you are mine. We stand united. Might it always be so.

CHORUS

Many years of happiness with this shining boy are promised them. Oh how touching!

EUPHORION

Let me hop and jump. I long to fly up into the sky. I can't wait.

FAUST

Careful, careful. Don't be rash, lest you meet with disaster and ruin us all.

EUPHORION

I won't stay on the ground. Let go of my hands and hair and dress. They're mine, aren't they?

HELEN

Oh think whose you are, think how it would hurt us to lose what the three of us have won.

CHORUS

Won, yes, but not for long, I fear.

HELEN AND FAUST

For the love of your parents keep this violence in check. Stay here in this rural spot. You adorn it.

EUPHORION

I'll do it for your sake. (*moving about among the chorus and inducing them to dance*) I float lightly in this gay company. Is the time right? And the step?

HELEN

Yes, excellent. Lead these beauties in a formal round.

FAUST

I wish it was over. These antics make me uneasy.

Euphorion and the chorus, singing and dancing, move in involved patterns

CHORUS

When you move your arms in that lovely way and shake your bright locks and trail your foot so lightly and twine your limbs, you win all our hearts. You've reached the goal.

Pause

EUPHORION

You are fleet-footed deer, suddenly appearing, close at hand, inviting play.   *page 165*

I am the huntsman, you are the game.

CHORUS

If you want to catch us, you needn't exert yourself. After all, our only wish is to embrace you, you fair creature.

EUPHORION

Off you go through the trees, over rough ground. If a thing comes easy, it repels me. I can only enjoy what I take by force.

HELEN AND FAUST

What exuberance! What rashness! No hope for moderation. Do I hear horns blowing across the woods and valleys? And this shrieking. It shouldn't be.

CHORUS *running in, one by one*

He ran past us, he despised us. He just seized the wildest one and is dragging her here.

EUPHORION *carrying a young girl*

Here I come dragging this sturdy girl along to enjoy her with violence. She resists me, but I kiss her mouth and press her to my breast and show her who is master.

GIRL

Let go of me. There's strength of mind in me too and a will as strong as yours. You won't soon overcome it. If you think I'm beaten, you're being over-confident. Hang on, you fool, and I'll burn you just for fun.

She bursts into flame and soars up

Follow me into airy spaces. Follow me into close caverns. Catch me if you can.

EUPHORION *shaking off the last of the flames*

I feel shut in among these rocks and bushes. This is no place for youth and vigour like mine. I hear winds and waves, but far, far away. I want to be near them. *He runs farther and farther up the rock*

HELEN, FAUST, AND CHORUS

Do you want to rival the chamois? You might fall. We shudder at the thought.

EUPHORION

I must go on mounting and enlarging the view. Now I know where I am. In the middle of the island, Pelops's island, close to continent and ocean.

CHORUS

Can't you stay peaceably in these wooded hills? We can search for vines, rows of vines on the slopes, figs and golden apples too. Oh stay, and be good, in this sweet country.

EUPHORION

Are you dreaming of peace? Dream if you like. The password is war and victory, sounding on and on.

CHORUS

Whoever in peace-time wants war back again must have abandoned all hope.

EUPHORION

May it inspire all the fighters this land has produced, men free and utterly fearless in danger after danger, careless of their lives, filled with unquench-
able fervour.

CHORUS

Look up. See how high he's climbed. And yet he doesn't seem small. He looks harnessed for victory in bronze and steel.

EUPHORION

No walls, no ramparts. Let each be sure of himself. A man's stronghold is a stout heart. If you want to live in freedom, go into the battle-field lightly armed. Women will become Amazons, children heroes.

CHORUS

Sacred poesy, let it mount to heaven. Let it shine, the fairest of stars, receding and receding, yet still reaching us and still delighting us.

EUPHORION

No, I'm not a child. I'm a young man armed. In company with the strong, the free, the brave I've shown my worth. Now off we go to tread the road to glory.

HELEN AND FAUST

Barely ushered into life, new to the joyful light of day, you climb dizzy stairs, seeking space and its dangers. Are we nothing to you? Was our lovely union a dream?

EUPHORION

Do you hear the thundering out at sea, re-echoing in the valleys, army against army, by sea and land, onset upon onset, pain and torment? Once and for all, death is imperative.

HELEN, FAUST, AND CHORUS

Oh, horror! Must it be?

EUPHORION

Should I look on from afar? No, I must share the suffering.

HELEN, FAUST, AND CHORUS

High spirits and jeopardy. A tragic fate.

EUPHORION

Nothing shall stop me. And now, see, a pair of wings unfolding. I must go. Don't rob me of this.

He throws himself aloft. His garments sustain him for a moment. His head is illuminated, trailing a beam of light

~~flew into sun~~

CHORUS

Icarus, Icarus. Oh the pity of it.

A handsome youth collapses at his parents' feet. In his death he resembles a known personage, but his mortal part disappears immediately. The aureole mounts comet-like. Dress, cloak, and lyre are left lying

HELEN AND FAUST

Cruel torment follows swiftly after joy.

EUPHORION *voice from below*

Mother, don't desert me in the dark kingdom. *pause*

CHORUS *elegy*

Desert you, no, wherever you may be. We believe we recognize you. When you take leave of life, all our hearts go with you; not so much lamenting as envying your fate. In good days as in bad your song and your courage were supreme.

Born into happiness, with high lineage and health and strength, you soon lost control, your early bloom scattered. Yours was a keen eye to view the world, a fellow-feeling for any warmth of heart, a passion for fair women, and a poetic voice all your own.

But nothing could stop you. Of your own accord you rushed into the fatal net, alienating law and order. At the last your noble ambition showed your integrity. You aimed high, but you failed.

Failed, but who succeeds? A vain question. Fate gives no answer to it on the day of doom when all are suffering and silent. Nevertheless raise your bowed heads and sing new songs. Earth has always begotten them and will beget them again.

Complete pause. The music ceases

HELEN *to Faust*
An old saw says that beauty and happiness cannot stay united. Sooner or later they part. And to my sorrow this is now borne out in me. The bonds of life are broken, and so in grief and pain I say goodbye, throwing myself in your arms for the last time. Persephone, receive my boy and me. *She embraces Faust. Her bodily part disappears, leaving the dress and veil in his arms*
PHORKYAS *to Faust*
Cling to what is left. The dress, keep hold of it. Demons already are plucking at it, eager to drag it down to the underworld. Don't let them. It may not be the divinity you lost, but it is divine. Make the most of this inestimable favour. Rise aloft. It will sweep you through the ether, above all that is commonplace, for the rest of your days. We shall meet again, far, very far, from here.

Helen's garments dissolve into cloud, surround Faust, raise him aloft, and pass with him

PHORKYAS *picks up Eurphorion's clothing and his lyre, steps forward, lifts them high, and speaks*
A lucky find, no matter what. The fire and flame is gone, I know. But I'm not sorry for the world. There's plenty of room for poets still, and poets' guilds and poets' grudges. I can't supply the talent, but at least I can lend the costume.
She sits down at the front of the stage, beside a pillar
PANTHALIS
Be quick now, girls, are we not rid of the incubus, the spell this old Thessalian hag threw over us all. Rid too of the tinkling music that was so jumbled, confusing the ear and, worse, confusing the mind. Down now to Hades where the queen with solemn step has gone already. Her faithful servants must follow her without delay. We shall find her at the throne of the inscrutable one.

Queens to be sure, are all right anywhere. Even in Hades they're up at the top associating proudly with equals, intimate with Persephone herself. But we background figures, deep in fields of asphodel, among barren willows and rows of poplar, how are we to pass the time? Squeaking and twittering like bats, a dismal, ghostly sound?

PANTHALIS
Whoever neither makes his name nor strives for higher things belongs to the elements. So away with you. For myself I crave to be with my mistress, the queen, again. Not merit only, faithful allegiance can preserve our person. *off*

ALL
We are returned to the light of day. Persons no longer, we feel it and know it. But back to Hades, never. Living nature claims us. We spirits have our claim on her.

PART OF THE CHORUS
In these thousands of branches that sway and tremble, rustle and whisper in the air, we gently, playfully, coax the springs of life up from the roots into the wavering twigs. We deck them lavishly with leaves, and then with blossoms, to grow and thrive unchecked. When the ripe fruits fall to the ground, people and cattle come at once in busy crowds to gather or nibble them, and everyone in sight is bowed to earth just as men bowed to the earliest gods.

SECOND PART
We stay close to these rocky cliffs and the smooth reflecting water. We move caressingly in gentle vibrations over the surface. And here we listen for every sound, bird-song, or fluting in the reeds, even Pan's dreadful shout. We always have an echo ready. A rustling sound. We rustle back. Thunder, then our thunder rolls and mightily repeats twice, three times, up to ten times.

A THIRD PART
Sisters, we, more mobile-minded, hasten away with the running brooks, drawn by the rich-looking lines of distant hills. Down and down we go meandering, watering first the meadows, then the pastures, then the gardens round the houses. Those pointed cypresses our waymark, towering above the landscape and the shoreline and the mirror of the sea.

A FOURTH PART
You others may go where you like. But we whisperingly haunt this hillside given wholly to vineyards. Here at any time we can see the vinedresser labouring devotedly for a dubious result. With hoe or with spade, heaping, trimming, binding, he makes his prayer to the gods, but first and most usefully to the sungod. Bacchus, the weakling, cares little about his faithful servants. He just rests or lolls in caves and arbours, trifling with a young faun, and eternally finding what he needs to sustain him in his tipsy reveries in skins and jugs and suchlike to right and left of him in the cool grottoes. But when the gods, and Helios above all, have done the airing and the wetting, the warming and the baking, and filled the cornucopia with all the grapes it will hold, then suddenly, where before there was only the solitary labourer, a great stirring of life begins, a rustling in every vine and a going from one to the next. A creaking of baskets, a clattering of pails, a groaning

under the loads all on their way to the great vat and the dance of the wine-pressers. And so the sacred wealth of grapes is rudely trampled to a horrid, foaming, splashing mess. Now the brazen clash of cymbals assails the ear, announcing the mysterious arrival of Dionysus with his following of goat-footed satyrs swinging their women, goat-footed too. Silenus's long-eared beast comes in with its outrageous braying. No respecting here of persons. The cloven hoof treads down all decency. Your senses are in a whirl, your ears are deafened. Drunkards feel their way to the cup, their heads and bellies filled to bursting. Apprehensions here and there only aggravate the tumult. The old skins must be emptied to make way for the new wine.

Curtain. Phorkyas rises to giant proportions, then steps down from her buskins, removes mask and veil, and reveals herself as Mephistopheles, ready, if need be, to supply an epilogue

scene 43

High mountains, rocky peaks. A cloud comes up, attaches itself, settles on a ledge of rock, and divides

FAUST *emerging*
Here at this outermost mountain-brink where, stepping cautiously, I can look sheer down into deepest depths of solitude, I relinquish the cloud-chariot that conveyed me gently over land and sea through the serene atmosphere and now, slowly disengaging itself, not scattering, begins to move eastward in a single mass. My eye follows it closely with astonishment, to see it dividing, shifting, changing with a wave-like motion. But surely now it is taking shape. Yes, there is no doubt of it. A wonderful giant form, a woman's form, reclining on a sunlit couch. Divine-looking. Like Juno, or like Leda, or it might be Helen. Majestic and how lovely too, but quivering to the sight. Already it has broken up and comes to rest across the eastern sky, a formless pile, like distant dazzling ice peaks, mirroring for me the deep meaning of those fleeting days.

But what is this delicate, shining wisp of cloud that comes and woos me, cool to the brow, refreshing, and now lightly, hesitantly, rises higher and higher and gathers into one? Am I deluded or do I see a rapturous image of what I prized and cherished most in youth and lost so long ago? A wave of my earliest emotions sweeps through me. Dawn-love it is. That buoyancy and zest. The first look, so quickly felt, so little understood, which, if one could only keep it, would outshine everything in worth. Beauty of soul, the essence of it, the gracious image shows me now. And it holds. It mounts into the higher air and takes the best of me along with it.

A seven-league boot clumps down. A second boot follows. Mephistopheles dismounts. The boots stride off

MEPHISTOPHELES
That was some walking, if you ask me. But what's your idea? Dismounting

in the midst of these horrors, these ghastly, grinning rocks? I know them well enough, though not just here, because, strictly speaking, this used to be the floor of hell.

FAUST

You're never at a loss for crazy mythology. Now you're at it again.

MEPHISTOPHELES *solemnly*

When the Lord God – and I know why – threw us out of the air into the lowest depths of hell where a central fire was blazing eternally, we had plenty of illumination, but we were in a very crowded and awkward spot. The devils all began to puff from above and below to put the fire out. There was an awful acid stink of sulphur everywhere and a pressure of gas so stupendous, that it burst through the flat crust of earth, thick as it was, with a great bang. And now it's a different story. What was once the bottom is now the top. They base on this the very theories they need to stand things on their heads. Anyway we escaped that hot imprisonment under the earth and gained the freedom and dominion of the air. An open secret, well-preserved, and not revealed to the world till later.

FAUST

Those mountains, noble as they are, have nothing to say to me. I ask neither why nor whence. When nature established herself, she neatly rounded off the earthly sphere, assembling the rocks and the hills, taking her pleasure in peaks and chasms, and leading down by easy stages to the foothills and the lowlands, where all is greenery and growth. Nature can rejoice in this without needing your wild upheavals.

MEPHISTOPHELES

That's what you say. You think it's all clear. But those who were there know better. I was there myself and saw the abyss boiling and flaming, and Moloch with his hammer shattering the rocks and hurling mountain-fragments all

over the place. The land is still littered with these erratic blocks. Who can explain the force that hurled them? The philosophers can do nothing with it. The rock is there and there we let it lie after cudgelling our brains to no purpose. But the common people in their decency have always understood and are not to be shaken in their belief. They know it's a miracle, and Satan gets the credit. This is the crutch of faith that brings the traveller hobbling to the Devil's Rock and the Devil's Bridge.

FAUST

Well, it's useful to have a glimpse of nature from the devil's point of view.

MEPHISTOPHELES

Let nature be as it may, what do I care? This is a point of honour: the devil was in on it. We are the ones to achieve greatness – tumult, violence, madness. Behold the sign. But, nonsense apart, is there nothing that satisfies you on this earth of ours? You're so hard to please. You've surveyed the kingdoms of the world and the glory of them in all their vastness. Is there anything at all you'd like to do?

FAUST

There is indeed. A great thing has taken hold of me. Guess what it is.

MEPHISTOPHELES

That's easy. Me, I'd seek out one of those big cities, with people scrabbling for food in the heart of it, twisted narrow streets, pointed roofs, a smallish market-place all cabbages and carrots and onions, butchers' stalls infested with flies, feasting on the fat joints. Plenty of bustle, plenty of stinks, all the day long. Then I'd have open squares and broad streets for my upper-class pretensions, and finally endless suburbs, unchecked by city walls, and there I'd ride around in a carriage, up and down, in all the noisy throng of human ant-heaps. And wherever I went, driving or on horseback, I'd be the centre of attraction, honoured by thousands, hundreds of thousands.

FAUST

That wouldn't do for me. One likes to see the people prospering and living well in their fashion, and even studying and getting educated. But in the end it only makes rebels of them.

MEPHISTOPHELES

Then I'd proudly build myself a fancy castle on some pleasant site with lovely gardens, woods, fields, hills, and lawns all round it, rows of trees and velvety turf, straight walks and shady seats well-planned, waterfalls tumbling over rocks, fountains of every kind, impressive here, petty and piddling in many another place. Then I'd build some intimate little cottages to house my pretty ladies and I'd spend endless time there in sweet seclusion. I said ladies, because I always think of them in the plural.

FAUST

Vulgar and up-to-date. Like Sardanapalus.

MEPHISTOPHELES

How is anyone to guess what you want? No doubt something vast and bold. You've just been travelling through the upper air, so I daresay you want the moon.

FAUST

Far from it. This earth is roomy enough for great deeds. I mean to astonish
the world. And I have the energy for it.

MEPHISTOPHELES
So it's fame you want. This comes from the heroic company you've kept.

FAUST
Not fame. Fame is nothing. I want action. I want property, power.

MEPHISTOPHELES
There'll be plenty of poets to sing your achievement to posterity and perpetuate your folly.

FAUST
What should you know of man's desire? You simply haven't it in you. With a nature like yours, all hatred and bitterness, how should you grasp the human need?

MEPHISTOPHELES
Have your way then. Let me hear the extent of your latest craze.

FAUST
The open sea arrested my attention. I watched it and saw how it mounted and mounted and then relaxed and spilt its storm-waves along the level shore. And this annoyed me. A man of free mind, who respects the rights of others, is always uneasy when he sees arrogance asserting itself immoderately, violently. And it was like this here. I thought it might be an accident and I looked again more closely. The waves halted, rolled back, and withdrew from their proud conquest. The hour will come and they'll do it all over again.

MEPHISTOPHELES *to the audience*
Nothing new in that for me. I've seen it for hundreds and thousands of years.

FAUST *excitedly*
The water comes creeping up, barren in itself, to spread its barrenness wherever it goes, in every hole and corner. Now it has flooded that desolate stretch of land and there waves upon waves run riot. Then they recede and nothing has been gained. It nearly drives me mad to see the elements so uncontrolled, wasting their energy so blindly. And here my spirit goes all out and boldly resolves to make this its battleground and prove itself the master.

And it is possible. With its fluid nature water can slip past any hillock. However much it rages, a slight rise can divert it, a slight drop can pull it down. Seeing this, I quickly made my plans: Get permission to exclude the imperious ocean from the shore, set limits to its watery expanse and force it back on itself. What satisfaction that would be! Step by step I thought it out. This is my wish. Help me to achieve it.

Distant drums and martial music
from behind the audience, on the right

MEPHISTOPHELES
I see no difficulty there. Do you hear those drums in the distance?

FAUST
Yes, war again. No man in his senses would welcome it.

MEPHISTOPHELES
War or peace, it's sensible to try and get what you can out of it. We all

watch for opportunities that favour us. Well, Faust, the opportunity's here. Seize it.

FAUST

Spare me this enigmatic jargon. Come to the point. What do you mean? Out with it.

MEPHISTOPHELES

I couldn't help observing *en route* that our worthy emperor is in great straits. You know what he's like. When we were entertaining him and put that paper money in his hands he thought the whole world was his. He'd been given his crown early in life and he drew the false conclusion, very comfortable for himself, that it was both easy and desirable to rule the empire and have his fun at the same time.

FAUST

A gross mistake. A ruler must find his reward in rulership. His heart is filled with a strong will and purpose, but no man must be able to fathom it. Only his intimates may share the secret. Then when the work is done, the whole world will be amazed, and he will retain his supreme authority and prestige. Self-indulgence debases.

MEPHISTOPHELES

He's not like that. He indulged himself, and how! Meanwhile the empire lapsed into anarchy. Great and small at one another's throats on every side. Brothers banishing and murdering brothers. Castles warring with castles, cities with cities, guilds with nobles, bishops with chapters and people. Merely exchange glances with a man and you were enemies. Your life wasn't safe in a church. It was all up with a merchant or journeyman, if he ventured beyond the city gates. People got bolder and bolder. You had to stand up for yourself, or you were a goner. Well, things dragged on that way.

FAUST

Dragged on, hobbled, fell down, got up, tumbled again, and rolled to a stop.

MEPHISTOPHELES

And you couldn't complain about it either. Everyone had his rights and was able to assert them. Any juvenile could play the adult. But in the end, the best people, the sound people, got fed up. They roused themselves in a body and said: Whoever can bring the country to order can rule it. The emperor can't and won't. Let us elect a new emperor who'll revive the empire, give us security, and wed peace with justice in a newly created world.

FAUST

That sounds like the priesthood talking.

MEPHISTOPHELES

Priests it was. Seeing to their own fat bellies. They had more to lose than any. The revolt spread and became respectable. And our emperor, whom we made happy, has withdrawn to this spot, perhaps to fight his last fight.

FAUST

I'm sorry for him. He was so kind and open.

MEPHISTOPHELES

Come. While there's life, there's hope. We'll have a look. Suppose we

rescue him from this narrow pass. Once out of it, he'll be safe henceforth.
Who knows which way the dice will fall. And if he has the luck, he'll
soon have a following.

*They cross the lower hills and inspect the disposition of the army in the
valley. Drums and martial music are heard below*

MEPHISTOPHELES
I see the position is well chosen. We'll join them and the victory's won.
FAUST
What's the good of it? Trickery, illusion, nothing else.
MEPHISTOPHELES
No, military cunning to win battles. Remember your purpose and keep your
mind on big issues. If we can restore throne and country to the emperor, all
you will have to do will be to kneel down and be presented with an endless
shoreline in fief.
FAUST
You've done so much, so why not go in and win a battle?
MEPHISTOPHELES
Not me. You'll win it. You're the commander-in-chief this time.
FAUST
That would be the limit. Issuing orders where I don't know a thing.
MEPHISTOPHELES
Leave it to the general staff, and the field marshal has nothing to fear. I know
what a mess war is and I've appointed my council in good time from among
the old giants. If you can assemble them, you're lucky.
FAUST
What's that over there? An armed force. Have you roused all the mountain
folk?

MEPHISTOPHELES
No, just the cream of the lot, like Shakespeare's Quince.

Enter the three giants

MEPHISTOPHELES
Why here the boys come! You see they're not all the same age. Not dressed the same way. Nor armed the same way. They'll serve you well. (*to the audience*) Nowadays everyone loves to see a knight in armour. And if these wretches are allegorical, so much the better.
RAUFEBOLD *young, lightly armed, gaily dressed*
Whoever faces up to me, gets my fist in his teeth right away. Cowards that run – I grab them by the hair.
HABEBALD *in his best years, well armed, richly dressed*
Empty scrapping. Not worth a thing. A waste of time. Get hold of what you can and let the rest wait.
HALTEFEST *old, well-armed, not in mail*
That won't get you far either. You can soon run through a great fortune. Getting hold is good, but keeping's better. Just you leave it to the old man and you'll lose nothing.

They all go downhill

scene 44 IN THE FOOTHILLS

Drums and martial music from below. The emperor's tent is thrown open. Emperor. Commander-in-chief. Retinue

COMMANDER-IN-CHIEF
It still seems to me that our strategy was well conceived when we withdrew the whole army into this valley. I have great hopes of success.
EMPEROR
We'll see how it goes. But I don't like this pulling back and this semblance of flight.
COMMANDER-IN-CHIEF
Look at our right flank, your majesty. The terrain is just what we could wish, the hills not steep, but steep enough to favour us and entangle the enemy. With our forces half-hidden in rolling country their cavalry won't venture in.
EMPEROR
I can only give my approval. It will be a test of strength, hand to hand.
COMMANDER-IN-CHIEF
Here in these flat meadows in the centre you can see our phalanx in good battle-spirit, their pikes flashing in the sunny morning mist. The rest a dark heaving square, powerful, thousands of them, eager for the fight. You can see how strong they are. I trust them to break their opponents' ranks.
EMPEROR
This is the first good view of them I've had. They look splendid. An army like that is worth double the number.

COMMANDER-IN-CHIEF
Our left flank speaks for itself. I have stout forces in the rocky cliffs covering the important pass into the valley. You can see their arms glittering. This is where I expect the enemy to be taken unawares and collapse in savage fighting.

EMPEROR
And there they come, those treacherous relatives that used to call me uncle, cousin, brother, and took one liberty after another till they undermined my royal power and authority. Then, with their quarrelling among themselves, they devastated the empire and now they've ended by joining forces against me. The populace wavered this way and that and finally drifted with the stronger current.

COMMANDER-IN-CHIEF
I see one of my trusty spies hurrying back down the cliff. I hope he has something useful to report.

FIRST SPY
We managed to work our way in among them, not without the usual risks, but our news is not very favourable. There are many who swear allegiance, as others have before them, but they plead inner disorder and danger to the nation and say their hands are tied.

EMPEROR
Self-interest always tells people to look after number one and forget about gratitude, duty, honour, and such. But don't you realize that when your neighbour's house is on fire your own house is bound to go too?

COMMANDER-IN-CHIEF
There's a second one coming down the hill, but slowly. He's worn out and trembling in every limb.

SECOND SPY
It was amusing at first to see confusion everywhere, but then, suddenly, a new emperor came on the scene and now the whole crowd is on its way under direction, following those spurious flags like so many sheep.

EMPEROR
A counter-emperor is all to the good. It makes me feel at last that I am the true one. I only dressed in armour as a uniform, but now it's converted to a higher purpose. At all our festivals, even at their most brilliant, I felt the lack of one thing – danger. You always favoured tilting at a ring, but my heart beat high and I was for jousting proper. If you hadn't been opposed to war I should be a shining hero by now. I felt powerfully fortified when I saw myself mirrored in the fire. The flaming element pressed me close and it seemed real and dangerous enough, though it was illusory. I've always dreamed vaguely of victory and fame. I mean now to make up for having failed so grievously before.

The heralds are sent off to challenge the counter-emperor. Faust in armour, the visor half-raised. The giants armed and costumed as before

FAUST
Here we come and trust we're not unwelcome. Caution can be useful even when not needed. You know the mountain people are deep in the lore of

nature and the rocks. The spirits left the flat land long ago and are more attracted by the hills, and there, in cavernous labyrinths, they're steadily at work on the gases and the metals, testing, separating, combining, with the sole purpose of making discoveries. And with subtle power of mind they construct transparent forms and read in silent crystals what is happening in the upper world.

EMPEROR

So I have heard and I believe you. But tell me, my good man, what concern it is of ours.

FAUST

May I remind you of the time in Rome when a dreadful fate awaited that Sabine necromancer from Norcia, who remains your devout and deserving servant. The twigs were crackling, the flames were leaping, the dry logs were all in place, mingled with pitch and sticks of sulphur. There was no hope for him, it seemed, from man or god or devil. But your majesty burst those chains of fire and saved him. He's eternally indebted to you and he thinks only of your welfare, forgetting himself from that day forward and consulting the stars and the depths on your behalf alone. He has enjoined upon us urgently to give you our support. Nature's resources are unlimited in that region and unimpeded, though the church in its stupidity calls it sorcery.

EMPEROR

On feast days when we're receiving and the merry guests arrive expecting to have a good time, jostling one another and crowding the halls, we welcome them all. This worthy man will be doubly welcome if he comes bringing strong support tomorrow morning when our fate hangs in the balance. Nevertheless you must hold back at this crucial moment when thousands are met to battle for me and against me. A man must be self-reliant and, if he claims the throne, prove in person that he's worthy of it. This ghost of a man who has risen against us, calling himself emperor, ruler, commander-in-chief, and feudal lord – let this fist of mine despatch him to the hell where he belongs.

FAUST

It can't be wise for you to risk your head in this way, no matter what. Isn't your helmet crested and plumed, protecting the head that fires our courage? Without the head, what use are the limbs? If the head weakens, they all weaken. If it is wounded, they're all wounded. They revive at once when it revives. The arm is quick to shield the skull, the sword parries and returns the stroke, the foot plants itself gaily on the slain man's neck.

EMPEROR

That's just what I burn to do. To set my foot on his proud head and make it my footstool.

HERALDS returning·

They received us with disrespect, brushed us aside, poured ridicule on our solemn announcement. 'That emperor of yours,' they said, 'is just an echo fading away in the hills.' 'Once upon a time' is how the tale begins.

FAUST

This rebuff entirely suits the wishes of your faithful supporters. There comes the enemy. Your men are ready for the fray. Order the attack. The

moment favours us.

At this point I withdraw and *to the commander-in-chief* leave it to you.
COMMANDER-IN-CHIEF
Very well. Let our right wing advance. The enemy's left is moving up the slope. We can trust our young forces to check them.
FAUST
Then permit this sturdy lad to join your ranks without delay and in their company show what he's capable of. *He points to his right*
RAUFEBOLD *stepping forward*
Whoever comes near me will have his jaws smashed, upper and lower. He won't get away with less. And if I come at him from behind his head'll be dangling loose from his shoulders in less than a jiffy. Let your fighters pile in with swords and clubs at the same time and we'll drown every man jack of them in his own blood. *off*
COMMANDER-IN-CHIEF
Next let our middle phalanx follow up, circumspectly, but with all its strength. Over there, a little to the right, our forces have already upset their plans.
FAUST *pointing to the middle one*
Allow this one to go with them. He's quick. He'll carry everything with him.
HABEBALD *stepping forward*
Let thirst for booty go hand in hand with heroism and we'll all make straight for the counter-emperor's tent and the wealth we shall find there. He won't be top dog for long. I'll place myself at the head of the phalanx.
EILEBEUTE *canteen-woman, snuggling close to him*
We may not be man and wife, but he's my boy all the same. And now we're running into luck. A woman's ruthless when she robs. She stops at nothing. So on to victory. All's fair in love and war. *They go off*
COMMANDER-IN-CHIEF
As was to be expected, they've thrown the weight of their right wing against our left. We must resist to the utmost the furious drive they're making to gain the narrow pass.
FAUST *pointing to the left*
Then please, sir, don't overlook this man. There's never any harm in adding to your strength.
HALTEFEST *stepping forward*
Don't worry about your left wing. You can trust the old man anywhere. What we have we hold. And in my hands it's lightning-proof. *off*
MEPHISTOPHELES *coming down the hill*
Look behind and see those men pouring out of the rocky chasms and filling the paths, all of them in full armour, with helmets, shields, and swords. A wall of strength at our backs, waiting for the word to strike.
Quietly to those in the know
You mustn't ask where this comes from. But I haven't been wasting my time. I've cleared out the armouries in these parts. There they all were, on horseback or standing, just as if they still were lords of the earth. Once they called themselves knights and kings and kaisers and now they're nothing but empty snail-shells for ghosts and devils to play about in and bring the middle ages back. It doesn't matter just which ones it is. They're serving the

purpose. (*aloud*) Just hark at the rage they're in, bumping into one another and rattling their tin armour. And I see flags fluttering on standards, longing for a fresh breeze. Remember this is an ancient tribe, only too eager to get into battle again.

Loud trumpeting from above. Confusion noticeable in the enemy ranks

FAUST
The skyline has gone dark with only here and there an ominous reddish gleam, repeated in the flashing arms and felt everywhere, in the rocks, the forest, the clouds.

MEPHISTOPHELES
Our right wing is holding well. And I can see that nimble giant Raufebold towering above the rest and very busy at his job.

EMPEROR
Where a single arm was raised, I now can see a dozen. It isn't just nature's doing.

FAUST
Did you never hear of mirages, like those on the Sicilian coast? There you see the strangest sights, hovering in full daylight halfway up the sky, all in their own peculiar haze. Cities shifting this way and that, gardens rising and falling, one image relieving another.

EMPEROR
But how disturbing. I see a flashing light playing at the tips of the long spears, flames dancing on the lances in the phalanx. This is too weird for my liking.

FAUST
Forgive me, sir, these are traces of spirits seldom seen now, the Dioscuri, gathering the last of their strength. Sailors swear by them.

EMPEROR
But tell me, to whom do we owe it that nature is assembling these rarities on our behalf?

MEPHISTOPHELES
To whom but that magician who has your welfare at heart. He's deeply concerned about the forces ranged against you. He wants to see you saved, even if it costs him his life.

EMPEROR
They were honouring me with a lively procession through the city. I felt I was somebody and wanted to show it. And without much reflection I took it into my head to let that old graybeard out into the fresh air again. I spoiled the game of the clerics, they didn't thank me for it. And now after all these years I get the reward for my happy impulse.

FAUST
Generous deeds bring rich returns. But look up. It seems he's sending you a sign. We'll soon see what it means.

EMPEROR
There's an eagle sailing high in the air and a griffin coming at it viciously.

FAUST
Watch out. It seems to me a favourable omen. Griffins are fabulous crea-

tures. Fancy its pitting itself against an eagle.

EMPEROR

They're circling round one another at a distance and now at the same moment they're turning to attack, each bent on destruction.

FAUST

See now, that wretched griffin's got the worst of it, drooping its lion's tail and collapsing into the trees, all tousled and torn.

EMPEROR

A remarkable sign. I accept it and hope things will go accordingly.

MEPHISTOPHELES *turning to the right*

A succession of thrusts by our men has made the enemy pull back and veer towards their right under pressure, and this has confused and exposed their left. Now our phalanx, swinging in that direction, has driven its spearhead into the weak spot. Both sides are going at it madly now, like a sea in storm. It couldn't have worked out better. The victory's ours.

EMPEROR *on the left, to Faust*

But look over this way. It seems dubious to me. Our position is in danger. I can't see any stones flying. The enemy has gained possession of the lower rocks. The upper ones have already been vacated. Now you can see them in large numbers coming closer and closer. They may already have taken the pass. Your wiles have failed. This is what comes of your unholy work. *pause*

MEPHISTOPHELES

Here come my two ravens. I wonder what they have to report. I'm afraid things are going badly with us.

EMPEROR

What are these ugly birds after? Coming straight at us on those huge black wings out of the heat of battle.

MEPHISTOPHELES *to the ravens*

Come and sit close beside me. Your advice can be trusted. With your protection our cause won't be lost.

FAUST *to the emperor*

You must have heard of doves that come from distant lands to nest and breed. It's the same here with a difference. The doves bring messages in peace time, the ravens in war.

MEPHISTOPHELES

Very grave news has come. Look, you can see what difficulties our men are in at the edge of the cliff. The enemy have seized the adjoining heights and if they take the pass, it would go hard with us.

EMPEROR

So you've fooled me after all. I've been uneasy ever since you got me in your clutches.

MEPHISTOPHELES

Don't lose heart. We aren't beaten yet. It's generally a close shave at the last, patience and cunning are called for. I have my reliable messengers. Let me take over.

COMMANDER-IN-CHIEF *arriving*

It's always gone against my grain to see you allied to these two. Jugglery is sure to let you down in the end. I can do nothing in the present situation. They started it. Let them finish. I resign and hand in my baton.

EMPEROR

Keep it till better days that may yet be in store. I shudder at this ugly customer and his trafficking with ravens. (*to Mephistopheles*) I can't give you the baton. You don't seem the right man for it. But take command and try to save us. Do what you can. *He retires into the tent with the commander-in-chief*

MEPHISTOPHELES

Let him keep his clumsy baton. It'd be no use to any of us. It smacked of the crucifix to me.

FAUST

What do we do next?

MEPHISTOPHELES

It's as good as done already. – Now, my coal-black cousins, my eager servants, off you go to the mountain lake, give my best wishes to the undines, and ask them to lend us their water-tricks. They have a women's knack, hard for you and me to grasp, of separating the appearance from the reality so that you'd swear it was the reality.

Pause

FAUST

Our ravens must have flattered those undines no end. Already the water's beginning to trickle. It's flowing strongly now down some of those dry rock-faces. They'll never win.

MEPHISTOPHELES

A rare surprise for them. Their boldest climbers are quite at a loss.

FAUST

I can see streams of water joining, gaining in strength, coming up again out of chasms twice the size they were. One powerful stream has arched high in the air and then spread out over flat rocks, plunging, foaming, this way and that. And stage by stage down into the valley. Any heroic resistance would be wasted here. Those big waves would wash them away. It frightens me to see such a fierce rush of water.

MEPHISTOPHELES

I can't see these deceptions. Only human eyes are fooled by them. But I can enjoy the curious spectacle. There they go, running away in crowds, thinking they're in danger of drowning and ridiculously going through all the swimming motions, and puffing and blowing, when all the time they're standing on dry ground. Total confusion everywhere.

The ravens have come back

I'll commend you to the master. But if you want to show that you're masters yourselves, make haste to the glowing smithy where the dwarf-folk are striking sparks from metal and stone. Ask them for fire, shining, flashing, exploding, the best they can devise. Sheet lightning far off, or shooting stars, you can see any summer evening. But lightning playing in the thickets, stars sputtering on wet ground, that's another matter. So talk them into it. It shouldn't be hard. Ask them politely first and force them, if necessary.

The ravens leave. The above is enacted

Now our enemies are in dense darkness, can't see a foot ahead, with shifting lights everywhere and sudden dazzling flashes. That's all very well. But now we must have some noise to frighten them.

FAUST

The empty armour that's lain so long indoors in those stuffy halls has come to life again in the open air. They've been rattling and clattering up there for some time. A strange falsetto note.

MEPHISTOPHELES

You're right. There's no holding them. They're fighting away just as in knighthood's golden days. Greaves and armlets renewing the old war of Guelphs and Ghibellines. They're used to it and they'll never be reconciled. There's nothing like party hatred to carry you through to a pandemonium when hell is celebrating. Listen to the noise, sometimes horrible like the god Pan shrieking, sometimes shrill and satanic, and sending a note of terror all down the valley.

Tumultuous noise of war in the orchestra, passing over finally into gay, military music

scene 45 THE COUNTER-EMPEROR'S TENT

Throne. Rich Setting. Habebald. Eilebeute

EILEBEUTE

So we did get here first!

HABEBALD

There's no raven could keep up with us.

EILEBEUTE

Oh, what a pile of precious things! Where shall I start? Where shall I stop?

HABEBALD

The whole place is so packed I don't know what to choose.

EILEBEUTE

This carpet's just the thing for me after all the hard beds I've slept on.

HABEBALD

And here's a steel-spiked club. I've wanted one of them for a long time.

EILEBEUTE

A red cloak with gold fringes. A dream of a cloak.

HABEBALD *taking the club*

This'll do a quick job. Knock him flat and move on to the next. You've packed a sackful and there's nothing any good in the whole lot. Drop the stuff and take one of these chests. This is the men's pay. Gold. Full of gold to the brim.

EILEBEUTE

It's a cruel weight. I can't lift it. I could never carry it.

HABEBALD

Bend over quick. Quick, I tell you. You're strong. I'll hoist it up.   *page 183*

EILEBEUTE
Oh dear. Oh dear. There it goes. My poor back's broke.

The chest falls and bursts open

HABEBALD
The good gold all spilt on the ground. Quick now and pick it up.
EILEBEUTE *crouching*
I'll grab an apronful. It'll be enough.
HABEBALD
That'll do. Now off you go. (*She stands up*) Oh, your apron has a hole in it.
Every step you take the money's falling through.
IMPERIAL GUARDS
What are you doing here? This is no place for you. Ferreting in the emperor's
property.
HABEBALD
We gave our services, and we're taking our share of the loot. It's the custom
in enemy tents and we're soldiers too.
IMPERIAL GUARDS
This won't do here. You can't be both a soldier and a dirty thief. The em-
peror must have honest men round him.
HABEBALD
We know what you mean by honest. You mean taxes. We're all on a level.
Here, give me that. To show we're buddies. (*to Eilebeute*) Beat it and take
what you can with you. They don't like us here. *off*
FIRST GUARD
Say, why didn't you swipe him on the mouth?
SECOND GUARD
I don't know. They were like ghosts. It took the stuffing out of me.
THIRD GUARD
I couldn't see straight. Everything was dancing in front of my eyes.
FOURTH GUARD
It was so hot all day, so close, so frightening, so ... I don't know what to call
it. You saw one man staying on his feet and the other falling. You fumbled
blindly and struck and down the fellow went every time. There was like a
veil in front of your eyes and noises in your ears, buzzing and roaring and
hissing. And on and on it went. And now we're here, somehow or other.
That's all I can say.

Enter Emperor with four princes. The guards withdraw

EMPEROR
The victory is ours. That much you can't deny. The enemy forces scattered
in flight across the plain. Here stands the empty throne and here, crowding
the place, the traitor's treasures with these carpets spread over them. And
now in our imperial dignity, with our own bodyguard round us, we await
the envoys of the nations. Good news, glad news, is coming in from every
side, assuring us that the land is quiet again and happy in its allegiance to

us. There may have been some ghostly forces involved in the fighting, but in the end it was we who won the battle. There can always be accidents that work in your favour. A stone falls out of the sky, blood rains on the enemy, magic noises come rumbling out of caverns, raising our courage, depressing the enemy's. The loser loses. Contempt is all he gets. The winner wins, re-joices, and thanks God. Not he alone. 'Lord, we praise thee,' comes from a million throats spontaneously. But now, most devoutly of all, I do what I seldom do. I look within. A happy young ruler may waste his days. But time teaches him to value them. And this is why, without delay, I ally myself to you four, you worthy custodians of our court and country.

To the first

It was you, sir, who shrewdly disposed our troops and struck boldly at the crucial moment. Carry on now in peace-time and do what is required. I appoint you High Marshal and invest you with the sword.

HIGH MARSHAL

Your army, faithful as ever, has been establishing order up and down the land. But once we have made our frontiers and your throne secure you must permit me on feast days at your castle to set the table for the banquet. I shall walk before you with the shining sword, the eternal token of your supreme majesty, and stand with it at your side.

EMPEROR *to the second*

You, a man of courage and of gentle manners too, I appoint High Chamber-lain. The duties are onerous. You will have complete charge of the household, where I know there is division among the servants and inefficiency. You must make yourself in their eyes the paragon of courtesy to all men.

HIGH CHAMBERLAIN

I shall earn your favour by carrying out your noble wishes which tell me to be helpful to the good people and to go easy on the bad, to be calm and clear-minded, dismissing all cunning and trickery. If you, sir, see me as I am, I cannot wish for more. May I be so bold as to picture that festive scene. When you come to the table, I shall pass you the golden bowl, hold your rings at the happy moment when you dip your fingers and give me a look of approval.

EMPEROR

I find it not easy to turn my thoughts from serious to joyful. But never mind. A lively start helps.

To the third

I choose you for High Steward, to supervise our game preserves, poultry yard, and manor farm. See to it that always month by month the choicest dishes are prepared and well prepared.

HIGH STEWARD

I shall make it my duty and my pleasure not to partake of a dish till it has pleased you. The kitchen staff will co-operate with you in bringing foods from afar and anticipating the seasons, always remembering that your own taste is for simple and healthy dishes, not for the unusual.

EMPEROR *to the fourth*

Since it has to be festivities we deal with today and nothing else, I appoint you, young man, my cupbearer. As High Cupbearer make sure that our cellar is well stocked with wines. For yourself, be moderate. Don't be led astray by the opportunities that come in merry company.

HIGH CUPBEARER

Young men, your majesty, if you give them responsibilities, quickly rise to the occasion. I too can see myself at that great festival. I shall deck out the imperial buffet with resplendent gold and silver ware. And for yourself I shall select the loveliest of goblets, of shining Venetian glass, comforting even to look at. It improves the wine and never intoxicates. People often rely too heavily on the virtue of this miraculous cup, but your moderation will save you from that.

EMPEROR

What I have bestowed on you you have now heard. It comes with authority in this solemn hour and you can count on it. The emperor's word is supreme and sufficient, but for confirmation we have to put it on paper and I must give you my signature. And now at the right moment comes the right man to draft the formalities.

Enter the chancellor-archbishop

EMPEROR

When an arch locks with the keystone, it can stand for all time. Here you see four of my princes. We have just dealt with problems of the court and the household. And now, turning to the empire as a whole, I rest the full weight and authority on the five of you. I intend you to rank above all others in property and I therefore enlarge your present territories from those of our recent enemies. Not only do I enrich you thus with fair domains. I also give you the right to extend them further by way of succession, purchase, or exchange. Further, I allow you full benefit of all privileges that pertain to your status. Judicially your verdict shall be final, and no appeal is valid. Then, fees, levies, taxes, of every kind, whether excise, transit, or escort, all are yours. Also royalties on mines, salt works, coinage. You see, to give you the fullest evidence of my gratitude I have raised you to positions second only to my own.

ARCHBISHOP

I thank you most deeply on behalf of us all. It strengthens us and strengthens you.

EMPEROR

I now have a further honour to bestow on you. I am still alive, eager to live and serve my empire. But when I reflect on my long ancestry it gives me darker thoughts and curbs my zeal. The day will come when I shall part from my dear ones. It will then be your duty to appoint my successor and solemnize his coronation. May that be a peaceful ending to these stormy times.

LORD CHANCELLOR

Humble in posture, proud in deepest heart, we bow before you, we princes, the first, the highest, on earth. So long as blood flows in our veins, regard us as a single body responsive to your every wish.

EMPEROR

To conclude then, let our deliberations be confirmed in writing and duly signed. Your possessions are yours outright with the sole condition that they are indivisible and, however much extended, must pass on undiminished to the eldest son.

LORD CHANCELLOR

I shall be happy to record this important statute on parchment for the good, of the empire and ourselves. The chancery will see to the engrossing and sealing and you, sir, will put your august signature to it.

EMPEROR

And now I can dismiss you, and leave you to reflect severally on this momentous day.

The secular princes withdraw

ARCHBISHOP

Stays behind and speaks with great solemnity
The chancellor has withdrawn, the bishop has stayed behind, warned by an inner voice to speak to you with fatherly affection and with deep concern.

EMPEROR

What can have alarmed you on this happy occasion? Speak freely.

ARCHBISHOP

It pains me grievously at this hour to find you, the emperor whose head is sacred, allied with Satan. True, you seem securely seated on your throne, but it is a mockery to the Lord in heaven and our holy father, the Pope, who, if he hears of it, will quickly inflict the severest punishment on you, shatter your wicked empire with his ban of excommunication. You must consider that he still remembers how on your coronation day you set that cursed sorcerer free, making your first act of pardon an offence to Christianity. But now beat your breast and lose no time in giving a mite out of your impious wealth to the holy cause. Listen to the voice of piety and endow the church with that stretch of hilly country where your tent stood, where evil spirits conspired to protect you and you lent a willing ear to the prince of darkness. The whole extent of mountain and forest, with upland pastures for grazing, clear lakes well stocked with fish, and all the water winding and cascading in countless rivulets down into the valley. Then the valley itself with its meadows and its undulations. In this way you will show your repentance and find yourself in favour again.

EMPEROR

I am so horrified at my offence that I leave it to you to set the boundaries.

ARCHBISHOP

First of all, it must be proclaimed immediately that this desecrated territory is to be devoted to the service of the church. In my mind's eye I can see strong walls rising, the early sunlight lying on the choir, the transept coming next, the nave extending and rising to the delight of all the faithful. Now I see them streaming devoutly through the great porch in answer to the bell that was heard for the first time over hill and dale, booming from the high towers. The penitent come here to start life afresh. At the consecration – may it be soon – your presence will be the chief adornment of the day.

EMPEROR

I trust this great undertaking will show the pious spirit that prompted it. May it glorify God and exculpate me. I am satisfied and already feel my spirits rising.

ARCHBISHOP

In my capacity as chancellor I must go through the formalities.

EMPEROR

Draw up a formal statement, deeding this property to the church, submit it to me and I will sign with pleasure.

ARCHBISHOP *takes his leave and turns back*

Furthermore, you must assign all the revenues from this territory for all time to the cathedral that is to be. Tithes, taxes, payment in kind. Vast sums are needed for maintenance and for administration. You must let us have some of your booty to speed the building on this desolate spot. Besides, you must remember, timber, lime, and slate will have to be brought from a distance. The people will do the hauling, as the pulpit will bid them, and the church will pronounce its blessing on those who give their labour. *off*

EMPEROR

That was a fearful sin I brought upon myself. Those wretched magicians have done me great harm.

ARCHBISHOP *turning back again and bowing obsequiously*

Forgive me, sir, you leased your shoreline to Faust, that disreputable man. But unless you penitently assign all the revenues from there too to the church, it will surely put its ban on him at once.

EMPEROR *annoyed*

But the land isn't there yet, it's still under water.

ARCHBISHOP

For those with justice on their side and patience the time will come. And your word will hold. *off*

EMPEROR *alone*

I might as well write off the whole empire.

scene 46

Open country

WANDERER

There they are, the dark old linden trees, as strong and sturdy as ever. And to think that I should set eyes on them once again after all my travels. It's the same old place, the cottage where they took me in, when storm and ship-wreck landed me on these dunes. A worthy couple they were, so kind and good. I'd like to tell them so and thank them. But they were old then. They may be gone now. It's a question. Shall I knock at the door or give them a hail? Greetings, if you're still there and enjoying the happy life you deserve after what you did for others.

BAUCIS *very old*

Hush, hush, stranger dear. Let my man finish his sleep. Then he'll be able to busy himself for the short time he's up.

WANDERER

Tell me, aren't you Mother Baucis? You must be. So I haven't come too late

to thank you for saving my life that time, Philemon and you. I was at the
point of death when you wetted my lips. I was young then.
Enter Philemon
And you are Philemon, who stoutly dragged my possessions ashore. I remember your quick bonfire and the silver sound of your bell. It was given to
you and Baucis to rescue me in that catastrophe. But now let me step outside and look at the ocean. Let me kneel and say a prayer. I am so moved.

He walks out over the dune

PHILEMON *to Baucis*
Quick now and set the table in the garden. Let him go and look. He'll get the
shock of his life. He won't believe his eyes.
Standing beside wanderer
Where you once had that grim struggle with wind and waves is all a
garden now, a paradise to behold. I wasn't young any more and I wasn't able
to give a hand, but as an ageing man I watched and saw them push the water
farther and farther back. The masters knew their job, but the men had to
take risks. They dug ditches, built dams, took land from the sea and made it
theirs. Look, one green meadow after another, gardens, villages, woods.
Come and feast your eyes. The sun hasn't long to go. Far off you can make
out the sails of ships heading for home tonight, like birds that know their
nests. That's where the harbour is now. The ocean's just a blue strip on the
horizon. To right and left of you the land's all thickly populated.

The three at table in the garden

BAUCIS
You haven't a word to say. You're hungry and you don't eat a bite.
PHILEMON
He wants to know about the prodigy. You like talking. You tell him.
BAUCIS
A prodigy it surely was. It bothers me still. There was something wrong,
something wicked, about the whole thing.
PHILEMON
Do you mean the emperor was wicked when he gave him the shoreline?
Didn't a herald proclaim it, riding past with his trumpet? It was quite close
to our dunes that the start was made. They set up huts and tents. And soon
there was a palace there with grass and green trees round it.
BAUCIS
The workmen toiled and slaved all day with pick and shovel and got no-
where. At night you could see lights moving, and the next day – there stood
a dam. Men's lives were sacrificed, you could hear them groaning in the dark.
Torrents of fire flowed down into the water and when the morning came
behold a canal. He's a godless man. He covets our cottage and our trees. He's
so domineering, he expects us to do what he tells us.
PHILEMON
Didn't he offer us a nice piece of property on the new soil?
BAUCIS
Don't trust that flat land. Stick to your high ground.

PHILEMON

Let us go to the chapel and watch the sun set, ring the bell, kneel and pray, and put our trust in the god of our fathers.

scene 47

Palace. Extensive formal garden. A large straight canal. Faust in advanced old age, walking about, meditating

LYNCEUS, THE WATCHMAN *through his megaphone*

The sun is setting. The last of the ships are running in. A freight boat is entering the canal to dock here, its masts erect, its coloured pennants waving merrily. The sailor's joy is centred in you. Fortune greets you at this crowning moment.

The bell rings on the dune

FAUST *starting up*

That cursed bell. It hurts me cruelly like a stab in the dark. Before my eyes my dominion is complete, but from behind vexation teases me, reminding me with taunting noise that my vast estate is not unblemished. I don't possess the linden trees, nor the brown cottage, nor the crumbling chapel. And if I wanted to rest there I should be terrified of ghosts. It's a thorn in the flesh, an offence to the sight. Oh, to be anywhere but here.

WATCHMAN *as above*

How nicely the freighter is coming in on the evening wind. Its pile of cargo in bales and boxes grows bigger and bigger every minute.

CHORUS
Now we've landed. Here we are. Hail to the master. Hail to the boss. *They disembark. The cargo is unshipped*

MEPHISTOPHELES
We've come through well. If the boss approves, it's all we ask. We set out with two ships and we've come back with twenty. What feats we performed, you can see from our cargo. The open sea frees the spirit. Who stops to think there? Quick action's what's wanted. Catching a ship's like catching fish. When you've caught three, you grapple a fourth. The fifth doesn't have a look-in. Might is right. You don't ask how, you ask what. If I know anything about the sea, there's a trinity here, a three-in-one, war, trade, and piracy.

THE THREE GIANTS
Not a word of thanks. Not a word of greeting. He pulls a face at what we've brought. This royal treasure. He thinks it stinks.

MEPHISTOPHELES
You won't get any more from him. You've helped yourselves already.

THE THREE GIANTS
That was just our pocket-money. Equal shares is what we want.

MEPHISTOPHELES
First you must set out the stuff in the halls. When he sees the wealth of it, he won't be stingy. He'll entertain us lavishly. The gay girls will be coming tomorrow. I'll look after them properly.

The cargo is moved away

MEPHISTOPHELES *to Faust*
When I remind you of your great good fortune you take it very gravely, very gloomily. Yet, as you can see, the plan was wise and has succeeded. The sea and the shore are at peace with one another, giving our ships quick and easy access to the open. Standing here in front of your palace, you can say that your arm encloses the whole world. And this is where it all started. Here stood the first log hut. We dug a ditch, where now the oars ply briskly. Your great purpose, the devoted labour of your men, have won the rewards of land and sea. Standing here ...

FAUST
Yes, here, here. It's the cursed here and now that weighs me down. I have to tell you, you man of many parts, that I find it intolerable. I'm ashamed of myself when I say it. Those old people will have to go. I want those lindens for my recreation. This handful of trees, that are not my trees, wrecks every-thing, wrecks my whole estate. I intended to build platforms there among the branches to let me survey the full extent of my achievement, the supreme achievement of the human mind, setting the nations constructively to work on newly gained land.

    This is the worst torture of all, to feel a lack with so little lacking. The sound of the bell, the scent of the lindens, stifles me like being in a tomb. The freedom of my mighty will is brought to nothing here in the sand. How

[handwritten marginal note: Pure selfishness]

shall I ever lift this off me? The bell tolls on, and I am beside myself with fury.

MEPHISTOPHELES

Of course, of course. There always has to be some one thing to sour your life for you. Don't we all know it? No man of breeding can bear to hear that tinkling sound, that damnable ding-dong that darkens the evening sky and gets into everything that happens from baptism to burial, making life seem no more than an idle dream between one silly note and the next.

FAUST

The stubborn way those people hold out mars all my splendid profit. It hurts me savagely to say it, but I have no choice. I give up trying to be just.

MEPHISTOPHELES

Haven't you been colonizing all this long time? Why make such a fuss now?

FAUST

Very well, go and evict them. You know the little estate I chose for them.

MEPHISTOPHELES

We'll pick them up and set them down. They'll be on their feet again in no time. And they'll forget the rough treatment when they see how lovely the new place is. *He whistles shrilly*

The three giants appear

MEPHISTOPHELES

Come and carry out the master's orders. And tomorrow we'll have a fleet festival.

THE THREE GIANTS

The master received us very coldly. A sweet festival will make amends.

MEPHISTOPHELES *ad spectatores*

What we're doing is an old story. Naboth's vineyard all over again.

Deep Night

LYNCEUS THE WATCHMAN *singing on the battlements*

Born with these eyes, appointed to watch, pledged to the tower, I like the world. I look at the distant, I look at the near. I see moon and stars, see forest and stag. And enduring beauty in everything. Content with it all, I'm at ease with myself. You happy eyes, when all is said, whatever you saw, it was lovely to see.

Pause

But I wasn't stationed up here for my own enjoyment. See what a horror confronts me in the night. Sparks flying in the dark clump of lindens. A conflagration spreading, fanned by the breeze. The mossy cottage burning inside. No help in sight and the need urgent. Oh, those dear old people, always so careful of fire, and now a victim of the fumes. What a disaster! The whole dark framework blazing red. If only they could escape this inferno. Tongues of flame are mounting in the leaves and twigs, the dry limbs catching and breaking off. Why must I have to witness this. A pity I'm so long-sighted. The little chapel is collapsing now under the falling branches. The writing

[handwritten marginal note: Faust's work through Devil]

flames have reached the tree-tops and the hollow trunks are glowing down to
the roots. *long pause. singing*
    What was always so pleasant a sight is one now with the centuries past.
FAUST *on the balcony, facing the dunes*
What plaintive notes are these that reach me from above, reach me too late
to be of use. It is my watchman grieving. And I too deplore what I did with
such impatience. But no matter. If the lindens are reduced to burnt stems
and cinders, we'll soon run up a look-out place, where I can gaze into the
infinite. And I can see the old couple housed in their new quarters, contented
in their last years and bearing no malice.
MEPHISTOPHELES AND THE THREE GIANTS *speaking from below*
Here we come on the high run. You'll have to excuse us. Things didn't go
smoothly. We knocked at the door and thumped at the door and no one
came. We shook it and thumped again and the old door gave in. Then we
shouted and threatened them and got no answer. They didn't hear; they
didn't want to hear. That's the way it is in such cases. But we lost no time
and quickly ousted them. The old couple didn't suffer much. They died of
shock. And a stranger there who showed fight was soon despatched. In the
short encounter sparks were scattered from the hearth and set some straw
on fire. Now there's a big blaze, a funeral pyre for the three of them.
FAUST
Were you deaf to what I said? I wanted exchange, not robbery. My curse on
this wanton deed. Share it among you.
CHORUS
It's often said: Obey your master. Yet if you stick to him and serve him
boldly, you've everything to lose, even your life. *off*
FAUST *on the balcony*
The stars are fading in the sky. The fire has sunk low. But a shivery breeze
is fanning it still, bringing a whiff of smoke with it. Haste on my part, over-
haste on theirs. But now what shadows are these coming?

Midnight. Enter four gray women

THE FIRST
My name is Lack.
THE SECOND
My name is Debt.
THE THIRD
My name is Care.
THE FOURTH
And mine is Need.
THREE OF THEM
The door is locked. We can't get in and we don't wish to. A rich man lives
here.
LACK
This makes me a shadow.
DEBT
And makes me a nothing.

NEED

From me they turn their pampered faces.

CARE

Sisters, you can't get in and you shouldn't. But Care can slip through the keyhole. *Care disappears*

LACK

Gray sisters away, away from here.

DEBT

I'll come along with you, side by side.

NEED

And I'll be close on your heels.

ALL THREE

The clouds are flying. The stars vanish at a breath. And now, over there, from afar, from afar, I see him coming, our brother coming, our brother Death. *off*

FAUST *in the palace*

I saw four of them come, and only three left. The sense of what they said I couldn't follow. I seemed to hear a word like breath and then another that rhymed with it, a dark word – death. It sounded muted, hollow, like ghost voices. I haven't won my way to freedom yet. If I could only get rid of magic, unlearn my incantations utterly, and stand face to face with nature as a man, just as a man, it would be worthwhile to be a man.

I was that once, before I probed the realm of darkness, damning myself and the world with impious words. The air is now so thronged with spooks and spectres there's no escaping them. The daylight hours may be all sanity and sweetness, but the night involves us in a web of dreams. We come home happy from the fields in springtime. A bird croaks. What does it croak: calamity. Beset, as we are, with superstitions hopelessly, there's always a something ominous that comes, a strange hint, a foreboding. It frightens us. We are alone. The door creaks and nobody comes in. *alarmed*

Is anyone there?

CARE

The answer must be yes.

FAUST

Who are you? Tell me.

CARE

I'm here. That's enough.

FAUST

Be off with you.

CARE

I'm in the right place.

FAUST *furious at first, then calmer, aside*

Look out now. No more magic spells from me.

CARE

When Care says a thing, whether heard or not, it reechoes in the heart. In one guise or another I make my cruel power felt. A disquieting companion by land or sea, not wanted, always at hand, cajoled one time and cursed the next. Have you never experienced me?

I've just raced through the world, seizing what I fancied by the hair of its head. If it wasn't good enough I let it go. If it eluded me, I didn't bother. I've simply desired and fulfilled my desire and desired again. And so stormed through life, at first in a big way, but now I move more wisely, warily. I've taken the measure of this earth we live on. Into the beyond the view is blocked. Only an idiot would peer in that direction, imagining there were men like him beyond the clouds. Why should he go roving off into eternity? Let him stand where he stands and look about him. The world always has something to offer to a man of worth. When he sees it he should hang on to it and shape his life accordingly. If there are ghosts about, ignore them. And find his pleasure and his pain in moving on and on, knowing all the time that he'll never be satisfied.

CARE

Once I get my grip on a man, the world is no use to him. A dark cloud settles down on him. The sun neither rises nor sets. With outer senses all intact, there are blacknesses within, depriving him of the very riches that are his and letting him starve in the midst of plenty. Happiness, unhappiness – a matter of caprice. Things to do, welcome or unwelcome, he puts them off, leaves them till tomorrow and tomorrow and never quite grows up.

FAUST

Rubbish. No more of that. I won't listen to it. Harping on that note, you might fool the wisest of men. You won't fool me.

CARE

Shall he go? Shall he come? He can't make up his mind. In the middle of the trodden road he totters and he fumbles, seeing more and more awry, getting more and more confused; a burden to himself, a burden to others; panting, choking, not quite suffocating; not yielding, not despairing, just rolling, unable to stop; thwarted, driven; relieved, oppressed; never sound asleep, never wide awake. All this fixes him where he is and prepares him for hell.

FAUST

You wretched ghosts, this is how you've treated the human race times out of number, turning even indifferent days into tangles of torment. Phantoms, I know, are hard to be rid of. The bond with them will never be broken. But your insidious power, O Care, I will not admit it.

CARE

Then taste it now in the parting curse I leave you with. Most men are blind all their lives. Now, Faust, at long last it's your turn.

She breathes on him. Off

FAUST *blinded*
The dark seems darker than before, but my inner light shines clear. No time must be lost in carrying out what I intended. The master's voice is needed here. Up from your beds, you labourers, every one. Let me see with my eyes what I so boldly planned. Seize your tools. At it with spades and shovels. The plot staked out must be finished now, and for strict discipline and speedy work I promise rich rewards. To complete a great project one mind is enough for a thousand hands.

MEPHISTOPHELES *as custodian, leading*

Come along, come along, you shambling lemurs, you half-begotten contrivances of bone and sinew.

LEMURS *in chorus*

> Here we are on hand at once, and as our wits half-tell us, there's a great piece of land going, and we're supposed to get it.
>
> The pointed stakes are waiting there, and the long chain for measuring. You sent for us to come and help. Why us, we can't remember.

MEPHISTOPHELES

This is no job for an artist. Just go by your own proportions. Let the lankiest of you lie down flat, and the rest of you ease the turf all round him. Dig out a longish rectangle, like those men dug for our forebears. Out of the palace into the narrow room. This is the stupid end it always comes to.

LEMURS *digging with droll gestures*

> When I was young and full of zest, I thought it very sweet. If there was merriment about, it got into my feet.
>
> But now old age has caught me up, and tripped me with his crutch. I stumbled at the door of the grave. Too bad it wasn't shut.

FAUST *coming out of the palace, feeling his way by the door-posts*

Oh how I love this clatter of spades. It's my men working for me, making the shore safe, checking the waves, setting limits to the sea.

MEPHISTOPHELES *aside*

You with your dams and piers, you're only playing into our hands. Neptune, the sea-devil, will have a great celebration over this. You haven't a ghost of a chance. We're in league with the elements and the end of it all is destruction.

FAUST

Custodian.

MEPHISTOPHELES

Here, sir.

FAUST

Use every means to get more workers. Treat them well, drive them hard. Pay them, entice them, press them. You must report daily on the progress of the ditch.

MEPHISTOPHELES *under his breath*

The way I understand it, it's not a ditch, it's a grave.

FAUST

There is a swamp, skirting the base of the hills, a foul and filthy blot on all our work. If we could drain and cleanse this pestilence, it would crown everything we have achieved, opening up living space for many millions. Not safe from every hazard, but safe enough. Green fields and fruitful too for man and beast, both quickly domiciled on new-made land, all snug and settled under the mighty dune that many hands have built with fearless toil. Inside it life will be a paradise. Let the floods rage and mount to the dune's brink. No sooner will they nibble at it, threaten it, than all as one man run to stop the gap. Now I am wholly of this philosophy. This is the farthest human wisdom goes: The man who earns his freedom every day, alone

deserves it, and no other does. And, in this sense, with dangers at our door,
we all, young folk and old, shall live our lives. Oh how I'd love to see that
lusty throng and stand on a free soil with a free people. Now I could almost
say to the passing moment: Stay, oh stay a while, you are beautiful. The
mark of my endeavours will not fade. No, not in ages, not in any time.
Dreaming of this incomparable happiness, I now taste and enjoy the supreme
moment.

Faust collapses. The lemurs pick him up and lay him on the ground

MEPHISTOPHELES
Indulgence never sated him, no happiness sufficed. One pursuit it was after
another, never the same. And now this futile, final moment of all, he wants
to cling to it. He stood out mightily against me, but time has conquered him.
There the old man lies. His clock has stopped.
CHORUS
Stopped. Run down. Silent as midnight.
MEPHISTOPHELES
It's all over.
CHORUS
It's finished.
MEPHISTOPHELES
Finished. A silly word. Why finished, I'd like to know. Finished and sheer
nothingness all one and the same. What use is this interminable creating,
this dragging creation into uncreation again? Finished. What does it point
to? It might as well never have been at all. And yet it goes its round as if it
was something. Give me eternal emptiness every time.

Burial

LEMUR *solo*
  O who has built so mean a house, with nothing more than a shovel.
LEMURS *chorus*
  You sorry guest in a hempen shroud, it's much too good for you, sir.
LEMUR *solo*
  And what about the furniture? No chairs, not even a table.
LEMURS *chorus*
  We had them on so short a loan. There are too many claimants.
MEPHISTOPHELES
Here lies the corpse and if the soul comes out, I'll quickly show it the blood-
signed title-deed. The trouble is there are so many ways now of outwitting
me. The old style is out of favour, and they don't like the new. The day was
when I could have managed this by myself, but now I need accomplices.

  Things are going badly with us devils. Established customs, ancient privileges, you can't trust anything any more. It used to be that the soul came
out with the last breath. I'd be on the look-out for it and, quick as a flash, I
had it in my clutch. But now it hesitates, loth, it seems, to leave its quarters
in that dismal corpse. I know the conflicting elements will bundle it out
sooner or later. But meanwhile I have to plague myself day and night with
when, how, and where. Death has lost its old vigour. You have to wait and

wait to see if it's really there. Many a time have I kept my eye greedily on the rigid limbs. And it was deceptive. The thing began to shift and stir again.

Making strange, mechanical, exorcising gestures

Come quickly, quickly now, you devils of the ancient cut, some with crumpled horns and some with straight. And bring hell's jaws along with you. I know that hell has many jaws and swallows its victims according to rank. But we aren't going to be so particular in future, even at this stage.

The horrid jaws of hell open, left

See there the tusks. And the raging flames pouring out of the arched gullet. In the murk behind I can see the city of eternal fire. The red surf comes foaming as far as the teeth and the doomed swim up, hoping to escape, only to be gulped down by this monstrous hyena and start all over again. There's lots more to be seen in holes and corners, so many horrors in such narrow space. You do right to strike terror into the hearts of sinners. They don't believe it's true, they think it's a sham.

To the fat devils with short straight horns

Now, you paunchy, short-necked devils with cheeks aflame, fattened on hell's sulphur, keep watch down here for a glint of phosphorus. That's the soul, the winged Psyche. If you pluck its wings off, it's just a nasty worm. I'll stick my stamp on it and then off with it into hell's whirlpool.

Watch the lower regions, you podgy ones. That's your special job. Whether this is where the soul resides, we're not so sure. But it likes the navel. So remember, it may slip out there.

To the scraggy devils with long twisted horns

You ninnies, you lanky dummies, keep combing the air all the time, with your arms extended and your sharp claws spread, so as to catch it if it flutters out. It won't be comfortable where it is now and it'll come shooting up before long.

Gloria, from above, right

THE HEAVENLY HOST

Envoys of heaven, follow us, follow, in easy flight, pardoning sinners, refreshing the dust, with loving-kindness for all creation, as you pass by, passing ever so gently.

MEPHISTOPHELES

Those wretched, harping discords, I can hear them, that boyish-girlish jingle so dear to the sanctimonious, coming down from above in this unwelcome blaze of light. You know that in darkest hell we planned to destroy the human race. Well, the foulest sins we invented are just what their piety thrives on.

They're hypocrites, the young puppies. They've robbed us of many a one that way, fighting us with our own weapons. They're devils too, only in disguise. If you let them beat you, you'll never live it down. So stand by the grave and hold your ground.

CHORUS OF ANGELS *scattering roses*

You dazzling roses, fluttering, hovering, spreading your fragrance, secretly

life-giving, winged with your twiglets, ready to blossom, be quick to burst
open.

Spring, come out in your greens and purples, bringing paradise to him
who is sleeping.

MEPHISTOPHELES *to the devils*

What are you ducking and dodging for? What way is this for hell's denizens
to behave? Back to your places, every one of you. They think they can snow
you under with their silly flowers. Blow on them and they'll shrivel up. Puff
hard, you puffers. – Enough now, enough. Your breath has blanched the
whole flight. But steady now. Close your mouths and noses. You've been
blowing too hard. You never know when to stop. Have you no sense of pro-
portion? You've not just shrivelled the stuff, you've set fire to it. Now it's
coming down on you in flames that sting. Huddle together and hold out. Oh,
they've given in, they've lost heart. They sense a seductive heat that is new
to them.

CHORUS OF ANGELS

These flowers angelic, these playful flames bring offerings of love and joy,
to gladden the heart, like words of truth in the clear sky, the heavenly host's
eternal daylight.

MEPHISTOPHELES

Oh damn it. The simpletons, standing on their heads, clumsily somersaulting,
plunging backwards into hell. I hope it roasts them. They well deserve it.
But I mean to stay where I am.

Beating off the roses in the air

Away, you will-o-the-wisps. For all your brightness, you're only messy
spots of dirt, when I get hold of you. Be off. Stop fluttering round me. You're
lodging in my neck like pitch and sulphur.

CHORUS OF ANGELS

What isn't yours, you must shun it. What is disturbing, you must reject.
But if we stung you, we must sting harder. Love alone leads lovers to heaven.

MEPHISTOPHELES

My head's on fire, my heart, my liver too. This is a more devilish element.
It's much crueller than hell-fire. So this is why unhappy lovers, when rejected, crane their necks in search of the one they wanted.

And it's happening to me. Why do I twist my head towards my sworn
enemies, the sight of whom I used to abominate? Some strange spirit has
come over me. I like the look of them, these darling boys. I can't abuse them
any more, something stops me. And if they can make a fool of me, I'll be a
fool forever. Those cunning youngsters attract me, though I hate them.
Tell me, aren't you too descendants of Lucifer? You seem to suit me, you're
so lovely, so kissable. It's all so easy, so natural, as if I'd seen you lots of
times before. And you're so enticing, you're getting prettier all the time.
Come nearer. Let me have a closer look.

CHORUS OF ANGELS

Here we are. Why are you running away? We're coming closer. Stay, if you
can stand it.

The angels close round and fill the stage

MEPHISTOPHELES *pushed forward into the forestage*
You call us the damned, but it's you who are the real witch-masters, seducing
both sexes at once. What a cursed thing to happen. Is this the element of
love? My whole body's on fire, making me hardly notice the agony in my
neck. You're floating about in the air, come down lower, work your limbs
a little less angelically. I know your solemnity suits you, but I wish you'd
smile a lover's smile for once. I'd be delighted. Just a twitch of the mouth,
that's all. You, the tall one, are the one I fancy. That clerical look doesn't go
with you at all. Why not give me a wicked one? And I'd like to see you not so
fully dressed. It would become you better. Those long robes are prudish.
Now the rascals are turning round. My, from behind aren't they fetching?

CHORUS OF ANGELS
Turn heavenwards now, you flames of love. And let the sinners be healed by
the truth, redeemed from evil, redeemed and happy, blest in the company of
all the blest.

MEPHISTOPHELES
Whatever has happened? I'm just like Job, my whole body a mass of sores,
making me shudder at sight of myself. And yet I triumph, when I look
deeper, and trust again in the stock I'm sprung from. The noble parts of the
old devil are unimpaired. That weird attack of sex has come out in a rash.
The flames are spent. And now I curse you all, as curse I should.

CHORUS OF ANGELS
Sacred fires, those they encircle will find the good life and share it with
others. All together rise and sing praises. The air is pure. The spirit can
breathe again.

They rise in the air, carrying off Faust's immortal part

MEPHISTOPHELES *looking round*
But what's this? Where have they gone? Those youngsters have taken me
by surprise and are off to heaven with their booty. That's why they came
meddling at this graveside. I've lost a rare prize, a unique one, the soul of this
great man. It was pledged to me and they've cunningly smuggled it away.

But where can I lodge an appeal? Who will procure me my rightful due?
I've been badly let down in my late years, very badly. And it's my fault. I
behaved disgracefully. A great effort gone with the wind, all because an
erotic impulse of the most absurd variety came over me. It puts me to shame.
Fooled at the finish. Me, the tough old devil that ought to have known better.

scene 48

*Mountain Chasms, Rocks, Forest, Wilderness. Anchorites at various levels
on the slope, clefts on either side of them*

CHORUS AND ECHO
A mountain side begins to show, tree-roots clutching the rock, forest stems
rising rank above rank, cascades splashing endlessly, deep caverns for

shelter, lions moving about, gentle, noiseless, honouring this sacred place, the abode of heavenly love.

PATER ECSTATICUS *floating up and down*

Joy that burns, love that sears, heart-anguish that scalds, divine rapture that foams. Arrows, come, pierce me. Lances, master me. Clubs, crush me. Lightnings, shatter me. Till all that is worthless is purged away and love's star remains for ever.

PATER PROFUNDUS *lower down*

The abyss at my feet rests on a deeper abyss. A thousand sparkling rivulets unite to form the dread waterfall. The trees soar upwards by their own strength. Each an expression of the almighty love that shapes and cares for all things.

There is a roaring everywhere as if the woods and rocks were in commotion. And yet the torrent sustains its happy flow down to the valley that it waters. The lightning strikes and clears the air of mist and murk.

These again are messengers of love, telling of the creative spirit that surrounds us. Would that it could kindle me, whose mind in cold confusion labours, with senses dulled and unremitting pain. O God, assuage my thoughts. Illuminate my needy heart.

PATER SERAPHICUS *in the middle region*

What morning cloudlet is this, floating through the swaying hair of the pines? I believe I know what it hides. Yes. It is a company of young souls.

CHORUS OF BOY SOULS

Tell us, father, where we're going. Tell us where we are. We know we are happy. Existence sits so lightly on us.

PATER SERAPHICUS

These are boys born at midnight, swept away from their parents with mind and senses barely started. A welcome gain for the angels. You can feel that one who loves you is near, so come closer. You have been spared any knowledge of the rude earth. I invite you to enter me. My eyes are adjusted to the world. Use them as your own and look about you. (*He takes them inside himself*) These are trees. These are rocks. Here is a great rush of water, shortening its steep path downwards.

BOY SOULS *from inside*

Powerful to behold, but gloomy. It fills us with fear. Good father, release us.

PATER SERAPHICUS

Rise to higher regions, growing imperceptibly, as God's nearness and purity gives you strength. It is in the revelation of eternal love, leading to beatitude and ever-present in the ether, that the spirit finds its nourishment.

BOY SOULS *circling around the highest summits*

Join hands in a ring. Sing sacred songs. Be happy, confident now that you will see the god you worship.

ANGELS *hovering in the upper atmosphere, carrying Faust's immortal part*

This noble member of the spirit-world is saved from evil. He who strives and ever strives, him we can redeem. And if love from on high is also his, the angels welcome him.

THE YOUNGER ANGELS

The roses given us by the women penitents helped us to win the fight, rescue this man's soul, and complete the good work. The devils weakened and ran when we pelted them. It was the anguish of love they suffered, not the familiar pains of hell. Even their old chief was stung to the quick. Rejoice, we have succeeded.

THE MATURER ANGELS

To handle a vestige of earth costs us an effort. It might be asbestos and yet it would be unclean. But when once the spirit welds itself with the elements, it is beyond the angels' power to separate them. Only love eternal can do it.

THE YOUNGER ANGELS

I feel a spirit-life near by, floating like a wisp of cloud round that rocky pinnacle. The cloud is lifting and now I see a lively group of boy souls, freed from the weight of earth, all in a ring, and revelling in the spring-like loveliness of the upper world. Let us put him in their company for a start, to grow along with them towards perfection.

BOY SOULS

We receive him joyfully in his chrysalid state. It will give us weight with the angels. Divest him of these earth-remnants. He is already handsome in his holiness.

DOCTOR MARIANUS *in the highest, purest cell*

Here the view is open, the mind uplifted. Women are passing upwards, our lady in their midst, star-circled. It is the queen of heaven in her splendour. *Enraptured*

Supreme mistress of the world, let me see your mystery under the blue canopy of sky. Do not disapprove of the sacred love I bear you in my man's heart.

At your command I am fearless. When you are gracious, the fire quietens. Virgin, mother, purity, our chosen queen, our goddess.

Light clouds play about them. They are penitent women, tenderly breathing the air around her, seeking grace. They in their frailty are allowed to approach you, the immaculate one.

A prey to their weakness, they are hard to save. Who has the inner strength to break the chains of lust? How easily the foot slides on a smooth decline. Who can resist the flattering breath, the seductive word and look?

The mater gloriosa passes by

CHORUS OF PENITENTS

You are ascending to the heights of eternity. Hear our prayer, you the incomparable, you the giver of grace.

MAGNA PECCATRIX

By the love that shed its tears on your son's feet, though the pharisees mocked, by the vessel that poured oil on them and the hair that dried them —

THE SAMARITAN WOMAN

By the well where Abraham once watered his flocks, by the cup that touched and cooled our saviour's lips, by the wellspring that flows from there through all the world in plenty and for ever —

MARY OF EGYPT

By the sacred place where our lord was laid, by the arm that thrust me from

the door, by the forty years of penance in the desert that I faithfully kept, by
the parting words of blessing that I wrote in the sand –

ALL THREE
We beseech you who permit women that have sinned greatly to come near you and as penitents recover and grow to virtue again eternally, grant your pardon to this poor sinner who fell once and fell in innocence.

UNA POENITENTIUM *formerly Gretchen, joining the others*
You the radiant beyond compare, turn your face to me in my happiness and be kind. My early lover, no longer troubled, has now returned.

BOY SOULS *approaching in a spiral motion*
He has already outgrown us in might of limb. He will reward us well for our care and devotion. We were cut off early, but he is experienced and will instruct us.

WOMAN PENITENT *formerly Gretchen*
In this spirit-company the newcomer hardly knows himself. He barely senses the fresh life beginning. This makes him already like the saints. See how he is shedding the last of his earthly self and, ether-clad, his primal youth and vigour emerges. Allow me to be his teacher. The new light still dazzles him.

MATER GLORIOSA
Come, rise to higher spheres. He will feel your presence there and follow.

DOCTOR MARIANUS *fallen on his face in prayer*
Look up to this saving countenance, all you that are softened with repentance, thankful now and ready to be transmuted into blessedness. Put yourselves at her service. Virgin, mother, queen, goddess, be gracious.

CHORUS MYSTICUS
Transitory things are symbolical only. Here the inadequate finds its fulfilment. The not expressible is here made manifest. The eternal in woman is the gleam we follow.

Faust never really repents

This book

was designed by

ALLAN FLEMING

with the assistance of

LAURIE LEWIS

University of

Toronto

Press

Pact o Devil:
If Devil can supply a high enough pleasure to satisfy Faust, Faust will then give him his soul.

Euphorion
Helen's + Faust's child. He dies; she goes to underworld with him.

Enjoyment in Deed in Creation